MODERN
BOUNTY HUNTING

For those who kept the candle burning, while I was out earning my way.

MODERN
BOUNTY HUNTING

A Real-Life Guide for the Bail Fugitive Recovery Agent

Rex Venator

Paladin Press • Boulder, Colorado

Modern Bounty Hunting:
A Real-Life Guide for the Bail Fugitive Recovery Agent
by Rex Venator

ISBN 13: 978-1-58160-476-4
Printed in the United States of America

Published by Paladin Press, a division of
Paladin Enterprises, Inc.
Gunbarrel Tech Center
7077 Winchester Circle
Boulder, Colorado 80301 USA
+1.303.443.7250

Direct inquiries and/or orders to the above address.

Visit our Web site at www.paladin-press.com

Contents

Warning

This book is not intended as an official training manual or a policy and procedure manual. It was not designed to replace instruction from qualified instructors on the methods and techniques involved in bail fugitive recovery, which can be a very dangerous profession requiring specific skills and training.

Further, bail enforcement laws differ in various states, counties, and municipalities.

It is up to you to know what the governing laws are in the various jurisdictions you may be operating in and to comply fully with them. Failure to do so can result in legal action against you.

Author's Note

A few notes are in order before I begin. First, my experience in bail fugitive recovery is in California, so that is my basis for legal qualifications, definitions, and examples. Since the legal authority for a private citizen to enforce a civil contract lies within the purview of each sovereign state, you must learn which laws are applicable to your anticipated area of operation. To help you do that, I include more specific details in Chapter 1, a chart of state laws in Appendix A, and suggested resources for further research at the back of the book.

Second, the names of all persons, agencies, and legal entities in this book have been changed to respect the privacy of the aforementioned parties and to protect recovery agents from "postoperation liability" (read: lawsuits, arrest, or fines).

Third, as in all other professions or fields, jargon abounds in bail fugitive recovery. We in the field generally refer to this as "bailspeak." I have tried to keep the use of bailspeak to a minimum, but the glossary in the back of the book will familiarize you with the terms you need to know.

Finally, although the hunted and the hunters come in both sexes, for brevity and clarity, here the masculine pronouns "he" and "him" will be used and should be considered gender neutral.

Preface

The term *bounty hunter* brings to mind an image of a larger-than-life Old West character with a rifle in one hand and a wanted-dead-or-alive poster in the other. That stereotype has been perpetuated by television and movies, but the nature of modern bounty hunting—though still colorful and challenging—is quite different. My intention in this book is to show you how the recovery business really works and, for those considering entering the field, to provide the best information available to make your entry safe and rewarding.

If you learn only one thing from this book, it should be that bail recovery work is very dangerous, often in ways you may not have considered. For example, have you thought about the possibility of being criminally charged, civilly sued, physically maimed, or even killed? Have you considered the ramifications of killing another human being, whether or not the taking of that life is justified? Can you live with yourself if some uninvolved person dies as a result of your actions?

As of this writing, I have knocked on more than 1,500 doors with the intention of arresting felony fugitives. With the exception of my pulling a hamstring during a foot chase, no one has been seriously hurt or injured during this time. I will make every effort to impart what is important—based on my training and experience as a law enforcement officer, a military policeman, a martial artist, and, of course, my 13 years in the private civil contract enforcement field—so that you too will have the knowledge to stay out of trouble. In short, I can provide you with the "maps," but it will be up to you to discover the "territory."

What exactly do I mean by maps and territory? Because these are important concepts in this book, the relevance of which may not be immediately apparent, allow me to elaborate by using an example based on a recent conversation with a colleague. In an intellectual discussion between Bill and me about parenting, the use of psychotropic drugs to control children came up.

"I believe that a child's lessons concerning right and wrong come from the learning of consequences at an early age—usually within the first five years," I said. "When I worked booking/intake at a large county jail, I could spot who hadn't been spanked as a child. Those people expressed strong feelings of entitlement and often yelled, 'You can't do anything to me!' during the booking process."

"How did you know they hadn't been spanked?" Bill asked.

"Because I asked, and they told me," I said.

Bill objected, "Look, I have a psychology degree, and I took the classes on how to raise children. I'm telling you that a person's personality is mostly hereditary and not situational. Those people are who they are, and how they were raised had nothing to do with it."

I respected Bill's education, but the simple fact was that he didn't have any children and I've got a whole tribe. "Bill," I countered, "you may have the *maps*, but I know the *territory* when it comes to raising kids."

Bill paused for a moment before conceding. "Yeah, I never thought about it that way. Many children who were not disciplined during the formative years may be the ones on Ritalin today."

"I don't know if that's the case, but if a child doesn't understand consequences, such as being reprimanded or spanked as the result of some action, then that person grows up without a concept of being responsible for what he does."

The concept of maps versus territory is universal: it can be applied to any subject. For the purposes of this book, you may draw certain *maps* about the bail fugitive recovery trade, but you won't know the *territory* until you get out there on the streets and use the *maps* contained herein to help you make quicker sense of the *territory* before you.

Okay, I can hear some grumbling about whether a "mere" 1,500 door-knocks qualifies me to write this manual. This skepticism is probably based on reports of "bounty hunters" racking up arrests in the thousands. Well, let's be realistic.

It is very difficult to get into the bail fugitive recovery business—and even harder to be successful at it. The bail agent, commonly referred to as a bondsman, is responsible for what his arrest agent does or doesn't do; consequently, he typically won't hire people who have never worked a forfeited bond or who present themselves as a liability in some way. Moreover, why should the bail agent pay someone hundreds or thousands of dollars to pick up a bail fugitive who is easy to find? The simple fact is that you will not be handed easy contracts. You will get contracts that are severely tainted by previous attempts to apprehend the fugitives, are days away from going into summary judgment, or are just plain hopeless— all instances where you are the last resort.

Bearing these facts in mind, do you really think a self-proclaimed bounty hunter, boasting of thousands of arrests, is being forthright about his arrest totals? I have spoken to people who claim to have made more than 3,000 bail arrests. These people would have had to average three arrests every day for three years to accrue that many arrests. Their claims just aren't credible.

My 1,500 door-knocks have resulted in the physical arrests of more than 300 felony bail fugitives and a comparable number of misdemeanor bail fugitives, and I have closed seemingly hopeless cases on legal technicalities in open court on another 100 or so cases. Those numbers may not sound spectacular to an outsider, but they are solid, and they can be verified.

Does every door-knock results in an arrest? Absolutely not. The above statistics reflect approximately 1,000 cases, but I was only able to close about 700 of them using various methods outlined in this book. Another 300 cases were terminal before I ever got them, meaning that they had been damaged by extensive pre-investigation, faulty motions filed in courts, or bonds written with little or no adherence to even the most basic of underwriting principles. Moreover, in an effort to save money, many of these cases weren't turned over to me until just weeks or even days before the summary judgment deadline; thus, there simply wasn't time to find new angles to work. Had I rejected many of these terminal cases, I'm sure my statistical success rate would be much greater, but I don't like to back down from a good challenge.

Why am I boring you with all these statistics about my door-knocks and arrest totals? Because these statistics illustrate just how tough independent contract work really is.

A distinction should be made here between independent contract work—which is what I do—and in-house contract work. I will refer to in-house bail fugitive recovery persons as *investigators* in an effort to keep the two groups distinct from one another.

In-house investigators are usually salaried employees or contractors who work exclusively for a specific employer. The cases in-house investigators get are typically just days—if not hours—old. As an example, let's imagine that a defendant on bail is supposed to appear in court on a specific date and time but does not show up. The judge presiding over the case will declare the defendant a no-show, issue a bench warrant, and order the bail bond forfeited. The case then goes to the court clerk, who issues and sends out a notice of forfeiture. The bail agent will receive the notice a day or two later, maybe make a couple of calls, and then shoot the case to the in-house investigator(s).

Frequently, the in-house investigator assigned the case will take an address straight from the bail application, go there, and pick up the wayward bail client. Thus, the in-house investigator—who often doesn't use his own money to work a case—may quickly build up impressive stats that are, in my opinion, rather hollow if one steps back and looks at the larger picture.

Let's take it a step further, shall we? The in-house investigator will inevitably run into a case that is just plain messed up. He will spend hundreds of hours logging in surveillance, running around, knocking on doors at bad addresses, and generally putting the bail fugitive on notice. He will use every trick he can think of, in the process alienating possible leads. Days turn into weeks and then to months. When the case is very close to summary judgment, the independent contractor—that's you—gets the call to try to make sense of the case, with little time left, the aftermath of uncooperative leads, and no up-front money to do the job. See how difficult bail recovery work is for independent contractors? Are you still interested?

No two cases are exactly alike. Each one will present a slightly different nuance based on the people and circumstances involved. Thus, I cannot provide you with a tried-and-true investigation formula that works every time. As mentioned, I will provide you with the maps, but it is up to you to apply them to your territory and your cases. Some bounty hunters spend much of their time using databases for their work, but not every bail fugitive can be tracked that way. I focus on old-fashioned door-knocking because I have found that this is the only way to get real-time human intelligence on the more elusive bail fugitives.

Last, throughout this book you will find "lessons from the street." The purpose of these real-life case studies is to show you that the instructive material is based on actual experiences and, therefore, worth your time to take seriously. They also illustrate that I am not perfect. As a bail recovery agent, I have made mistakes from time to time. I can laugh at my mistakes now because they did not result in tragic consequences. It is my sincere hope that you will be open to the tactical information presented here and that you learn from it so that you can avoid making the same mistakes I did.

INTRODUCTION
A Brief Description of the Bail System

I don't want to get bogged down in a long, drawn-out history of bail enforcement, but you need a basic understanding of the bail system and its players before you can appreciate what a bail fugitive recovery person is and what he does.

Simply put, when a person is arrested for a crime, he may be eligible for release from jail until the adjudication of his criminal case, depending on whether the offense he is charged with is "bailable" or not. The statutes vary from state to state, but basically there are four ways of getting out of jail:

- Cite and release—generally speaking, certain offenses require defendants to be booked, but they are released after signing a "cite and release" form and promising to appear as directed (sometimes referred to as "citing out").
- "Own recognizance"—by agreeing to appear at a specified time and place defendants who are not considered flight risks are sometimes released without security being posted.
- Cash bond—by depositing a cash bond or securities in the amount of the bond, defendants (or in conjunction with private individuals acting on their behalf) may secure their own release.
- Bail or appearance bond—by executing a surety bond with one or more commercial bond companies, defendants enter into a contract with the company or companies to appear in court as agreed.

The appearance or bail bond is what we deal with in this book.

Bail is the system of guaranteeing that the person released from jail (the defendant) will appear in court when he is scheduled to do so. It is an agreement between the government entity holding jurisdiction over the accused and the accused and his depositor of bail. The *bond* is money (or something of value) put up to guarantee the defendant's appearance in court; if he misses his court appearance, the

1

judge will order the bond forfeited. The amount of the bond varies, depending on the seriousness of the crime committed and the reliability of the person accused of the crime. A judge or magistrate sets the amount.

WHO DOES WHAT?

Bounty hunter, bail enforcement agent, bail fugitive recovery person, bail runner—these are all terms for a person who tracks down bail fugitives. But the bail process involves more than just the "hunted" and the "hunter." To understand the recovery business, you need to understand the roles of the various players.

- Bail agent—a person or entity licensed by a state (in California by the department of insurance) to transact bail for an insurance company and is backed by the same surety/insurance company
- Bail bondsman—a person who files with the state to transact bail without a surety and does so with his own assets.
- Bail enforcement agent—commonly viewed by the media and public at large as a bounty hunter. *Bail* signifies what area of law the private citizen is working under, *enforcement* characterizes what type of action is employed, and *agent* is taken directly from case cites and codified law(s).
- Bail fugitive—the principal who is out of jail on bail and fails to appear.
- Bail fugitive recovery agent—someone who receives written authorization by the bail or depositor of bail and is contracted to investigate, surveil, locate, and arrest a bail fugitive for surrender to the appropriate court, jail, or police department; or any person who is employed to assist a bail or depositor of bail.
- Bail runner—in those states that specifically prohibit freelance bounty hunters or bail enforcement agents, a bail runner, who works for only one bail agent at a time, is often permitted. A bail runner is contracted to investigate, surveil, locate, and arrest a bail fugitive for surrender to the appropriate

court, jail, or police department. Most states require bail agents to provide a list of all bail runners they employ.
- Bounty hunter—historically, private citizens who sought out wanted criminals for cash rewards were called bounty hunters, and, today, some people continue to identify themselves as bounty hunters—primarily on reality television shows. California law describes a person who is qualified to enforce private civil contracts as a "bail fugitive recovery person," BFRP for short.
- Depositor of bail—a person or agency that has deposited money or security to secure the release of a defendant.
- Indemnitor—commonly called a cosigner, this person signs the bail bond contracts and other documents, wherein he is personally guaranteeing the appearance of the accused and agrees to be responsible for the total penal amount of the bond or bonds and all necessary expenses.
- Independent contractor—bail fugitive recovery person (a bail agent or bondsman is authorized through a state license to transact bail bonds, whereas a bail fugitive recovery person who is not a licensed bail agent cannot bail people out of jail but can enforce the private contract between the parties by physically arresting a bail bond client and returning that person to the proper authority: city, county jail, or court).
- Surety—California Civil Code §2787 defines *surety* as one who promises to answer for the default of another, and it is defined similarly in other states.

So how does the bail system work? Typically, a person is arrested, taken to jail, and booked, and then, depending on the bail schedule set by the judges in the county in question, bail is set.

The arrested person—now called the *defendant*—will most likely have access to a telephone to call someone for help. The defendant can either call a bail bond company or have his outside contact, usually a friend or family member, make the calls. Many jails provide a list or board with contact information for bail bond companies.

If negotiations are successful, then a bail agent or bondsman goes to an agreed-on meeting place (normally the jail where the defendant is being held) to meet with a co-signer to have all the paperwork filled out. Some bondsmen will allow a defendant to co-sign for himself, depending on the situation and the character and trustworthiness of the latter.

The bondsman will submit a bail bond face sheet along with a power of attorney, and the defendant is subsequently released.

Sometimes, the defendant or his family doesn't have enough money to have a bond posted in the original bail amount. When the defendant appears in court, the judge or magistrate may lower the bail, keep it the same, or increase it, or occasionally the defendant may be released on his own recognizance. In many cases, the bail will be reduced, and the bond can be posted at a lower rate that the family can secure.

WHAT HAPPENS IF THE DEFENDANT FAILS TO APPEAR?

If at any time the defendant fails to appear as directed by the court without a good excuse, then the bail bond will be forfeited and a warrant for the arrest of the defendant issued.

Most bondsman will try to resolve the problem diplomatically at first, and this works more often than not. However, there are always those defendants who are actively on the run.

Payment on the forfeited bond will be due in a set period, which varies from state to state (see Appendix K). When the time to pay the forfeited bond draws near, a bondsman who has failed to close the case himself will call a bail fugitive recovery person, who specializes in troubleshooting problem bonds.

If the surety or his agent surrenders the defendant to the proper authorities before the bond comes due, then the forfeiture will be vacated and the judge hearing the case will exonerate the bond, which means that the company is off the hook for the defendant and the defendant must secure another bail bond or return to jail.

Forfeited bonds that cannot be corrected with simple phone calls will require a more proactive approach, such as physically locating the defendant, arresting him, and booking him at the jail in the county where the charges originated.

Larger bail bond companies may have in-house, salaried investigators who work on problem bonds full time. Independent bondsmen normally have someone to whom they've awarded contracts in the past work the forfeited bond.

In either case, the defendant will be systematically tracked, located, identified, arrested, and surrendered whenever possible. That's what bail fugitive recovery is all about.

PART ONE
It's the Law

CHAPTER ONE

Fugitive Recovery Laws

Before attempting to establish yourself in bail recovery work, you must determine whether bail is even legal in your state, under what conditions, and whether you meet the criteria.

Every state has some provision for recovering bail, but not all allow "bounty hunters." Appendix A summarizes the various state laws governing bail recovery. At the time of this printing, four states—Illinois, Kentucky, Oregon, and Wisconsin—outlaw commercial bonding, public bail systems, or bounty hunters. Three states—Florida, North Carolina, and South Carolina—have banned "free-lance" bounty hunters, but allow "bail runners" who work for one bail agent at a time. Thirteen states—Arizona, California, Connecticut, Indiana, Iowa, Louisiana, Mississippi, Nevada, New York, South Dakota, Utah, Washington (effective December 2005), and West Virginia—require bail recovery agents to be licensed. Seven states—Arkansas, Colorado, Georgia, New Hampshire, Oklahoma, Tennessee, and Texas—have enacted legislation regulating bail enforcement agents in various ways.

If you have access to the Internet and want to conduct more in-depth research on bail recovery legislation, you can go to the Web sites listed in the Resources section at the back of the book. Particularly useful is the Fugitive Recovery Network's site (www.fugitive-recovery.com), which provides more details on the laws in all 50 states, including the following:

- Applicable state laws and court rulings
- Licensing requirements for bond agents and bail recovery agents
- Forfeiture provisions to the surety and agent
- Time period between the forfeiture notice and payment
- Forfeiture defenses
- Remission period
- Bail agent's authority to arrest
- Bounty hunter provisions

Just remember that laws are in a constant state of change, so be sure to correctly identify whether or not the laws cited for your state are in fact current.

Certainly, the Internet is a big help in researching bail recovery laws, but in my opinion, the best place to start your legal research is at your local law library, which is generally found in the courthouse in the county seat. For example, in my area, San Joaquin County, the best-equipped law library is located at the courthouse in Stockton.

At first, you may find yourself overwhelmed by the expanse of books filled with legal jargon. However, in most states legislation concerning bail bonds is found in the sections on criminal procedures and/or insurance. A few states have a division of licenses, and statutes relating to licensing criteria likely will be found there. Once you've found the section pertaining to penal/criminal codes and or insurance/licensing regulations, pull the book that contains the section or sections covering "bail" and start scanning for the areas you should study.

Keep in mind that in each state, counties, parishes, cities, towns, and a variety of law enforcement agencies may have slightly different laws or mind-sets when it comes to bail fugitive recovery agents. It is up to you to discern and define the jurisdictions of the different agencies with which you must work and to comply with the specific laws and regulations of each.

Most states, but not all, define who can be a bail recovery agent. The most common criteria are as follows:

- Minimum age (usually either 18 or 21)
- Proof of completion of mandatory training requirements and/or passing of examination
- U.S. citizenship or legal residency
- State residency (usually 6 months to 1 year)
- No felonies or convictions for violent crimes (criminal background check, with finger-printing, required)
- No mental health problems that would interfere with the ability to perform the duties of the job

For example, in California prior to January 1, 2000, any person of "suitable age" and with no felony convictions could be given an authority-to-arrest form, a court-certified copy of the bail bond, and begin the hunt. This is no longer the case. Now you must be at least 18 years old and carry proof that the following criteria have been met:

- Completion of an 832 PC course approved by the Peace Officer Standards and Training Commission
- Completion of 12 hours of classroom education pursuant to California Insurance Code §1810.7
- Completion of a power to arrest course pursuant to California Business and Professions Code §7583.7
- Or possession of California private investigator license pursuant to Chapter 11.3 of Division 3 starting with Business and Professions Code §7512

In California, if you don't have private investigator's license, you will have to find a community college offering the one-week 832 PC course, which costs around $100. Next, you apply at a security company, take the powers-to-arrest test, get your B&P 7583.7 slip, and then respectfully decline the job. Finally, contact one of the prelicensing bail agent schools and sign up there or check the California Department of Insurance Web site at www.insurance.ca.gov for more information on other schools. This two-day course will run you around $400. For other states, a simple Internet search using the key words *bail licensing* should do the trick.

Once you've got all of your certifications, make miniature copies, laminate them, and slip them into your dedicated wallet (one you use only for bail work, which is discussed in more detail later). Stick the originals in a file folder and keep them in your "mobile office" for viewing if necessary.

LESSON FROM THE STREET

It had been a long night of hopping from city to city in search of three bail fugitives. We were all tired by the time we were ready to launch our last residential inspection, so we parked at a convenience store, had a passer-by take a couple of group photos of us for posterity, and called the local dispatch to advise the cops of our intentions. The dispatcher told us to wait where we were for a supervisor.

A few minutes passed before a marked patrol car arrived. The driver, a Hispanic man with distinguished gray hair at the temples and sergeant stripes, pulled up to where we were standing.

"You guys bounty hunters?"

Jerry replied, "No, sir, bounty hunters chew tobacco and have three first names; we're bail agents."

The sergeant looked us over. I caught his name tag. He was the same sergeant who had arrested one of my contemporaries a month earlier for failing to have all of his documents in order.

"Let me see your 1299 Certs," he demanded.

My whole team withdrew their dedicated wallets and began handing the sergeant miniaturized, laminated copies of all of our 1299 certifications [see page 15 for more on 1299 certifications, which are required in California before a recovery agent can attempt an arrest] and even certifications that weren't required.

"Okay, okay," the overwhelmed sergeant conceded. "How do you read these?" Jerry handed him a pocket-magnifying sheet of plastic. The sergeant examined a couple of certifications and said, "Happy hunting."

The patrol sergeant, at the very least, would have run us out of town and, at the very worst, moved to arrest my whole team had we not been in compliance with 1299.

You will most likely not be asked to produce your certifications, but, if things go wrong, you can bet any part of your anatomy that the local deputy district attorney will heavily scrutinize your whole operation.

Get legal before you take on that first case, and make certain you carry all the requisite certification with you.

CHAPTER TWO

Your Legal Authority to Arrest

You shouldn't attempt to make bail fugitive arrests without a working knowledge of the laws under which you will be making arrests as a private citizen.

The bail bond is considered to be a legal contract between party one (the government entity holding jurisdiction) and party two (the person accused of the crime and his sureties, who agree to pay the amount of the bond if the accused fails to appear in court as specified). The bondman's right to rearrest a person out on bail pending trial derives from medieval common law and has been upheld by various U.S. courts, including the U.S. Supreme Court. In 1873, the U.S. Supreme Court in *Taylor v. Taintor* (83 US 366, 21 2ed 287) held that a defendant released on bail is regarded as having been delivered to the custody of the depositor of bail, that is, the surety. Moreover, the court held that a surety's dominion is a continuance of the original imprisonment and that the surety, or his authorized agent, without new process since none is needed, may apprehend the defendant.

> *[The sureties] whenever they choose to do so may seize [the bail fugitive] and deliver him up in their discharge; and if this cannot be done at once, they may imprison him until it can be done. They may pursue him to another state; may arrest him on the Sabbath, and, if necessary, may break and enter his house for that purpose. The seizure is not made by virtue of new process. None is needed. It is likened to the rearrest by the sheriff of an escaping prisoner . . . The bail have their Principal on a string, and may pull the string whenever they please, and render him in their discharge.*
> —*Taylor v. Taintor* (83 US 366, 21 2ed 287)

Since the relationship between the surety and the principal is a private contractual one, an original right derived through the State, *Taylor v. Taintor* held that a surety can travel to other states and arrest a principal and return him to the state where his bond was executed, without having to establish jurisdiction. The surety can discharge himself of the obligation of the bond by surrendering the principal at any time, even before forfeiture of the bond. The right to pursue fugitives across state lines conveyed by this case does not extend to foreign countries.

> *Bail have no power to arrest the principal in a foreign country. But, as between the states of the American Union, the bail of one held to answer in one state may arrest the principal in another state, and no requisition is necessary.*
> —*Nicolls v. Ingersoll*, 7 Johns (N.Y. 1810)

Until recently, the common law principles granting sureties and their agents power and authority have been modified very little. It must be noted, however, that the 1873 decision and many of the subsequent court decisions upholding it were written for a different time and sensibility. Excesses by some bounty hunters and the vagueness of the language have led to some fixes by various courts and legislatures.

The federal Uniform Criminal Extradition Act (UCEA), passed in 1937, established the formal extradition process used by state law enforcement and judicial agencies for returning criminal fugitives from the state where they were apprehended to the state where the crime took place. All states except Missouri and South Carolina have adopted the UCEA. How does UCEA apply to the recovery of bail fugitives? At least one state (Oregon) has applied UCEA to bail fugitives. This means that the fugitive is entitled to a formal extradition process before he can be returned to the state where his bond is held.

Even in states that don't extend UCEA coverage for bail fugitives, out-of-state recovery agents may be severely restricted in whether and how they can arrest bail fugitives. Most states require notification of local law enforcement agencies of the presence of out-of-state recovery agents and their intent to arrest, and some states (e.g., Arizona and Louisiana) force out-of-state agents to contract with a licensed bond agent in the state where the apprehension takes place. For example, I meet the requirements to make bail arrests in California, but I am not licensed in Nevada or in any other state, so, despite *Taylor v. Taintor*, I cannot arbitrarily cross a state line and make a bail arrest.

The law by its very nature is in a constant state of change; therefore, it is your responsibility to properly research your intended area of operation to determine whether or not you have the lawful right to cross into another state and make a bail arrest. It is up to you to know the laws and to comply with them.

LESSON FROM THE STREET

I answered the telephone one afternoon to find Jenny on the other end of the line completely frantic. It turns out that her husband had been jailed after admitting to charges related to sexually molesting his granddaughter.

"Please, Mr. Venator, you have to help me; no one else will," she begged, sniffing.

Jenny and her husband, Phil, had no money to post the bond, but Jenny offered Phil's coin collection to hold until the bail bond premium was paid. Jenny also offered to put her house up for collateral.

It sounded good, so I drove on over to Jenny's house, where I inspected the coins, and we signed the appropriate papers. Later when I arrived back at Jenny's with Phil I explained that they had 90 days to pay up or the coins would be sold. Well, 90 days came and went, so I sold the coins, which appraised at around $2,500.

Later Phil called and threatened to sue me for selling his "$30,000 coin collection." He also wanted me to remove the lien on his house so he could get a "$50,000 loan." At this point I figured the loan was to either hire an attorney to sue me or skip out on the bail.

I ambled on over to the county recorder's office and found that Phil and Jenny were actually upside down on their mortgage, thus leaving my $100,000 bond unsecured. I decided to surrender Phil before he had a chance to abscond.

My team and I donned black business suits instead of tactical gear, since I didn't view Phil as dangerous. I didn't want to come off as intimidating, so it seemed appropriate to make the arrest in professional business attire. The arrest and surrender went without a hitch. But shortly thereafter, Jenny and Phil sued me in small-claims court, asserting that my actions were illegal and had caused financial losses because he had to secure another bail after I surrendered him. They also wanted to be paid for a bail premium that was never collected in the first place!

In court on the appointed day it was just my luck to draw a knee-jerk, liberal judge who felt it was okay to dispense with the rule of law in favor of ruling from the bench. His veins noticeably protruded as he screamed at me, "What gives you the right to enter these poor people's home and arrest one of them?" Pausing, he then asked, "And why were you all dressed in scary black?"

The hearing was for two separate small-claims suits totaling $10,000, so it was important that I convince the judge that my actions were legal. I explained that the "scary black" worn on the night of the arrest was also my attire in court that day, and I, with confidence, began to recite various cases and codes that outlined my authority to arrest. My argument prevailed, and the judge dismissed both cases against me.

Whether you're explaining your presence in a city to an ignorant officer or your right to arrest to an equally ignorant judge, you need to be able to present your authority to arrest accurately and articulately.

CHAPTER THREE

Legal Documents to Acquire and Carry

As already mentioned, the documents you must have to lawfully arrest a bail fugitive differ in form and nomenclature from state to state, but they include some version of the following:

- A *court*-certified copy of the bail bond or
- An affidavit of undertaking provided by the bail agent
- An authority-to-arrest form provided and signed by the bail agent

The surety insurance company prints documents, not the bail agent. Moreover, the department of insurance must be notified prior to any surety issuing any form to any of its bail agents. In addition to the above documents, you should have the following items before making any arrest attempts:

- Booking photo of the bail fugitive (do not rely on a Polaroid from the bail agent)
- Copy of the bail application
- Copy of the notice of forfeiture from the court clerk
- *Court*-certified copy of any warrant(s) on the bail fugitive
- 1299 certification (California Penal Code Section 1299.08[a] through 1299.08[d]) or equivalent in your state

Remember, you are *not* a bail fugitive recovery person without the mandatory documents in your possession at the time of arrest or attempted arrest. Failure to have the mandatory documents can subject you to criminal charges, which again vary from state to state, but could include:

- Felonious false imprisonment

- Conspiracy
- Assault and/or battery
- Burglary
- Kidnapping

Also don't forget that you can carry a weapon only if you are legally eligible to do so and the arrest you are attempting is a lawful one (see Chapter 5). An unlawful arrest could lead to a weapons charge as well.

You will encounter people in this trade who scoff at the necessity of having these legal documents when attempting to apprehend a defendant. My strong advice to you is to ignore these people.

LESSON FROM THE STREET

I dislike hunting bail fugitives during the day because they're typically not home and the streets are crowded. In this case, however, our only lead consisted of a positive employment check at a computer software company. The bond on this bail fugitive was $50,000, and I desperately needed the commission.

I knew that all of my documents were in order, but when I got stuck in traffic, I decided to call the court for one final last-minute check on the bail fugitive. The clerk informed me that the bail fugitive had not only appeared in court that very morning, but that his case had been dismissed. I immediately notified my team that the hunt was cancelled. Even though my documents were in order, arresting the bail fugitive would have been unlawful, subjecting my team and me to severe liability.

The lesson here is to always perform one *more* last-minute check to ensure that the bail fugitive is still wanted. The situation described in this example is not uncommon in this business.

CHAPTER FOUR

What Is Your Legal Liability?

Any person who has been stripped of his financial assets or spent any time in jail should have a fair understanding of liability. But you might not be aware of all the ways your actions can make you legally liable if you don't follow the appropriate laws.

- You could be arrested for false arrest, kidnapping, assault or battery, or even homicide if someone gets killed. If convicted, you could be imprisoned and/or fined. In addition, you could end up with a criminal record, possibly limiting your career options and making you ineligible to own, possess, or have custody and control of a firearm.
- You could be held responsible for property damage whether or not an arrest goes wrong.
- You could be arrested and maybe even charged with trespassing or incur other civil penalties for being too aggressive at a third-party residence.
- You could be sued civilly.
- You could have a restraining order placed against you, which also could affect your ability to carry a weapon, enter into certain professions, qualify for business or professional licenses, etc.

From my years in this field, I can spot liability where others cannot. I have pointed out liability, been told to stow it, and later had these skeptics admit that my concerns were correct. It is important that you hone your ability to spot potential trouble every second that you are working on a case.

After deciding to go full-time in bail fugitive recovery, I bought some books and a video on the subject, but the references to liability in them were very vague. One indicated somewhat nonchalantly that bounty hunters "might occasionally" get arrested while working a case. The mentality of being OK with getting arrested was particularly troubling to me.

Most uninitiated people don't differentiate between getting arrested and being convicted. The latter has far-reaching consequences inconsistent with most careers worth entering these days. This goes for bail fugitive recovery as well. I know of good people who cannot pass a background check based on a minor mistake made decades earlier. I can help you spot and avoid such trouble so that your record remains clean.

I literally spent two solid weeks in the law library obtaining a working knowledge on the legalities of hunting bail fugitives as a private citizen before attempting to apprehend anyone. My efforts have paid off on numerous occasions, as they have kept me from being sued or arrested or incurring any other postoperation liability.

You would be remiss in entering into this trade without doing your own homework. But, whereas it took me weeks of running around just to get a feel for the trade, you can gain tremendous insight by simply reading this book and following the maps I include. Of course, that doesn't mean that I have done all your homework for you.

While working bail fugitive cases, you will frequently encounter law enforcement personnel and lawyers, and most of these hard-working professionals will be completely ignorant of the bail laws under which you are working. You need to know these laws completely so you can explain to them why the laws authorize you to do your job. It'll make your job easier and earn you valuable allies for future operations. I cannot impress upon you enough how important it is to learn your trade to the last detail.

LESSON FROM THE STREET

We found a well-lit parking lot in the city of Unicorn because we didn't want to draw the attention of the local police. The convenience store lot was ideal for resting and gathering my customary fuel source during long nights of hopping from city to city: Mountain Dew and Kit Kats.

Our target house had been discovered only

hours earlier during the inspection of another target location and had not been reconnoitered. I sent Tom, one of my arrest agents, ahead to do a cursory drive-by in his foreign car because official-looking cars (I drove a Ford Crown Victoria Police Interceptor) tend to spook people in certain neighborhoods.

My partner Jerry broke out the case file on our fugitive and initiated contact with the local police dispatcher. Jerry provided the dispatch operator with all the details required by law, and I heard Jerry ask for a civil standby. Jerry approached me and said, "Dispatch says that they don't have any officers available to assist. What do you want to do?"

"How long until they do?" I asked.

Jerry furrowed his brow and grunted, "About 45 minutes or longer."

I decided that we were good to go without police support. It is nice to have the local heat with you, but it isn't always possible.

Jerry notified the dispatcher that we would be attempting a bail arrest within 10 minutes and supplied all the information on our team: target location; number and descriptions of team members; clothing worn by team members; make, model, and license plate numbers of vehicles; and descriptions of suspect.

Tom returned and popped the trunk on my car. He unhitched and swung the grease board from the trunk and retrieved a grease pen from one of the many bags in the trunk. He then drew a map detailing the target structure, the streets, obstacles, and everything else we needed to know. All of us then set our cell phones to ring police dispatch if needed.

I surveyed our arrest team, which consisted of five seasoned agents. The breakdown of assignments would be as follows:

- I would knock on the door, gain permission to enter, and then control the inhabitants found there. (I've been denied entrance only once in 1,500 tries.)
- Jerry and Tom—heavily armored (Kevlar helmets, Level IIIA vests with Level IV ceramic plates, knee and shin protectors, Kevlar groin protectors, ballistic face shields) and equipped with various search tools (e.g., mirror and flashlight attached to a pole) to look in closets, cabinets, under beds, and in cluttered living quarters—would enter after me and conduct a systematic, two-man search of the dwelling.
- The fourth agent would maintain security around the front of the structure.
- The fifth agent would watch the rear of the structure.
- Agents four and five would also respond inside the dwelling if needed or, since they were carrying the least amount of equipment, would pursue the fugitive with the intention of directing the balance of the team (or law enforcement personnel if any showed up) in the pursuit.

I met with Jerry in front of the target structure while the rest of the team conducted a tactical withdrawal. It took us less than five minutes to gain permission to enter and search the house—our guy was not there.

Suddenly, a marked police cruiser arrived, and a rather large, unidentified patrol sergeant stepped out of the car.

I greeted him, "Hello, sergeant. What can we do for you?"

"Are you guys peace officers?"

I could tell from his tone that this wasn't going to be a "smoking-and-joking" session. I holstered my flashlight and approached him with my gloved hands extended away from my body at a slight angle. "No, sir. We're bail agents."

The sergeant pulled up on his sagging duty belt and demanded, "What gives you the right to come over here and serve a warrant?"

Here we go, I thought. This guy clearly had no concept of bail law, and now he was going to try to arrest us on something.

I quoted various California penal code sections along with case law, but he wasn't impressed. In fact, I could see that his brain was working to put a case together against us. If you have ever been, or even applied to be, a police officer, you know how cops are. (I have tested for approximately 30 different agencies.) Cops inherently refuse to change their minds once a course of action has been chosen. During police oral boards, you'll score high, whether or not your answers are correct, if the panel fails to make you change your mind on any given scenario. You'll fail if you answer "A" and then are forced to change your answer to "B."

At this point, my job was to sit back, observe, and determine how to keep the sergeant from deciding to arrest my team. Although any such action on his part would have been highly improper and grounds for a civil suit, I wanted to avoid this unpleasantness before any minds were made up.

Meanwhile, Jerry had broken out his unabridged California penal code book (the abridged version that cops carry doesn't have the sections on bail and bail fugitive recovery persons) and was giving the sergeant an instant class on bail law. I turned around and noticed 19 fine-looking police officers, one K-9 handler and his beautiful German shepherd, and the fact that these smiling officers were getting closer.

Although totally correct in his argument, Jerry was doing just that with the sergeant—arguing.

(As a former law enforcement officer, I can give you this piece of advice: when dealing with cops as a bail fugitive recovery person, you *never* argue because they're always going to win, even if they're completely sideways on the issue. At the very worst, you'll be arrested. You may not be charged, but why risk it?)

The sergeant was red in the face, shaking, sweating, and looking for the chance to bust my team. He waved his finger at Jerry and shouted, "You will not come into my town and disturb anyone! I don't care what book you pull out!" (I thought it odd that a field supervisor would cast aside the book he is hired to enforce.) "You have no right to approach this house!"

I decided to intervene. "Excuse me, sergeant."

He glared at me.

"I respect your position, and, with your permission, we will now leave your city."

"But . . ." Jerry started.

I cast Jerry a look signaling that my decision was final. "We're leaving."

Had it not been for our ability to present the laws pertaining to bail arrest clearly, concisely, and with confidence, I am convinced that the sergeant would have wrongly arrested my team out of sheer ignorance. Of course, the whole matter would have been dropped ultimately, but it made no sense to push the sergeant at that time since my goal on any recovery job is to *make* money, not *spend* money on attorney fees. Besides, the fugitive wasn't there anyway.

The lesson is that you should be able to intelligently articulate the applicable laws and regulations should you ever be questioned by law enforcement officers, as well as able to judge when it is worth fighting and when it is best to walk away and avoid legal entanglements. This book will help you with both.

CHAPTER FIVE

Firearms and the Law

In the bail fugitive recovery trade a gun is a defensive tool carried to protect and preserve human life. It can be carried while making or attempting to make *lawful* arrests only, provided that you can legally possess the firearm in the first place.

Again, the laws of the state and municipality where you will be working must guide your actions concerning the carry and use of firearms. Make it your first priority to have a working knowledge of the gun laws before taking steps to make an arrest while carrying a firearm.

Under federal law you are prohibited from possessing a firearm if you

- have been convicted of a crime punishable by imprisonment for a term exceeding one year;
- are a fugitive from justice;
- are an unlawful user of or addicted to any controlled substance;
- have been adjudicated as mentally defective or been committed to a mental institution;
- are an alien illegally or unlawfully in the United States or an alien on a nonimmigrant visa;
- have been discharged from the armed forces under dishonorable conditions;
- have renounced your U.S. citizenship;
- are the subject of a restraining order against an intimate partner or child of that partner;
- or have been convicted of a misdemeanor crime of domestic violence.

The city and state where you live or intend to work may also have laws regarding the possession and use of firearms. It is up to you to research these ordinances and comply with them. You should have a current, unabridged penal code book from the state where you intend to work. It is a valuable resource that you will use regularly in your work. Note, however, that the penal code does not exempt bail fugitive recovery agents from firearms laws that apply to all citizens of the state.

The following are my general recommendations on firearms carry by those in the bail recovery field:

- I advise that you carry your weapon exposed, but if your state issues concealed carry permits and you are granted one, you can carry your firearm concealed. Be advised, however, that the agency that issued your permit is most likely not aware that you are using it for employment purposes. Therefore, you could lose your permit after questioning by a cop on the street who decides to call the issuing agency for a "heads-up." In California you can be charged with carrying a concealed weapon if you are found to have a weapon directly under your control and that weapon is capable of being concealed.
- Your weapon should be unmodified. There are thousands of laws pertaining directly to firearm modifications, and these laws change constantly, so play it safe and keep your weapon stock.
- The only way to transport a weapon safely is in your trunk, unloaded, locked separate from the ammunition, which should also be locked in the trunk. Don't use a glove box for transporting a weapon.
- Choose your ammunition carefully. On one hand, you don't want to have to explain to a jury why you killed someone with the hottest, fastest, meanest load you could find. Yet, you don't want to get killed because your ball ammunition failed to stop an aggressor. I suggest that you use something in the middle; your local gun dealer can help you in this area. Be sure to cycle your intended ammunition through your weapon before carrying it on the job, so you don't get into a firefight with ammunition that doesn't feed properly in your weapon.
- Always draw and use a weapon responsibly. You could be charged with brandishing a firearm if you draw your weapon in a rude, angry, or threatening manner in the presence of another. In other words, don't break out the handgun for the sake of flexing your muscles.

- You should know that possession of any instrument that decreases the report of a firearm is a felony, so don't try using a silencer.
- In some states (including California) you cannot possess a mounted riflescope that enables you to detect targets in the dark. As always, check your local gun laws for guidance on using night-vision on rifles. In short, do not get caught with any night vision equipment that can be made to fit on your rifle.
- Make sure that your teammates can also legally possess a firearm. You don't want to get into a shooting situation with a teammate who shouldn't have had a gun in the first place.

By this point you're probably scratching your head and wondering what you *can* do. Well, if doing so is legal in the first place, you can carry a weapon exposed when making or attempting to make a lawful arrest. Now this is a very crucial point: the arrest you are attempting must be lawful. (I will expound on making a lawful arrest in more detail later.) You may also carry a loaded firearm, when it is otherwise lawful, if you believe that you are in immediate, grave danger and that the weapon is necessary for the preservation of your life.

If you are pursuing a defendant from one state to another, you must also check the firearms laws of any state you enter to make sure you are still legal, especially when it comes to concealed carry. If you are an off-duty or retired law enforcement officer, you should be aware of the provisions of the Law Enforcement Officer's Safety Act. Signed into law in July 2004, this federal law exempts qualified current and retired law enforcement officers from state and local laws prohibiting the carrying of concealed handguns. Note that the law does not exempt officers from federal firearm laws; therefore, you cannot carry firearms on airplanes, into federal buildings, on federal property, or in national parks. Other areas are also restricted: (1) in localities where *state* law (not *local* law) allows private persons or entities to prohibit or restrict the possession of concealed weapons on their property, and (2) the state can prohibit concealed weapons from being carried onto state or local property.

A "qualified" active law enforcement officer is someone employed by or retired from a local, state, or federal law enforcement agency who meets the criteria established in the law. A current law enforcement officer must (1) be authorized to carry a firearm, (2) have statutory powers of arrest, (3) meet the standards of his agency to use a firearm, (4) not be under the influence of any drugs or alcohol, and (5) not be the subject of any disciplinary action. A retired officer must (1) have retired in good standing with at least 15 years service and for reasons other than mental instability, or have been retired because of a service-related injury; (2) have not forfeited his retirement benefits; (3) be able to legally own a weapon under federal law; (4) meet the same proficiency standards required of an active-duty law enforcement officer in his state, and (5) not be under the influence of drugs or alcohol. For more information on the Law Enforcement Officer's Safety Act, check the Web site of the Law Enforcement Alliance of America (www.leaa.org).

If you have your documents in order, have checked to make sure that the bail fugitive is still wanted, know that the fugitive is a dangerous shooter, and are attempting to arrest the bail fugitive at a known crack house, then I'd say you're pretty well covered. It all boils down to common sense and your ability to decipher firearms laws.

LESSON FROM THE STREETS

"Hurry! He's packing his bags as we speak!"

The bail agent was frantic, and I hadn't been in the trade long enough at the time to be sure what was what, but the call came and I rolled. At this time I was without backup, so I called my brother, who was going to meet me at the assigned site.

I met with the bail agent and got all of the

necessary documents. The bail agent told me that the bail fugitive had skipped on an $8,000 bond, and he was presently at home.

"So why don't you go get him?" I asked.

The bail agent began sweating and breathing heavily, and his pupils were dilated. Something had triggered an adrenal response.

"I tried to pick him up with some help, but he screamed that he had a gun and tried to run us over with his truck," the bail agent confessed.

I thought about it for a second. "You think he's at home?"

The bail agent threw his hairy arms in the air. "Yeah, I just called him, and he said, 'Come and get me.' C'mon, Rex, you gotta help me."

A short while later I knocked on the door. A man answered, but he didn't look like the booking photo, as usual. "Hi, may I speak to Charlie Logan?"

"Yeah, that's me, what do you? . . ."

I drew my weapon and yelled, "Let me see your hands!" Charlie raised his hands. I wasn't playing games with this guy, so I pushed him back first against the nearest wall. "Turn around and face the wall."

"Ah, fuck that," Charlie said while pushing at me.

I used my nongun hand to withdraw a stun gun. I placed it on his chest with the probes facing up and let the sparks fly.

His eyes lit up in sheer fright. "Hey, whoa!"

"Turn around." The loud sparks humbled him, so it wasn't necessary to actually stun him; I only wanted to get his attention.

I noticed that Charlie's wife was standing just inside the entryway of the house and screaming into the telephone. "Please hurry; the home invaders are kidnapping my husband!"

This incident happened in 1992 when there

wasn't any requirement in California to notify the police before attempting an arrest. Besides, the bail fugitive was reportedly packing to leave, so I had to move quickly.

The first police officer pulled up while I was escorting Charlie to my T-Bird. In light of the circumstances, my brother and I assumed the felony stop position until the matter could be straightened out.

It was a very hot day, and the bail fugitive sat in a closed-up police cruiser for more than an hour, while a gaggle of the city's finest pored over penal code books covering the top of a police car and the watch commander made phone calls to verify that our guy was in fact wanted. Eventually, the cops handed us our fugitive, who was then put in the backseat of my car. For security reasons, my brother and I placed our weapons in the trunk in plain view of the cops.

One of the wiser police officers approached us and said, "Oh yeah, you guys do have permits for these weapons, right?

Here we go, I thought. "Check Penal Code 12031(k)," I said confidently.

"12031(k)," the police officer yelled to his partners.

They all started flipping pages in the code book and ultimately flashed the thumbs-up sign.

"Okay, you gentlemen have a good day," the watch commander offered.

Knowing the laws concerning bail enforcement work has helped me more than once, and it is vitally important when it comes to firearms.

WEAPON RETENTION

Deciding to carry a firearm for your work involves more than simply researching and complying with the relevant laws. It also means that you must be capable of keeping your weapon out of the hands of the bad guys you are attempting to arrest.

You have probably heard stories of police officers being killed with their own weapons. These stories shouldn't be ignored by anyone considering bail fugitive recovery work.

One of the deputies in the sheriff's department where I used to work was transporting a prisoner to the county hospital when the prisoner quickly snatched the deputy's service revolver out of the department-issued, simple thumb-break holster. Fortunately, the deputy was able to slap the weapon out of the prisoner's hands. The prisoner then ran into the hospital, where a fight ensued, and hospital workers helped control and restrain him.

Retention Holsters

As a result of this incident, the sheriff's department issued Level III retention holsters to all its badge personnel—me included—and introduced mandatory combat shooting and weapon retention training. It's one thing to fire at paper targets while standing still, but running over and between obstacles while firing is a whole different thing.

To demonstrate, with a standard laser pointer mark a wall that is more than 20 feet away while trying to keep the dot stationary. You'll notice that the red dot bounces around like an insect leaping off a hot light. Now, do 30 or so jumping jacks or skip rope for a minute or two and then try the laser dot again. You'll notice that keeping the dot still is much more difficult when you are winded. Running from barricade to barricade while firing at thin, metal knock-down targets is far more difficult that one could imagine with no frame of reference. This type of training followed the gun grab at the hospital along with weapon retention training.

As I said, the department also issued us Level III retention holsters. The directions, as best as I can recall, suggested drawing the weapon past the three-lock system 200 times before using the new holsters on duty.

The first time I used the Level III retention holster on the range, I noticed that it took just a fraction of a second longer to get the weapon out of the holster and to put it into action than it took with the thumb-break holster. After passing the range course with the new holsters, it was off to the mats, where we each yanked at holstered guns and tussled with each other trying to get someone else's gun while retaining our own.

It was at this training course that I learned how keep my weapon in the holster once a would-be gun-grabber made his move by reaching for my weapon. From there, I learned how to trap the attacker's offending hand or hands and to knock the attacker off balance. Based on the techniques I learned in that course, I later mastered various pain and compliance techniques to subdue and eventually handcuff attackers.

Now, on a good day these compliance techniques usually work, but on a bad day, things may not go as planned. I would consider anyone trying to take my weapon as posing an imminent threat to my life and act accordingly. If I lose my gun, I assume that the new owner may take my life with it; therefore, I will fight to retain my weapon under such circumstances like my life or the lives of my partners depend on it.

I can recall my first day of qualifying at the sheriff's gun range after being issued the new holster. My score dropped slightly because of the delay in drawing my weapon, and at first I didn't like the new holster. However, with time spent on the range, I found that I felt more confident using a holster that offered me protection from gun-grabs.

I later took what I learned from these weapon retention sessions and incorporated the information into the training program for my new trainees.

Interview Stance

You should use the interview stance when dealing with street contacts or a bail fugitive. The interview stance is where you stand with your nongun-side foot forward of your gun-side foot. The point is to keep your weapon as far away from the interviewee as is possible. Moreover, weapon retention techniques begin from this seemingly nonthreatening, balanced stance.

LESSON FROM THE STREET

Jerry had asked me to help him make an arrest to close one of his contracts. I agreed, so we traveled to Timberlake, where we notified the local police of our intentions. Several police officers made contact with us, smoked and joked, and offered to station themselves just around the corner in case we needed them. Department policy prohibited them from helping us directly, so I gave them a spare radio to listen to our radio traffic.

This was Jerry's case, so he went first. He gained permission to enter and search the house. I followed him in. The house reeked of urine. The bail fugitive was sound asleep on the living room couch. Jerry cleared the house of any dangers while I stood over the sleeping fugitive.

Directly behind me was a young girl sleeping on the floor. She woke up and appeared to be scared, so I withdrew a stuffed toy (I carry small toys with me to soothe any small children who may be startled by my presence) out of my tactical vest and gave it to her. Behind my right shoulder Grandma watched from a second couch. The living room made for tight quarters. The front door was behind me, and the bail fugitive was trapped. I only hoped that he wouldn't fight.

Jerry signaled that he was ready, and I woke the bail fugitive, who sat up suddenly and looked shocked. As usual, I was about to begin my "these handcuffs are just procedure until we figure things out" speech when Jerry suddenly declared, "You're under arrest!"

I thought, *Oh shit.*

The bail fugitive stood up, looked at the front door, at me, at my gun, at the front door, at me, at my gun, and I knew it was on.

The couch hadn't been cleared of any weapons, so I countered the bail fugitive's move. He quickly—and I mean quickly—grabbed at my gun. I caught his offending arm, trapped the hand reaching for my gun onto my holster, and used my left shoulder to strike his left shoulder while pushing down on his hand. I performed a disco-like move and got behind him. Jerry jumped in, and before long we had him handcuffed, in the car, and turned over to authorities.

His reaching for my gun wasn't personal.

The bail fugitive did what he thought he had to do, and I reacted accordingly. His efforts to snatch my weapon were not likely to succeed, at any rate. First, he had to get past my training and experience. Second, his tugging would have been fruitless, since my weapon could not be drawn the way he was pulling at it. Had I been wearing a standard holster, his efforts might have succeeded.

Of course it would have been better if Jerry hadn't announced our intentions immediately, but in this work it's all about reactions.

CHAPTER SIX

Use-of-Force Guidelines

It is reasonable to assume that at some point a bail fugitive will resist your efforts to help him find the way back to court, so it is in your best interest to have a plan to make him do what he obviously doesn't want to do. This plan should include how you will use force, if it proves necessary. As with all legal aspects of this job, the laws governing the use of force vary from state to state and from city to city. It is your responsibility to know the laws and comply with them.

Generally, what use-of-force plan would be better to explain—should it become necessary—than one with which the police, the district attorney's office, and a jury are familiar? Therefore, the following is based on a typical use-of-force policy by which the cops on the street are governed.

Force is defined as follows: overcoming resistance by the exertion of strength, weight, and power. The following is a guideline for its use.

- Use only the minimum amount of force and restraint reasonably necessary to establish and maintain control of person who displays violent, threatening, or resistive behavior.
- Never use physical force as punishment.
- In every case in which force is necessary, use good judgment in how that force is applied.
- If you believe that bodily injury is about to be inflicted upon another person, you may use such force as is reasonably necessary to prevent injury to that person.

The degrees of escalating force are as follows:

A. Verbal direction
  1. Telling a bail fugitive what to do
  2. Designating one person as spokesman to ensure that all directions are clear and authoritative

B. Show of force
   1. Confronting or surrounding a bail fugitive with superior numbers
C. Leading by the arm
   1. Always exercise caution when taking anyone by the arm
   2. Fight can easily begin here
D. Arrest and control techniques: guiding by the arm, low-profile handcuffing for compliant fugitives, high-risk handcuffing for those who resist, wristlocks, wrist take-down to prone control, prone handcuffing, and all-out fights to gain control and restrain
E. Any means
   1. Used to defend against immediate, life-threatening aggression by any person who attempts to cause you or another person great bodily injury or death

Of course, before putting your entrepreneurial little hands on anyone and using reasonable force to arrest and detain him, you had better be damned sure you've got the right person and that person is still classified as a fugitive.

Whether his account was true or not I cannot say, but a person—claiming to be a bail enforcement agent—claimed that he used an electronic device to shoot a fleeing bail fugitive for the purposes of ending a foot chase! Now, in one foot chase (described in Chapter 7) I engaged a person who turned out to be the brother of the bail fugitive in question, and I can only imagine the problems I would have encountered, following an unlawful use of force, such as using an electronic device on a third party. In the example I described, the guy was dirty for something and most likely had warrants out for his arrest, or he wouldn't have run, and therefore he didn't complain.

As of this writing, controversy is mounting about the use of electronic devices, which can sometimes result in death, even though they are classified as less than lethal. Therefore, as a bail enforcement agent, I am disinclined to use any weapons whose use may later be questioned.

Before using any defensive devices (with an emphasis on the word *defensive*), you would be best served by conducting an in-depth study of how the law in your state addresses such weapons as batons, pepper sprays, pepper balls, beanbag projectiles, rubber bullets, and electronic devices.

When I say "in-depth study," I'm not talking about a cursory review of simple criminal or penal codes; I'm talking about locating and studying applicable case citations involving the use of less-than-lethal devices by private citizens. You may be able to find such references at your local law library or on the Internet.

My studies indicate that less-than-lethal devices are not to be used offensively. What I mean by this is that a bail enforcement agent should not walk up to a suspected bail fugitive and summarily spray him with pepper spray to begin the arrest, as was alleged in one news account, with charges pending against the agent at the time of this writing. Batons, pepper spray, pepper balls, beanbag projectiles, rubber bullets, and electronic devices cannot—in my opinion—be lawfully used to force a bail fugitive who is resisting arrest into submission.

If, at any point, you or another person is in imminent danger of great bodily harm or death—and cannot escape—then the use of less-than-lethal devices may be justified to end the aggression. Of course, if things get bad enough to employ less-than-lethal devices, then the use of a firearm to protect life may be the last best resort. My mentioning less-than-lethal devices and defensive firearm use in the same sentence indicates where I stand on justifiable use of less-than-lethal devices. I place less-than-lethal devices just below the use of deadly force and would employ such defensive devices only in the most critical of incidents.

The justified use of force also includes going hands-on with a bail fugitive. I've seen training footage where the students are trained to rush a *suspected* bail fugitive, push him against the wall, search him, and then place handcuffs on him. The problem is, how do you know if you have the right person? If that person has not committed a crime in your presence, then why are you using force on him? If you take the described action against an innocent party, you may end up facing serious criminal charges.

Do less-than-lethal devices have a place in the bail enforcement agent's arsenal of defensive tools? The answer is yes and no, depending on your state laws and the attitudes of law enforcement in your intended area of operation. As you can see, however, this is a complex question with too many variables for you to simply and blindly incorporate less-than-lethal devices in your operations without first doing your homework.

Whether or not you subscribe to my interpretation of less-than-lethal device use is up to you, but don't forget that I have been doing this specialized work for nearly 13 years with no postoperation liability whatsoever.

LESSON FROM THE STREET

A bail agent, and master bounty hunter, requested my assistance in apprehending a man who failed to appear earlier that day. The bail agent didn't have any collateral on the bond, which is common, and he had learned that his client was planning to vacate the area.

We pulled up to the house in a rural section of the county. The target location was a single-story structure on approximately five acres of land with overgrown foliage, making the approach hard to see at night.

I noticed a large, unmarked moving-type truck near the house. We were walking past the truck when it suddenly became clear that it was being loaded with crates of vegetables. We couldn't see anyone inside, but we heard the unmistakable voices of a hurried crew.

We walked up the ramp of the truck, entered, and came face-to-face with our bail fugitive. He was out on bail for assaulting someone with a knife and had a history of the same offense, so I had worn my body armor on this warm night. We proceeded with caution and drew our weapons.

The bail fugitive pretended not to see us.

"Drop the crate," my partner said.

"The rest of you get out of the truck," I said to the rest of the crew, and they all rushed past us and got off the truck.

My partner yelled, "Drop the crate and turn around!"

The bail fugitive stared for a moment and then tossed the crate at my partner. I quickly holstered my weapon and rushed toward the fugitive, and, sure enough, he produced a box cutter as he advanced toward my lettuce-covered partner. I quickly crowded the fugitive before he could put the box cutter into action. As he tried to push me away, I tied up his arm and slapped the back of his hand, causing him to drop the box cutter.

Grasping the back of his neck, I ordered him to get on the ground, but he was strong. My partner had recovered from the salad attack and put his bearlike hands to work, and, before long, the bail fugitive was on the ground screaming out this "injustice" and that "wrong guy" claim. Nevertheless, he was subsequently booked into the local jail without further incident.

My partner and I were there to make a lawful arrest. The bail fugitive drew a weapon and resisted to the extent that we had no choice but to put our hands on him. Technically, I could have shot him when he lunged toward my partner with a box cutter, but I chose to avoid using lethal force. The choice was mine and mine alone. Luckily, I made the right choice. Will you?

PART TWO
Are You Cut Out to Be a Bail Fugitive Recovery Person?

CHAPTER SEVEN

What Training Do You Need?

At the time of this writing there are two television shows loosely focusing on bail enforcement, and I understand that a third one is in production. My opinions on these "reality shows" notwithstanding, "reality" varies greatly from the geographical locations shown on these shows to the rest of the country. In any case, it is safe to assume that these programs will tantalize some viewers, who will then look into how they might enter into the business of hunting felony fugitives for profit.

Don't kid yourself that bail enforcement is an easy way to make money. First of all, as noted earlier, bail enforcement is a tough trade to enter, and I'm here to tell you that the job is tough—very tough. Arresting bail fugitives is mission specific. There is no other profession that will by itself prepare you for this work, but a combination of past training can help you transition more smoothly and safely into it.

Perhaps the most effective way to acquire the right skills for this job is by serving an apprenticeship under an established pro. Of course, you must be careful to ensure that your mentor has a proven record of success and has never been arrested, criminally charged, or sued. Otherwise, the apprenticeship may not last long simply because you too could get into trouble with the law.

Of course, it might not be easy to find a mentor who is willing to take on an apprentice. Another option is to attend a commercial training academy or course. A number of organizations offer bail enforcement training online or through seminars. I cannot comment on these organizations or their training since I have not attended any of them. But it might be worth your time and money to check out certification programs in your area. Many states that license recovery agents require specific training courses, so be sure to check to see if this is the case in your state before enrolling.

There are many noncertification training courses that teach useful skills for the aspiring recovery agent, such as investigative techniques, skip tracing, firearms training, the safe and legal use of nonlethal weapons, etc. I am a student of many subjects, and I like to attend classes for my own edification. If a training school or course doesn't work for you, you can always use training books and videos to acquire or enhance your skills. Look in the Resources section in the back of the book for some ideas you might pursue.

Many of the people choose this line of work because of the skills they have acquired from previous jobs or training experiences. Specifically, the training that one gets in the martial arts schools, law enforcement, or the military can be invaluable to the recovery person.

MARTIAL ARTS

Martial arts training is excellent to have in your background; it can teach you practical self-defense moves, fighting strategies, submission holds, weapon-disarming techniques, as well as how to defuse hostile situations. As a bonus, if you're serious about your training, you can stay in excellent physical condition and keep your reflexes razor sharp.

I am a mixed martial arts fan. I love to watch practitioners of the different styles get together and compete against one another. In the early days Brazilian jiujitsu dominated the sport. Today a hybrid system of fighting has evolved to the point that no one style is superior to the others. In short, you have to be able to do it all: box, grapple, kick, and apply and escape submission holds.

The fighters who compete in these events are superb athletes who are frequently being evenly matched, but there is still a winner. Oftentimes the difference between the winner and the loser is conditioning. The winner's cardiovascular endurance is often superior to the loser's.

My martial arts background consists of taekwon do (mostly kicking), Western boxing (punching and being punched), aikido (standing joint manipulation and energy redirection), and Brazilian jiujitsu (a combination of Japanese jiujitsu, American freestyle, collegiate, and Greco-Roman wrestling). I would love to compete in mixed martial arts competition, but the younger guys would probably dominate me with their speed and cardiovascular advantage.

During my 20-plus years of martial arts training, I learned that stand-up cardio is not the same as grappling cardio. For example, in 1996 when I faced my first Brazilian jiujitsu opponent (who was only 16 years old), I could spar stand-up for 12 two-minute rounds with no rest between rounds, so I thought I was in good shape. I was wrong. I became absolutely exhausted within two minutes of fierce grappling and was used to dust the mats.

I was so impressed by the Brazilian system that I devoted all of my training to learning the basics. A year later, I went back to my stand-up buddies, took each one down, and forced submissions at will. I then tried to stand-up spar with them. I could not compete with them standing because of immediate exhaustion.

I now incorporate a variety of exercises designed to help me win a street confrontation whether it is on the ground or standing. In other words, I am determined not to lose a street fight because of fatigue.

Most bail skips will not resist your efforts to arrest them, but, as any cop will tell you, there is always that one fugitive who will fight as if his life depends on hurting or killing you. Although unlikely, especially if you approach people properly, you may someday find yourself fighting for your life. You want to make sure you are ready and able to defend yourself. If attacked by an unarmed assailant, you must gauge your response to the level of attack that you are being subjected to. For example, it would be considered excessive to use your boxing skills to subdue a smaller, weaker bail fugitive or launch a crippling Muay Thai kick at the thighs of a mouthy bail fugitive.

This isn't a self-defense or combat conditioning manual, and there are lots of excellent books and videos on the subject you can get (check out www.paladin-press.com). Briefly, for fugitive recovery work what you need to be able to do is the following in rapid succession:

- Run one mile in under 10 minutes
- Box for 5 minutes

- Wrestle for 10 minutes while retaining your firearm(s)
- Run another half-mile in under 5 minutes

You are probably thinking that I am suffering from acute delusions, but the above outlined routine is based on a series of actual events, as illustrated in the following scenario.

You approach a structure with the intention of simply asking the occupants some questions. The bail fugitive, who is watering his lawn, sees you and runs. You chase him. He leads you on a prolonged foot chase. You round a corner and see that he is cornered. The fugitive suddenly starts boxing with you. It turns out that he is a better boxer than you, so you take him down. You can feel him grabbing at your weapon. Unable to restrain him and retain your weapon at the same time, you disengage. Then you notice that he has been joined by two of his brothers. Remembering that you are under no obligation to arrest a bail fugitive—that $500 commission isn't worth tens of thousands in legal fees, jail time, serious injury, or death—you run. The three men give chase. You manage to escape.

If this scenario sounds far-fetched, then you probably are not suited for bail fugitive recovery. In any case, the recommended combat conditioning routine is based on real experience. Frankly, it is better to be in shape and not need it than to need it and not have it. The by-product of being able to do the suggested routine is excellent health. Helpful though it is, being a martial arts practitioner doesn't automatically make you a good recovery agent.

LESSON FROM THE STREET

My partner Jerry and I met at 0200 hours in Marion. We had decided in advance that our bail fugitive, Rick, would be available for a face-to-face in the early morning hours.

As usual, Jerry called the local heat to request a civil standby, but the policy of that agency was not to help recovery agents. Jerry acknowledged the agency's position and advised them of our intentions and all other relevant details.

The neighborhood was in a serious state of disrepair. The quadraplex needed exterior repair—I suspect that there was no homeowners association to keep up on the gardening. Luckily, the streetlights were largely intact and operating properly. But the lights illuminated a serious problem with the structures: most were missing house numbers. We would have to guess which unit was the target location and approach it under some pretext.

By now it was 0300 hours, and people were still out milling around the neighborhood as we parked near the suspected location. We exited our vehicles, making sure not to slam the doors. I approached an unidentified male who was standing on the front lawn. He wore long hair, dirty jeans, and no shirt. He stood as still as a statue.

"Good morning, sir. I hate to trouble you, but I am unclear on the address of this structure," I said.

The man didn't move or look at me.

I continued, "Could you tell me where 1234, unit 2 is?"

The man barely moved his mouth and refused to look at me as he whispered, "Keep walking to the door on your left side of the building."

"Thank you," I responded in an unsure tone.

Jerry took a cover position, and I readied myself to initiate contact and then pressed the doorbell. A loud crash erupted above me. I looked up in time to see a man, wearing only blue jeans, jump out a window onto the first-story roof and disappear out of my view. I raced to the front of the structure and saw the man running to the opposite side. I maintained visual contact by following along the structure on the ground and then saw, with my own eyes, the guy jump off the first-story roof, land on his feet, and bolt into the darkness. The runner matched the description of our bail fugitive, so I gave chase. Jerry ran around the opposite side of the building to cut him off.

I caught up to the man and was about to tackle him, when suddenly I felt a sharp sting in my right hamstring, and my leg wouldn't work properly. Suddenly, the neighborhood filled with people taking out their trash, watering lawns, and doing other uncommon things at 0305 hours, which was a good thing for Jerry and me. As it turned out, these neighbors kept pointing out the fugitive's trail as he fled. Thirty minutes later, following these directions, we arrived at a structure four units away from the original target. Our fugitive was reported to be in there.

I covered the front, while Jerry talked his way inside. While I was watching and listening for the guy to crash through another window, Jerry requested my assistance over the radio. Ignoring the hamstring problem as best as I could, I ran into the building, up the stairs, and into one of the bedrooms. Jerry had found our man hiding in a closet.

The guy's physical characteristics were identical to the fuzzy booking photo and matched the description we had. He even had the identical tattoos described in court documents, so, naturally, we were skeptical when he claimed to be Ray, the bail fugitive's brother (a very common claim). We got him out of the closet, placed handcuffs on his wrists, and made our way downstairs just in time to run into approximately 13 of his male family members.

Jerry and I managed to talk our way out of the structure with our prisoner in tow and his family members following close behind. We finally reached our vehicles near the first

structure, but the tension was acute. I told "Ray" to call off his family if he really was Rick's brother. He did just that, and Ray's wife brought out family photos showing Rick and Ray together. I decided to go by a general rule: when in doubt let the prisoner go.

I took the handcuffs off Ray and asked him why he ran. He replied, "I don't know." Yeah, right.

"We'll be back later on," I promised Ray. (We kept our promise, as you can read in Chapter 15.)

This lesson illustrates how important it is to maintain good physical conditioning and the consequences of not doing so. The afternoon before this incident I had grappled and kickboxed with some buddies. Later, I went home, showered, ate dinner, and rested on the sofa for a while before I had to meet Jerry for the action just described. I woke up, showered again, got dressed, and headed out to meet Jerry. In retrospect, after my workout I should have warmed up with a light walk on the treadmill, stretched, and then taken a shower. But I didn't, and therefore my hamstring was very tight, which led to my injury when I had to chase the fugitive.

Despite being injured, however, I was able to drive on because of my regular fitness routine. My leg was black and blue for two weeks. Now, as a direct result of this incident, I always warm up and stretch before attempting any arrest.

An incidental, but equally crucial, lesson here is to make sure you have the right person before you take him into custody.

MILITARY

Military training is also desirable for anyone interested in entering bail fugitive recovery. I was trained and served as a military policeman in the U.S. Army Reserves, so my training combined aspects of both military and law enforcement and has proved useful to me in this trade, including the areas of restraint and control, officer safety, and liability awareness.

While a military background is definitely useful, I have had some problems with military-trained bounty hunters. People straight from the armed services come from a highly structured environment, where most everything is done according to rules and regulations with little deviation. Conversely, as I've said, each case in the bail enforcement field is unique, requiring a freethinking mind-set that is adaptive to the particular circumstance. Being flexible and taking the time to do things the right way for the circumstances will keep you out of jail, the hospital, the morgue, and civil court.

Military training is different from that suited for bail recovery work in terms of its goals. Military personnel are trained to protect *us* by killing *them*. This doesn't work for most civilians. For example, you deliver bail fugitives to the jail in the same exact condition as you found them whenever possible.

On the plus side, military training instills discipline, professionalism, and personal maturity into trainees, as well as specific skills that are useful in the bail recovery field, including:

• Weapons use and maintenance (e.g., firearms, chemical)
• Map reading and orienteering
• Hand-to-hand combat
• Signaling and communication

LAW ENFORCEMENT

I served for eight years as a corrections officer for a county sheriff's department, and this experience has helped me tremendously in my current occupation. Not only did I develop apprehension and restraint skills, on the job, but I also learned how to do the administrative part of the job well, and the latter has been invaluable. When I started my business, I already knew how to fill out and read the

various types of paperwork that are critical to tracking down, arresting, and surrendering bail fugitives, as well as interfacing with law enforcement officers as part of my job as a private bail recovery agent.

Police training is ideal for bail fugitive recovery work, but it also has limitations as well. You can do things as a police officer that you cannot as a bail fugitive recovery person and vice versa.

First of all, cops enjoy certain protections afforded by their office: so long as they are operating within the scope and mission of their duties, their agencies will back them in the event of legal problems. Bail fugitive recovery agents are acting as private citizens enforcing a civil contract.

Cops can be more furtive with people suspected of being in violation of the law, but recovery agents can only be furtive with the specific bail fugitive being sought and not third parties. For example, you, as a private citizen, do not have the protection of a city or county government; moreover, cops are tasked with detecting criminal behavior and may investigate suspects surreptitiously. A bail enforcement agent is only lawfully able to arrest the person listed on the authority-to-arrest form unless, as a private citizen, he intends to make a citizen's arrest as prescribed by law. However, being able to rattle someone without violating his rights or breaking the law is a specialty that former cops enjoy and may be able to employ as an investigative tool in private recovery work.

I've had to counsel new trainees from civilian law enforcement not to be so pushy with street contacts, because as recovery agents they do not have the same leverage as they did as street cops. Police officers can go to a judge for a search and/or arrest warrant. This legal document enables them to kick in doors, throw everyone on the ground, and tear the area apart. Bail fugitive recovery agents cannot do that.

On the other hand, recovery agents can arrest a person without a warrant; police officers cannot arrest a person without just cause or a warrant. In most states, an authorized bail agent can arrest a bail fugitive without any legal process because the bail bond contract is between private parties and therefore is a civil matter. I will get into this in far greater detail later.

People with prior law enforcement experience can bring invaluable skills to the bail enforcement field, including but not limited to the following:

- Interviews of potential informants
- Confidence gained from experience in hostile situations
- A working knowledge of lawful behavior
- Weapons training
- Control, restraint, and handcuffing expertise
- Familiarity with shoot/don't shoot scenarios
- Experience with court appearances
- Proper procedure for making felony fugitive arrests

• • •

Each type of training outlined in this chapter—training academies, martial arts, military, and law enforcement—is excellent for specific purposes, but none can totally prepare a person for bail fugitive recovery work. The best way is to find a seasoned bail fugitive recovery person who has been in the trade and learn from him. The more aggressive types will ignore my advice and strike out on their own. I think it is fantastic if you can do that, but I haven't met any successful bounty hunters who did it without help. Good luck!

LESSON FROM THE STREET

Rob seemed like a squared-away young man, so I decided to try him on one of my contracts. I parked my car in a shopping center lot during a busy part of the day so that the trunk lid would hide the fact that we were getting our firearms ready to attempt an arrest.

I slid my gun holster onto my belt and removed my weapon from a mounted lockbox in

my trunk. I cleared the weapon by pulling the slide back and verifying that it was empty. In doing so, I pointed the weapon at my spare body armor strung up in the trunk of the car, so that any accidental discharge (it has never happened to me, but you never know) would strike a Kevlar panel and likely be stopped.

Rob held up his weapon so that it was pointed at the nearby shopping center and dropped the slide, despite my instruction to clear his weapon into the vest mounted in the trunk.

"No, no, no!" I yelled. "Put the gun down in the trunk, and let's talk." I paused for a moment to calm myself down. "Exactly why did you point your weapon at that crowded shopping center and drop the slide?"

Rob didn't miss a beat. "That's how I was trained to clear my weapon in the army."

"I was in the army, too, Rob. I don't recall being trained to clear my weapon by pointing it at women and children."

Rob bit his lower lip, looked at the kids and parents going about their day. "Yes, don't you remember pointing your weapon downrange to clear it?"

Okay, he was going to argue about his point even though his position was seriously flawed and without any factual basis in military training whatsoever. I waited to respond.

"You clear your weapon by pointing it downrange," Rob insisted.

I decided not to take my magazines out of the second lockbox mounted in the trunk. This incident needed to be worked out. Gesturing to the shopping center, I asked, "Does this look like a fucking gun range?"

"Well, that's how I was trained," Rob proclaimed.

"Under what circumstances would you shoot

someone, Rob?" I asked. We had had this conversation before, but I wanted to see what he had retained.

"I would shoot to wound if . . ."

"Excuse me," I interrupted, "shoot to wound?"

"Yeah," Rob said quizzically.

"No, Rob. We do not shoot to wound or fire warning shots or anything of the sort." I took another deep breath. "You will only discharge your weapon if you are in immediate danger of being killed or to protect someone from being killed. Under

those conditions you shoot only to stop the aggression of the person or persons who are presenting the imminent danger. You aim center mass. Your weapon is a tool to defend you or another human being from being killed. It is not for scaring, warning, capturing, or pointing at fucking shopping centers. Do you understand?"

The author uses a spare set of body armor to clear his weapon in case of an accidental discharge. Note the two combination lockers above the vest that are used for lawful transport of a firearm.

"But in the army . . ."

"You are no longer in the army." I looked around and began putting my gear away. "Rob, we're going to call this off and go home."

As I drove home, I wondered how Rob had managed to convince me that he was suited for this work. It then occurred to me: under times of stress, which is what Rob was experiencing as a result of attempting his first arrest, he reverted to his original training. It is widely accepted that, when stressed, people will react how they were trained to react. Rob had no training other than what he had learned in the army.

As a result of this incident with Rob, I personally train each new bail fugitive recovery person before allowing him to go into the field. The training includes bookwork from my in-house training manual, written tests, unarmed self-defense, arrest and control techniques, handcuffing, weapon retention, shooting at a local gun range, specific scenario-based instruction, house-clearing drills, and competitions on the paintball field against a professional team for a final lesson in humility.

During all phases of the training, the trainees are trained to react just as they would during an actual arrest attempt. This reminds me of a story once told to me. It goes something like this . . .

A police officer had a premonition that a suspect would someday hold a gun to his back, so he decided to learn how to disarm such a person. He had his wife play the bad guy and had her point an unloaded gun at his back while he practiced the disarm technique over and over. In fact, he became an expert at this technique. Each time he disarmed his wife, he handed the unloaded weapon back to her and started over.

One day a bad guy did hold a gun to this police officer's back, and, just as he had trained, he effectively disarmed the bad guy. And just as he had trained, he then handed the gun back to the bad guy, who shot and killed him.

Remember, under times of great emotional stress, you will respond according to how you trained; therefore, your training must be comprehensive and realistic at all times.

CHAPTER EIGHT

How Do You Relate to People?

The best indicator of whether you are cut out to be a recovery agent might be how you relate to other people. In this business, you deal with people all the time—bail agents, teammates, police officers, court clerks, attorneys, family members and friends of the people you are pursuing, as well as the bail fugitives themselves. It helps tremendously if you can get other people to help you do your job. To do this you have got to be able to get them to talk to you, to tell you things about your fugitive that you can't find out on your own. In large part, how people respond to you is determined by how you treat them. I cannot impress upon you enough how important it is to treat people right. You must not mistreat anyone while pursuing bail fugitives.

Remember that you are acting as a private citizen enforcing a private contract between private citizens. The bail fugitive may or may not accept your efforts to arrest him as a legal part of the criminal justice system. The bail fugitive may see your efforts as nothing more than another attempt to take his freedom away, and, if he is looking at going through narcotics withdrawal or doing substantial prison time, you had better use every advantage at your disposal.

Throughout your preliminary and main investigations, it is advisable to smile when interacting with people. Smiling puts people at ease right out of the gate. You should come off as cordial and polite when dealing with court clerks, store owners, apartment managers, street people, and others.

In this business, a lot (if not most) of your interaction with others is initiated through the door-knock, and the best time to do this is at night—when most people are home. The problem is that most people will be suspicious of your presence at their door in the middle of the night.

The trick to door-knocking is behaving like you belong there while apologizing for disturbing the occupants. You should speak clearly and immediately establish a rapport with the first person you encounter. Identify yourself and offer to show the warrant for the person you intend to arrest. If you do a good job, you will gain permission to enter the structure, provided that you come across as trustworthy in your behavior and your appearance.

At all times you should be prepared for hostile behavior. I've been invited into places only to have the occupants suddenly turn angry. If this happens, remember, you are there as a private citizen attempting to enforce a civil contract between private parties, so be flexible in how you handle yourself.

You should know that some defendants and cosigners lie on the bail applications about their addresses. This means that you will be executing door-knocks—usually late at night—on third-party addresses. These third-party locations must be treated with extreme caution. Most legal problems for bail recovery agents come from acting too forcefully against third parties at bad addresses. You must approach each address as if it is incorrect and at the same time with strict adherence to agent safety rules.

In addition to checking addresses and developing leads, you will also come into contact with people at motels, strip malls, and around the neighborhood. During all your efforts to find useful information, it is important to know when to use the disarming smile and when to play it tough with people, which may alienate you from potentially good contacts but intimidate an otherwise reluctant party to squeal. I have found that projecting sincere concern for the bail fugitive and those who have pledged assets on his behalf, such as the grandma who is going to lose the house her deceased husband built with his own hands, works best for my team and me.

Finally, never forget that the bail commission is not worth risking your life or career for. If a cosigner demands that you get off his property, then do it calmly and politely. Afterwards, post wanted posters all over the neighborhood, talk to neighbors, and even establish a surveillance post right in front of his house. This will get old real fast for the co-signer, and taking this type of action can trigger a break in your investigation.

CONTROLLING HOW YOU REACT TO HOSTILE PEOPLE

Effective people skills are more than just knowing how to get people to talk to you; they also are about how you react to other people. Some people go into emotional meltdown when they are yelled at in an aggressive manner. Others cannot maintain a professional demeanor once a slight has been perceived. People with an inability to deal calmly with hostile people will be immediately handicapped in the bail fugitive recovery trade.

In most cases you will be treated the same way you treat others. I know of some people who cannot approach people without each encounter turning into a full-blown argument. They make lousy recovery agents.

How you handle hostile behavior is determined by many factors, beginning with your childhood. You may not be able to handle a verbal attack if you have a history of being physically attacked or injured after being yelled at. Your reaction to this type of stimulus may be to retreat into a passive self-preservation mode. In this event, you will not be able to make an arrest, which may be required. If you were trained, maybe by an authority figure (parent), to react submissively to aggressive behavior, your reaction to a stressful situation is more that of a scared child than a bail fugitive recovery agent.

On the other hand, you may react too aggressively to hostile behavior because you are now an adult who can thrash an abusive person you view as an authority figure.

It is in your best interest to check your ego and pride at the door when confronted with an angry person. In most cases, you'll find that a yelling person is just trying to save face and not appear to be weak to his family or friends, so let him yell.

One of the things I do is lower my tone and even speak softly to a person who is yelling at me. This forces that person to turn on his ears to *hear* what I'm saying. If he strains to hear, there is a chance to reason with him, and that might make him lower his voice and listen. If he won't try to hear you, then a fight is likely. You may want to consider leaving to avoid a legal problem.

If it is possible, steer the subject away from whatever the person is yelling about. Be cordial, avoid arguing, and then go back to your original point once things calm down.

If it is safe to do so, change your body language—while maintaining balance—to a less threatening posture or break up the flow of the challenge by asking the person to look at your files. By doing this, you have involved him in a secret, and a good secret turned into a conspiracy will get everyone on the same side, whether or not the person knows it.

If you are incapable of defusing a hostile situation, then perhaps you don't have the temperament for bail fugitive recovery because hostile people come with the territory. This area gets tricky, which is why I require my contract workers to undergo oral stress testing and psychological screening. You may not even be aware of how you deal with hostile people. I suggest that you talk to people who know you. Ask them how they perceive you during times of stress. The time to find out is now, not during a street confrontation.

LESSON FROM THE STREET

Peter, who at the time was a bored associate with a rather distinguished law firm, contacted me with an enthusiastic wish to moonlight as a bail fugitive recovery person. He struck me as sincere, so I put him through the paces: stress oral, psychological screening, and written test. Peter passed with flying colors.

As a bonus, Peter's martial arts prowess was impressive because of his extensive kajukenbo (combination of karate, Japanese jiujitsu, and Chinese boxing) background. During one session as he was beating me at stand-up, I shot in, took him down, and choked him into submission. Despite being pulled to the ground, where his training provided little help, Peter never panicked

or lost his temper. I thought this boded well for him as a bail fugitive recovery agent.

Peter completed the first several phases of training within a couple of months. Accordingly, I advanced him to field training. Peter accompanied me on several uneventful arrests, and he performed as expected. As a part of my training program, everyone must learn how to work every position during the arrest operation. Peter performed well as rear security (covered the back escape route and provided support as needed), front security (covered the front escape route, provided cover for the team during exfiltration), and as a member of a two-man search team (went in behind the door-knocker and systematically searched the dwelling for the suspected bail fugitive). It was time for Peter to initiate the door-knock.

The door-knocker holds a very dangerous job, comparable only to that of the search team. Knocking on the door is where the whole arrest operation can go very wrong. It is the door-knocker's job to make first contact with the occupants, identify the team, determine if grounds exist to force entry, obtain permission to enter the structure, establish and maintain a rapport with the occupants (this is where a person can decide to file a suit if you mishandle the process or use strong-arm tactics), gather all occupants in a central location for safety reasons, maintain control of and interrogate all the occupants while the search team does its job. It is also the door-knocker's responsibility to make sure the field interview cards are filled out, either by him or the occupants.

The night of Peter's inaugural door-knock was perfect for hunting. The moon was bright enough that we could see but not so bright as to silhouette us as we approached the target location.

Our bail fugitive had a reputation for being one bad dude with multiple restraining orders filed against him by various people. He was so scary looking that most people who saw his booking photo panicked.

When I approached Peter at the staging area, a well-lit fast-food restaurant parking lot, he seemed excited. "Peter, the intelligence dump on this guy suggests that he can be a problem. I think that I should knock on the door tonight."

Peter's face dropped. "I know I'm ready," he said.

Peter *was* ready to receive some pending cases to investigate, but I couldn't give him those cases until he was checked out on the door-knock. Peter knew this.

"C'mon, you're going to be right there if I choke," he pleaded.

"Peter, this guy even gives *me* the creeps."

The whole team was listening by now. It was important for them to have confidence in Peter, and replacing him as door-knocker would jeopardize his standing with them.

"Okay, I'll take up a position on the search team. I won't begin the search until you get control of any and all occupants."

"Right on," Peter replied.

The target location was situated in a tract of dilapidated homes with an alley at its rear. The rear security person was instructed to park his vehicle in the alley facing the rear of the target location, to stand at least 30 yards away from the vehicle, and to use the remote to control the floodlight aimed at the target location. Upon radio notification from the door-knocker, rear security would use the remote-controlled floodlight to give the appearance of greater numbers (bail fugitives usually won't run into a blinding light where an unknown number of arrest agents may be), but position himself safely away from the vehicle since the light could become a target for gunfire.

Our requests for a police civil standby were denied, so we opted to move in on our own.

The initial approach was textbook. Everyone took up his position without incident. Peter stood on the porch to the side of the front door. He looked back at me to get the go-ahead to knock. The door was ajar, so I motioned for him to hold. Peter would not get checked out on the door-knock tonight.

I took the lead while Peter trailed Ed, the agent behind me. We entered the house stealthily. The condition of the house was indescribable. Floorboards were missing, garbage was piled up, and the counters were cluttered with items that looked like they had been untouched since the early 1900s. Luckily for us, our bail fugitive was zoning on the couch in the living room. The needle on the couch near his arm suggested that he had just injected himself with a drug (probably heroin based on the works, which meant his reaction would be less volatile than if the drug was meth or another stimulant). I covered the fugitive while Peter and Ed quietly cleared the rest of the structure—there was no need to wake up our friend just yet.

Peter stood next to me while Ed covered our backs. The layout of the house was so bizarre that it was possible that the search team might have missed a shooter hiding in a pile of trash. I surveyed the immediate area around the fugitive and could not see any weapons. I moved the needle with my gloved hand to avoid any accidental sticks. I looked at Peter, and he motioned that he was ready.

I touched the bail fugitive, hoping to handcuff him without waking him up. He suddenly leapt up, and I jumped back (much like the characters in the movie *Seven* when the seemingly dead guy on the bed took a deep breath and moved) since maintaining distance is a crucial part of agent safety. Peter did not move. I drew my weapon into a low ready position with my finger alongside the trigger well.

"Let me see your hands!" I yelled, but the bail fugitive just glared at Peter. "Move out of the way, Peter!" I instructed. Peter didn't appear to have heard me.

"Status!" Ed yelled.

I put my back against Ed's back to comfort him. Ed was maintaining cover of our rear, so he could not turn around. "Move, Peter!" I commanded. Peter stood immobile. The bail fugitive kept his hands at his sides and stared at Peter in an intimidating manner. The waist-high clutter blocked me from getting the right angle if a shot was necessary. I signaled that I needed help by keying my radio mic, "10-87 (come here) code 2 (now)."

The bail fugitive slipped his right hand behind his back and started to stand up. I holstered my weapon and used my left arm to push a rigid Peter out of the way. At the same time, I used my right forearm to knock the bail fugitive back onto the couch. He kept trying to reach around his back. "Get the fuck off me, you motherfucker!" he yelled.

"Stop resisting," I ordered. I shifted my eyes and could see that Peter was still standing, still just watching. "Ed, I need your help," I said.

Ed broke rear cover and gained control of the large bail fugitive's left arm while I tried to secure his right arm. "Give me your arm!" I demanded.

I pulled his arm out from between him and the stained, smelly sofa, and a huge hunting knife came out with it. "Knife!" I yelled.

The bail fugitive bucked and managed to knock Ed away. He used his right arm to pull at my duty belt, looking for my gun. His strength was notable for a presumed heroin user; I could feel that he was stronger than me, so I disengaged by jumping back.

I kicked Peter back with my left foot because he was still frozen in place. Ed was struggling to regain his footing from the pile of garbage he had landed in. The bail fugitive used this opportunity to get up off the couch and lunge at me with the knife. I parried the knife hand, redirected his forward movement, and bent his wrist to take him down. The force of the technique caused him to lose the knife. He pulled me down and tried to get on top of me. I swept him over onto his back, mounted him, and immediately found myself fighting to retain my weapon as he yanked for it. Fortunately, I wore a Level III retention holster. By then the rest of the team had entered the house and helped me restrain the bail fugitive.

At the time our sedans didn't have prisoner partitions, and the crazy bail fugitive tried to open the door and jump out on the way to the jail. He was unsuccessful and was booked into the jail without further incident, with the exception of making death threats against my team and me.

Debriefing was a solemn task. The team knew that I would have to dismiss Peter, and he knew it too.

I cannot explain what happened with Peter, and the psychiatrist who examined him was at a loss as well. Peter had excelled at everything I threw at him to prepare him for that moment. I knew that he had never been in a physical fight, except for martial arts sparring, but nothing could have revealed his propensity to freeze during a real-life situation—with the exception of a real-life situation.

How do you react under severe stress? Do you know? You should before getting into this trade.

CHAPTER NINE

Understanding the Adrenal Response

Staying calm and rational is key to surviving harrowing experiences. Freaking out isn't helpful—if you tend to lose your composure under pressure, then reconsider your career path.

The adrenal glands shoot adrenaline into our systems when a dangerous situation is perceived. Perhaps your adrenal glands fire off whenever you are about to knock on a front door in search of a dangerous bail fugitive. Or maybe your adrenals fire once you realize that the person you're talking to is the bail fugitive being sought.

In some regard this is perfectly normal, but at some point, I believe, you can actually damage your adrenal glands. For example, if my adrenal glands were to fire every time I approached a bail fugitive's front door, I might at some time experience adrenaline rushes when approaching any front door.

One of my former coworkers was yelled at and then attacked by jail inmates over and over. After 18 months of this, he started initiating sudden attacks on anyone—not just inmates—who yelled at him. Why? I believe that his adrenals had been damaged, and being yelled at triggered an adrenaline rush at inappropriate times. Our bodies are not set up to withstand repeated adrenaline rushes. At some point there is going to be a breakdown. Therefore, you must train to reduce the adrenal response during times of stress.

One way I've found to control the adrenal response is through martial arts training, which teaches you how to stay calm during a physical confrontation. You will know if you're experiencing an adrenal response if your vision tunnels during a search or if things seem to be moving in slow motion. This is not the state to be in when searching a bedroom for a bail fugitive known to carry weapons.

It's acceptable to be afraid, so you don't want to suppress this emotion unless it becomes overwhelming—and if this happens, you should reconsider your chosen trade.

Finally, it is advisable to establish and maintain an indomitable will to survive. Visualize what can go wrong and how you plan to troubleshoot the problems. Be in good shape at all times. Falling into a state of biomechanical disrepair will cause you to feel psychologically and mentally inadequate and vulnerable.

The bottom line is to *think* like a human being and not *react* like an animal.

LESSON FROM THE STREET

Our team of five had just surrendered two bail fugitives, and we were looking for the final one. We approached the target house, which was located in a farming community. There appeared to be some sort of ramshackle development along the sides of the single-story house.

None of us had been to this place before. We had only learned of the address an hour earlier in a neighboring city, so we were hitting this one cold without any surveillance. This was also our first night with the new radio headsets we sported. So far they had worked so well that getting along without them seemed impossible.

I talked my way into the house, but the search yielded nothing. We decided to split up and check around the perimeter of the house. One team member stayed in front and coordinated the search. The remaining four split up into two teams and systematically searched the property.

Before long it became clear that we had entered a complex of assorted shacks, trailers, wrecked vehicles, and tents, all of which seemed to house dozens of migrant workers, who were now out and about.

My partner and I found a one-bedroom house with four guys playing cards and drinking beer. We engaged the crew in casual conversation before eventually focusing on our fugitive. My partner noticed more people coming and decided to step outside and question them.

A few minutes passed with no word from my partner, so I tried radioing him for an update. There was no response, but I pretended that he had answered me and made up an excuse to leave the house. I stepped outside, but my partner was nowhere to be seen. I tried radioing him repeatedly with no response.

Just then, I realized that about a dozen men—all carrying picks, shovels, and hammers—were following me. One of them babbled something about my being at the wrong place and asking the wrong questions. I became increasingly aware that the property was huge and that I had become entangled in a maze of improvised living quarters, with a ballooning mob on my tail. I felt an adrenaline response but maintained a calm exterior—I think.

This whole scene was reminiscent of the *Frankenstein* and *Aliens* movies wrapped into one. First, my team members seemed to have been picked off one by one, and then the pitchfork- and torch-bearing farmers were on the warpath after me. Suddenly, another set of men bearing chains and two-by-fours cut me off. I was carrying a Para-Ordnance .45 with 10 rounds and another two clips of 10 rounds each, and I feared that this was going to turn into a shooting situation.

I kicked my way through a wall of rose bushes and found myself in a freshly plowed field. My attempts to contact my team by radio remained futile. The various groups of men debated how best to deal with me, and it sounded like some were clanging their farm tools together in anticipation. This was not good. At that instant, I heard my partner talking to another team member over the radio. I made contact and eventually found my way out.

After the whole team congregated in front of the target house, I learned what had happened to my partner: he had spotted the bail fugitive, begun a chase, and had tried futilely to advise me by radio. The bail fugitive ran right into the second search team, who apprehended him and made their way to the target house, still unable to raise me by radio.

The lesson here? I was pursued by one band of armed men, intercepted and confronted by yet another batch of armed men, cut off from radio contact with the rest of my team, and forced to charge through a wall of rose bushes to get away. Even though I was outnumbered and seemed to be in dire straits, I like to think that I maintained control because I had trained myself to do so.

Although this was just an isolated incident, you need to plan how you will deal with adverse conditions, so that when they arise—and they will—you can handle them.

PART THREE
Taking Care of Business

CHAPTER TEN

Starting Your New Business

When first starting my bail fugitive recovery business, I ran up my credit cards obtaining computer equipment, guns, a sedan, restraints, body armor, business cards, stationery, handcuffs, duty belt leather, raid jacket, and more. The only thing missing was clients. The accumulated debt made things rougher at the start than they had to be. I recommend that you start out slowly, keep your purchases minimal, and use the income you make to invest in your business. When you are running a one-man operation, you don't need all the bells and whistles.

Starting your own business is an involved process. You have to find a place to operate (at first this will probably be from your garage or spare room) and equip it, name your business, figure out how to handle taxes and insurance, design and order business stationery and cards, and outfit yourself with the proper attire and tactical equipment. And, most importantly, you have to figure out how to find clients.

WHAT'S IN A NAME?

The name you pick for your new business is vitally important when it comes time to advertise. The name should sound professional and relate to the nature of your work. It should also be nonthreatening to potential clients, police officers whose assistance you solicit, or district attorneys or jurors you might have to explain your actions to in the future. Avoid anything like "Bring 'em Back Alive Bounty Hunters." Most recovery agencies make sure that they include the terms *bail bond recovery, bail fugitive recovery,* or *bail enforcement* in their business names. If the phone directory is one of your primary advertising tools, you might want to consider where your name will fall in the alphabetical listing of similar companies. For example, AAA Bail Fugitive Recovery comes way before Zapato Bail Fugitive Recovery and may yield more cold-call inquiries.

After deciding on a name, you need to check to make sure that the name isn't already in use. In most states, the function of registering business names is done by the secretary of state's office. Check there first, and a representative can direct you to the proper office.

After selecting the name of your business, you will need to file for a business license. In California, it isn't necessary to file an application for "doing business as" with your county if you use your actual name in the business name. For example, if you call your business Andy's Fugitive Recovery Service—and your name is Andy or you use any part of your legal name—then you don't need to file a doing-business-as application. But if you call your business Bond Recovery Group and no part of your legal name appears, then you will have to file a fictitious business statement with your county, publish your new business name in a local paper for six weeks, and whatever else your municipality requires for such businesses. Check with your local government to get the rules for businesses in your area.

BUSINESS LICENSE

Obtaining a business license allows you to open a business checking account and claim tax deductions for business expenses. The process for doing this varies from city to city. Check with your city government for the applicable forms, restrictions, licenses, and fees.

Be careful not to list your actual home address on any of the applications if possible. The city records are public record, and whatever you do list will be available to anyone.

BUSINESS CARDS AND STATIONERY

You will need business cards and letterhead. It is important to design a neat, professional card with a telephone number that is not likely to be changed. Avoid overcomplicating the layout of your business card and letterhead. Black print on white paper works best. Having the cards and stationery professionally printed is expensive and unnecessary. You can design and print them from your own computer and

printer or have a friend with a computer do them for you.

INSURANCE

Despite my experience in bail recovery, I can't offer you any guidance in terms of obtaining insurance for your new company. If you can find a company willing to underwrite your bail enforcement company, that is great—if you can find one that will underwrite your bail enforcement company *and* is still around once you've finished reading this book, then send me an e-mail to let me know (rex@uenforcebail. com).

Bail enforcement is a high-liability trade, and there may not be any bail enforcement companies that are actually insured. Some people obtain insurance for their private investigation firms, but I suspect that their application for insurance omitted certain facts concerning the bail enforcement aspect of the firm's activities.

You most likely won't be able to obtain insurance for your bail fugitive recovery business. Your only protection is to do things right. Now, there is an upside to not being able to get insurance—believe it or not—if you work with five bail enforcement agents and only one is insured, whom do you think the civil lawyers will focus on? That's right, the guy with the deep insurance pockets backing his actions. The downside is that your personal assets will most likely be frozen pending the outcome of a civil action.

OFFICE EQUIPMENT

I strongly recommend that you get a computer and printer if you don't already have them. You will also need Internet access and an ability to print wanted posters, which I'll discuss in Chapter 14. Internet access is important because of the search engines, investigative tools, and e-mail it provides. Check with the Internet service providers in your area for local availability and costs.

You will need working space to organize your files and spread out documents. A kitchen table may work temporarily, but as soon as you can, get a desk and a file cabinet. All of this equipment is most likely depreciable, but check with your accountant.

TACTICAL EQUIPMENT

This is an area where the gadget lovers are going to have a ball. There are literally hundreds of pieces of equipment that you're just going to have to have, but probably don't need. I can't chastise you too much about being a gadget freak, because I am guilty of acquiring equipment that is not really necessary but that does come in handy surprisingly often.

At the very minimum, you need some sort of reliable transportation and at least one set of handcuffs with a handcuff key. Personally, I wouldn't try to arrest someone with just any type of car. The sedan I now use to transport prisoners is equipped with a Plexiglas spit guard, side bat wings, and antikicking board, and the backdoor door handles and windows are not operational.

I always carry at least two sets of handcuffs—or at least I try to. On more occasions than I care to admit I have forgotten to recover my handcuffs from fugitives once I turn them over to local authorities. I now have all my hand-cuffs engraved with my name and phone number for easier retrieval. Some re-covery agents use flex cuffs, which are a lot cheaper.

Recommended equipment specific to bail fugitive recovery agents is as follows:

- Reliable four-door sedan with a prisoner partition (sedans are generally considered safer and have the room to install a "cage" and your equipment)
- Handgun with speed loaders or spare magazines
- Backup weapon (the fastest reload is a second gun)
- Holsters (hard shell is preferable to collapsible in case you have to put your weapon in the holster to free your hands to handcuff a fugitive, because it is easier to slide your handgun into a hard-shell holster and then lock it in)
- Two sets of handcuffs, available online or at your local police supply store (Peerless handcuffs are my first choice)
- Waist chains
- Shackles
- Cell phone
- Two-way radios
- Level IIIA body armor
- Raid jacket
- Eye protection
- Kevlar helmet

- Tactical vest
- Two three-cell Mag flashlights
- Backup mini-flashlight
- Tactical boots
- Gloves
- Rapid deployment bag
- Pepper spray
- Stun gun with holster

Every now and then the job may call for equipment such as this third-generation night-vision setup.

Occasionally, you may need really specialized gear, such as night-vision equip-ment for low-light situations, but these items are expensive and not essential when you are first starting out.

Now, you're

probably thinking that acquiring all this equipment is a bit extreme. Some of it is essential for safety reasons. For example, you really shouldn't try to make an arrest without body armor. Perhaps you should consider the fact that you are embarking on the trade of hunting felony fugitives, not a defenseless animal that cannot attack you with a firearm, knife, booby trap, or send his homeboys after you. Make sure you have the proper equipment before you hit the streets.

ATTIRE

Like I've said, each case is unique, and therefore how you approach the arrest is contingent on what your preliminary investigation has revealed about the intended arrestee. For example, going after that third-striker with a history of violence who has barricaded himself inside a building may warrant full tactical gear: Kevlar helmet, eye protection, Level III body armor, backup weapon, pepper spray, and even police support if available. The accountant who failed to appear on a driving on a suspended license case could be arrested at work, and normal street clothes or a suit would be more appropriate for this occasion.

Another aspect of choosing your attire is whether or not you want to blend in with the neighborhood. I've done work in some areas where driving by slow in street clothes would draw fire from gang members taking preemptive action to a perceived drive-by shooting. In these cases, I did everything I could to look official, including being fully uniformed and driving a Ford Crown Victoria with spotlights. In one situation, I was searching a house when a man suddenly emerged from a bedroom and was clearly getting ready to charge me with a broomstick. His attack was immediately forestalled when he looked down at my shoulder patch, which read "Bail Agent." I can say with complete certainty that he would have attacked if I had been dressed in everyday attire.

Looking official has its place, and blending in is also critical in some situations. If you will

be interacting with professionals (e.g., law enforcement or court personnel, attorneys, business owners), a business suit is in order. It will be up to you to decide how you will dress for the specific case you are working.

Of course, your choice of attire must be in compliance with any state regulations. For example, several states prohibit a bail recovery agent from wearing any apparel or badges that appear to be those of a law enforcement officer, so that recovery agents won't be mistaken for police officers. Other states require that the recovery agent wear either a badge or article of clothing that clearly identifies him as a bail enforcement agent or whatever the preferred term is in that state. Research the law in your state and make sure your apparel and equipment are legal.

LESSON FROM THE STREET

I received 17 contracts from the same bail agent, who was visibly shaken after receiving all the forfeiture letters in the same month and realizing that the bail applications all bore false information.

After preliminary investigation, it quickly became clear that the fugitives were all couriers in a drug ring and that they had used the same bail agent with no intentions of showing up in court. Once out on bail, they simply melted away, amid rumors that they intended to return to Mexico. I knew it was going to be difficult to find these fugitives, but that's the life of an independent contractor.

In addition to their occupation and their bail agent, all the bail fugitives had one more thing in common: they all listed the same attorney on their bail applications. Unfortunately, the attorney turned out to be bogus, but recurring references in the various files led me to an apartment in a rather large city.

The apartment was fairly sanitary, but the distinctive odor of dirty diapers and spoiled formula indicated the presence of small children. In any case, I felt sorry for the woman and her two small children. After some brief cajoling on my part (including paying to have her telephone service resumed), she sold me the information on the bail fugitive. It turns out that her former boyfriend, the bail fugitive I was hunting, had run up the bill on calls to Mexico and taken off with her car. We made a deal on what the information was worth to both of us.

The team and I were somewhat concerned about the neighborhood. We had done work in that section of the city, and tensions between the local gangs were evident. But when we went in at 0330 hours on a Tuesday morning, the target street was surprisingly quiet. We approached the target house from separate directions, parked six houses away on both sides, and walked in. The house was dark, and, if the informant's car hadn't been out front, I would have guessed the place to be a dead end.

After notifying the local heat that we would be attempting a bail arrest, we decided on a stealth entry if at all possible. All five of us circled the house. I quietly whistled at the backyard gate to see if there were any furry, four-legged trouble spots that needed to be circumvented. There was no response.

I found an open side door to the garage. Just then, my primary flashlight blew a bulb. Luckily, I had my backup mini-flashlight. I got the message from my bone-transducer mic (a mic that fits just in front of the ear and allows the wearer to hear radio traffic through the bones in the ears instead of the eardrums, which means he maintains full use of both ears while radio traffic is silent) that two of my guys had entered the house through a sliding door in back. I made my way into the garage, which was set up with makeshift partitions. I heard someone moan, but it was not until my eyes slowly adjusted to the darkness that I realized that the garage was housing numerous persons.

A commotion in the house seemed to mobilize the people in the garage, so I flicked on the overhead light. It was disgusting. A dozen or so men were practically piled against each other, fully dressed, and all of them were in desperate need of a personal hygiene workshop. Their moving around stirred up an overpowering odor.

I checked my radio to see if the other search team needed assistance and was advised that they were questioning dozens of occupants scattered throughout the three-bedroom house. Announcing my intentions loudly, I walked around the garage scrutinizing the men until I noticed one guy hiding his face with his blanket. I asked to see his face. He refused. I demanded to see his hands, and he complied. I told him to put his hands down to his sides, palms down. He complied without showing his face, but I was actually looking for a cloverleaf tattoo on the back of his left wrist, which was there in plain view. While my partner backed me up with his service weapon, I pulled the blanket off the fugitive and placed handcuffs on him.

Meanwhile, a second person appeared from behind a hanging blanket to protest my arrest of the fugitive. I couldn't believe it: a second bail fugitive had jumped right in my face. My partner hooked him up on the spot.

A more detailed search yielded a total of five bail fugitives (one more was too iffy to take) and a loaded double-barrel shotgun on the windowsill I had passed by to enter the house. Ostensibly, my uniform prevented the men from firing the shotgun. It was a good night.

The lesson here? First of all, I used both sets of handcuffs, my backup flashlight, my uniform, a radio, and, no one could tell for sure, but my Kevlar helmet may have saved my brains from fertilizing the grass near the fence.

If not prohibited in your state, it is fine to mimic some of the equipment used by the cops. These professionals are out there to arrest offenders, and their equipment suits bail fugitive recovery agents as well. Look at it this way: would I be writing at this very moment if I caved under the wannabe badgering of my contemporaries and crossed that window in street clothes? I can't say for sure, but what do you think?

TAXES

After you've received your business license, the write-offs for bail fugitive recovery businesses are fairly substantial. Think about it.

- Your office on wheels is deductible—though I'd advise you not to claim a 100-percent deduction on the car. The fuel, maintenance, equipment, and repairs are all deductible.
- Your office equipment can be deducted on a depreciating scale.
- You can write off postage and copying expenses.
- You'll have telephone and cell phone write-offs.
- You can deduct any travel expenses (e.g., motel, food).

Before setting up your business you should talk to a good accountant about your business operations, especially your taxes. If you can, find one who has worked with a business similar to yours. That can save you a lot of money in tax deductions, as well as in penalties and late fees that you will have to pay if you screw up your taxes. And it can keep you from being audited, believe me. Just know that most tax preparation people have no clue about what

a bail fugitive recovery person does. You'll need to instruct him about the ins and outs of your business so he can determine how various tax laws affect you.

LESSON FROM THE STREET

In the beginning, my knowledge of how to keep books for a business was seriously lacking, but as time went on I learned the ins and outs. Then I got an audit notice from the Internal Revenue Service (IRS).

I had never been audited before, so I brought everything I could think of to the meeting: wanted posters, receipts, bank statements, videos of arrests, and everything else related to my business.

The IRS auditor assigned to my case, Stephanie, was soft spoken, polite, and one hell of an interrogator. She made me feel like I could tell her anything.

As it turned out, the person who prepared my taxes had erroneously indicated sold goods when there weren't any such transactions and, despite my instructions not to, claimed a 100-percent deduction on my work car, both of which sparked an audit after the taxes were filed electronically. I also learned that equipment could not be deducted for the amount purchased. According to Stephanie, I should have depreciated the value of my equipment and spread out the deductions over five years.

In the next cubicle I could hear one of my fellow taxpayers yelling about [Nelson] Mandela being falsely persecuted and how "whitey [was] trying to keep the black man down." My fellow taxpayer was being grilled over the same tax issues as I was, so I couldn't see where his ethnicity had anything to do with his audit. I did overhear that he too had claimed 100-percent business use for his vehicle.

Thumbing through my vehicle travel log, which recorded mileage, gas and oil consumption, repairs, destinations, and other information related to my business, Stephanie challenged me, "So, Mr. Venator, show me proof that you were in Hollister on April 6, 1997."

I thought for a second. Then it occurred to me that I had got lost in Hollister and had to buy a road map. I had kept the receipt for the map, and, as a way to remember what the receipt was for, I had written the details on the receipt.

"Okay," I responded excitedly. I moved my boxes around and found the envelope containing the receipt. I pulled out the receipt and handed it to her. "There you go."

I could hear the same challenge being put to the taxpayer in the next booth: "So, prove to me you drove to San Jose on May 13, 1997."

"What the fuck are you talking about?" my fellow taxpayer mumbled.

"Please watch your language," the IRS guy warned.

"How in the fuck am I supposed to pull proof of that? This is racism! I bet if I was white you wouldn't be asking me these fucked-up questions!" Security guys started circling around the next cubicle.

While this excitement was going on in the next booth over, Stephanie matched up the two-year-old receipt with my vehicle logbook. It was a perfect match.

"Okay, what next?" I asked.

Stephanie closed my logbook and gave me a 95-percent deduction allowance on my office car. I took a small hit for incorrectly deducting business equipment, but, all in all, the audit went really well. At least it went better for me than it did for my fellow taxpayer, who was crying when I departed the building.

Start your business off right by maintaining good habits. Keep all of your receipts organized and don't mess around with the books. You'll have fantastic write-offs as a direct result of your bail fugitive recovery business, and, if you're doing it part-time, your expenses may be deducted from your regular income. Most important, make sure that you get good tax advice from a professional going in, and then follow it.

CHAPTER ELEVEN

How to Get That First Contract

Let's turn the tables for a moment here and pretend that you are a bail agent, not a bail fugitive recovery person. Knowing that you are responsible for what anyone you hire does or doesn't do, are you really going to trust everything you have accumulated to just anyone who claims to be a bounty hunter or recovery agent? Hell no! So you don't hire a recovery agent right away.

You will probably spend a month or two making phone calls or visiting cosigners yourself. At some point you may even start threatening legal action. One month turns into two and then five and a half. The trail is getting cold. You rush over to the courthouse and file a motion to extend time. You appear in court and get the extension, but do you scramble to find the bail fugitive? Not really. Before you know it, it's been almost another six months, and in three weeks you'll have to pay the county $20,000. As the bail agent on the hook, what do you do? Desperately look for a bail fugitive recovery agent, of course.

Now back to reality: you're an aspiring recovery agent who's trying to land his first contract. Most likely, on your first case you'll be handed a file or a jumbled pile of paperwork that is dated, missing vital information, and not really much help at all. The bail agent who hired you or some of his in-house staff have probably spent a little time on the case, but their efforts effectively burned what few leads there were to start with. Phone numbers are disconnected or assigned to different people, and, most likely, anyone you contact is just going to be pissed off from the previous contacts.

So how do you go about busting your ass to be handed this honor? And make no mistake—you will end up working hard to get this first mess.

Contrary to the oft-heard assertion that skips are "pouring into your area from other states," I suggest that you not waste your time and money trying to get business from out-of-state bail bond companies. In fact, you should really just concentrate on areas within a day's drive in normal traffic.

Do not use your local telephone book to cold-call bail agents. You will quickly find that many of the listed numbers ring the same bail agent, and he will get annoyed. I used to get a dozen or so telephone calls a week from people wanting to become bounty hunters. After a while, I started asking for a credit card number to cover all of the questions they were asking. The interruptions were really a bother.

You may want to go to your county jail or courthouse and ask for the bail bond book. Many counties keep track of who is bailing whom. Make a list and call the companies that seem to be doing most of the bail work.

Don't make a pitch over the telephone; request an appointment. At this point you should know that bail agents are not reliable at keeping appointments. They're typically on call 24 hours a day, seven days a week. And if given the chance, they'll take off and collect thousands of dollars in cash instead of keeping an appointment with you. Be patient.

Plan what you are going to say ahead of time. Wear a suit and be neatly groomed. Be prepared to produce your training certificates. Most of all, be prepared to have your knowledge tested.

You should have a business card and maybe a brochure to leave with the bail agent. After your appointment, send the bail agent a follow-up letter thanking him for his time. You may not get a contract right away, but often this type of contact will lead to contracts.

Bail agent offices are frequently located in the same neighborhood or area of the city, so when you leave the first bail agent's office, cruise by the other offices and speak with the bail agents or just drop off your information.

You can also contact your state department of insurance (or whichever department has jurisdiction over bail in your state) and purchase a CD with all the names and addresses of the bail agents licensed in your state. Filter out the ones that are out of your area.

Use your new computer to make a mail merge list of all the bail agents you want to contact. Create a letter that outlines your professional qualifications and have the computer insert all of the names and addresses onto your cool letterhead and business enve-lopes. Buy a roll of stamps and mail them. Your name and company will be out there. (See Appendix B for examples of letters.)

Finally, avoid getting small contracts spread over several counties. At one point, I had about a dozen contracts of less than $5,000 each spread over seven counties. The time and expense to investigate these cases properly far exceeded any possible return. You're working on a commission basis, so be wise about the work you take. But also recognize that you may have to go upside down on a case or two at the beginning to prove yourself to bail bond company owners. A case may cost you more than it is worth, but if it leads to bigger and better things, then why not? Like I said before, this is one tough trade to break into without help, but it can be done if you're willing to work hard to establish yourself.

LESSON FROM THE STREET

I had sent out 500 letters with absolutely no results whatsoever. Tired of waiting around for a response, I rode my bicycle to the gym and sparred with some of the guys, weight trained, and swam; rode over to a fast-food place for calories; and staggered through my front door.

My message machine was blinking. I figured it was Mom making sure my diet contained all the necessary food groups and that my arm was sore from getting the new season's flu shot.

I hit the shower, got dressed, and plopped myself onto the couch in front of the TV, where I fell asleep watching Captain Kirk fight the lizard man. The ringing phone jarred me out of a deep sleep. Disoriented, I finally found the phone. "Hello," I slurred.

"I would like to talk to Mr. Venator," a female voice said.

"I'm Rex Venator; who's this?"

"I need some recovery work."

I didn't know what to say. I was still disoriented, and this was my first recovery call. I mean, what do you say when a caller wants you, a private citizen, to hunt down another human being?

"Er, uh, okay." I finally stammered.

I cleared my throat, shook my head, and repeated, "Who is this?"

I must have sounded drunk or stupid. The bail agent wasted no time in making her evaluation. "Oh, just forget it!" she said and disconnected.

"I send out 500 hundred pieces of mail, and I blow the first and only call!" I chided myself.

I didn't have Caller ID, so I couldn't call her back. Then I thought maybe she was the one who left the message, so I hit the button to listen.

"Hello, this is Gerald Wilson with Bail-A-Lot Bail Bonds. I was hoping to speak to a Mr. Venator. You may return this call at . . ."

"Wow," I said to myself. Not wanting a repeat of the previous call, I washed my face and got a glass of water before returning the call.

"Bail bonds," the man on the other end said.

"My name is Rex Venator, and I am returning a . . ."

"Rex, can you meet me now?"

That would mean abandoning the *Star Trek* marathon, but bills were due, and I had no clients. "Sure, where would you like to meet?"

Mr. Wilson suggested a restaurant in his town two counties away.

"How will I know you?" I asked.

"If you're going to hunt for me, you had better be able to pick me out," he said.

At the time I was on a very strict diet, and the smell of greasy food was somewhat unsettling to my stomach. The restaurant was nice and clean, but I would have preferred to meet with Mr. Wilson at his office.

Mr. Wilson entered the restaurant with his wife, a spectacularly lovely lady, who drew glances from all the male patrons. Mr. Wilson, who was wearing a Hawaiian shirt, was healthy looking and had a bright smile.

I stood up from the booth and introduced myself. Mr. Wilson sat down with his wife, Mary, and we exchanged some brief pleasantries.

"So," Mr. Wilson began the interrogation, "how many bail skips have you caught?"

Mr. Wilson struck me as an intelligent reader of character, and, bearing in mind that I am a terrible liar, it made no sense to embellish my experiences to a man capable of detecting my lies.

"Aside from making countless arrests as a uniformed law enforcement officer and as backup for an out-of-state bail agent, this is actually my first solo meeting with a bail bond company owner."

Mr. Wilson studied me for a moment. Mary smiled politely at me and said, "You look awfully young. Do you mind if I ask your age?"

I provided my age and other biographical information, which seemed to satisfy them. Mr. Wilson, unbeknownst to me, had run a full make on me and was himself a former cop out of the same county as I had been.

Mr. Wilson quizzed me on whom we knew in common. *So far, so good*, I thought.

"So what do you know about bail?"

I had spent two weeks in my county law library (time well spent) and two hours watching a bounty hunter movie starring Steve McQueen (time not so well spent, in terms of learning the bail business, as it turned out). I soon found out that I didn't know as much as I thought. Mr. Wilson grilled me on numerous bail topics, schooled me on others, and asked about my investigative techniques.

"I would begin with the telephone directory, courthouse, and neighbors," I began.

"What if all that obvious stuff has already been done?"

"I have a knack for spotting seemingly trivial items and making something out of them," I replied.

"But you've never worked a solo case before," Mr. Wilson countered.

"I'm a trained investigator."

"Yeah," Mr. Wilson reasoned, "but you're used to having access to government information sources. Now you don't."

"A computer can only tell you so much. I will get out there every day and beat the street until something gives."

"Are you going to carry a gun?"

Ah, I thought, *a trick question.* "If I think it is necessary." I had no clue at this time whether or not I could legally carry a gun.

"What law says you can carry a gun?"

Got me. "I don't know."

Mr. Wilson pulled out a penal code book and slid it across the table toward me. "I have to run to the head. You find me a law that says you can carry a weapon while arresting a bail skip."

Mr. Wilson returned after five minutes or so, and I was still thumbing through the book without much success. Mr. Wilson took the book, flipped through the pages, and pointed out a section. "How do you interpret that?"

I read the section—12031(k)—and racked my brain trying to see if it was applicable or a test question. "It would appear that anyone could carry a gun while trying to arrest someone."

Mr. Wilson, Mary, and I continued this conversation for about 90 minutes. Suddenly, Mr. Wilson pulled two files from under the table and handed them to me.

"I'm going to give you a try," he declared. Thus began a business relationship and a friendship that survive to this day.

I closed the two cases he handed to me, but I have to admit that it was a tremendous amount of work, with many learning experiences (read: minor mistakes).

I can't predict whether you will be subjected to this type of first meeting, but I can confidently predict that any bail agent will hire someone who knows the information imparted in this book over a new bail fugitive recovery person who does not.

Since that day, countless bail agents have contacted me for meetings, but it has been my impression that most had made up their minds to hire me before making that first phone call. I don't know why, but I've never met with a bail agent who did not hire me on the spot. It could be reputation or desperation, who knows?

Bail recovery is a highly complex field. Finish this manual, learn the lessons, follow the instructions, and you'll ace your first interview.

CHAPTER TWELVE

Dealing with Those Crafty Bail Agents

Mr. Wilson turned out to be a fair, honest, and reputable businessman, but there are a number of people posting bail bonds who aren't. The following examples illustrate various unethical behaviors.

A new bail fugitive recovery person asked me to help him with his first case. We met the night of the hunt, and, after reviewing his documents, I informed him that the bail agent had given him a forged certified copy of the bail bond, making any arrest attempt illegal. The bail agent had cooked up a bail bond face sheet and used his own stamp. I suspect that the bail agent was either too lazy to go to the courthouse, or the actual bond was worth much more than the forged one.

In another case, I spent two solid months and hundreds of dollars putting information together on two separate bail fugitives whose cases were four counties away. I faxed in a status report that both cases would be closed within 12 days. The next day, the bail agent called and mysteriously terminated my contracts.

He said, "Yeah, just send me what you got." I sent him exactly what he sent me—nothing.

A week later, he called and put me back on the cases. A couple of hours after that, some guy called, wanting me to drive four counties away to give him my files on the two cases. It turned out that the bail agent thought he could symbolically put me back on the cases and have two months' worth of investigation happily turned over. I refused.

As a result, the bail bond company took a $187,000 hit five days after an informant had called me to tell me where both fugitives were staying. The bail agent, for some reason, opted to scheme instead of just paying me and ended up losing—big time.

Another time a bail agent used me to bring in a dangerous bail fugitive on an $8,000 bond while knowing that there was another bond on the same fugitive for $25,000. I should have collected $3,300 for surrendering the bail fugitive, instead of $800, but I was not aware of the second bond because of the hurried nature of the arrest.

Never let a bail agent tell you how to operate. It's fine to pretend that you are being supervised, but, remember, the bail agent called you out of desperation. He is probably about to go bankrupt and feels that he has nothing to lose—and this is true if you're the one taking all the chances and shelling out the up-front money.

Before jumping on the case, take the time to visit the courthouse holding jurisdiction over the bond. Pull and study the bail fugitive's file. Check for any other active cases on the same bail fugitive. It's a good place to start your investigation, and you'll quickly figure out if the bail agent is trying to screw you out of some cash.

Bail agents will frequently request status reports concerning your progress. This is fine, but you must be intentionally vague and even misleading in your reports; furthermore, do not give the bail agent precise information on your investigation. You are spending your time and money on the case. The bail agent may use your information to arrest the bail fugitive and deny you your commission.

Always specify in your contract with the bail agent that you will receive payment for *causing* the exoneration of the bond rather than just *arresting* the bail fugitive. You may very well find the bail fugitive already in custody. It is reasonable to charge 3 percent of the penal amount of the bond if it cost you time and money to track him down in jail. This detail should also be specified in your contract or at least worked out ahead of time with your client.

The bail fugitive may turn himself in because he knows you are looking for him. This is especially common if your search involves members of his family. For example, if you woke up Grandma and Grandpa in the middle of the night to search their retirement home, they may either convince the fugitive to surrender or he may decide on his own to do so, either to spare them further inconvenience or to spare himself further humiliation. This is very common. If it costs you time and money to cause the self-surrender, then you should be paid for making it happen. Again, work out this detail ahead of time.

Finally, always assume that you are being used by the bail agent, who will try to screw you out of your hard-earned money at every turn. Not all bail agents are like this, but I've been burned enough to be wary.

LESSON FROM THE STREET

I had two contracts sitting on my desk from a bail agent named William. I performed the usual surgery on the files, which consisted of eliminating the obvious. I logged on to a couple of Web sites and found one of the fugitives in jail. I called the jail and confirmed that the bail fugitive was in custody. Next, I called the bail agent to advise him.

"That's great news," William replied. "You know what I'm going to do?"

"I have no idea," I answered.

William cleared his throat. "I'm going to send you a check for $25."

Another character-building experience, I thought. "Okay, you have a good day," I retorted.

I turned to the other contract, hoping for a better outcome for me. Two weeks of traipsing all over two states yielded a firm address in a rural California county. I called William and gave him specific information on my intentions for that night.

The road was barely visible with the high beams on. The team and I drove for more 30 miles without seeing a light or another motorist. Finally, we found a gas station where we could refuel and study the road map. It was time to hit the most probable location for the bail fugitive thus far.

After several passes, we identified the address. It turned out to be a prefabricated house sitting on approximately five fenced-in acres of heavily wooded hillside. It quickly became clear that my city experience was about to be tested.

I sent one of my team members up the dirt driveway of an adjacent property to watch over us. This watcher was wearing high-end night-vision goggles so he could relay intelligence from a hidden flanking position. The remaining four of us waited for the signal from the only team member who could see in the dark.

"R-1, R-2," the watcher radioed.

"R-1," I replied.

"Go."

The team and I unhitched the fence, pushed it open, and began walking up the hill. The approach was approximately 300 feet as far as I could tell. Suddenly, my watcher warned over the radio, "Dogs!"

Approximately eight dogs rushed us from up the hillside. They were a ragtag bunch of small and large breeds, and they set upon us very quickly.

"Stun guns and Mace!" I yelled.

We all let the sparks fly from our high-watt stun guns and sprayed Mace at the dogs' barking faces—it worked. We continued to move up the hill.

"Gun!" the watcher yelled over the radio. We all turned tail and made our way for the gate down the hill.

"Man with a rifle pointed at you—run!" the watcher alerted us.

I veered right, turned to look up the hill, and saw only darkness. Meanwhile, the dogs got brave and started nipping at our heels. With some degree of effort, we managed to get out of the fenced-in area and closed the dogs in.

"I see a man running into the woods," the watcher advised.

I got on the radio and asked for more information, but whoever was running into the woods was out of sight.

"He's gone," my watcher reported. "Guy with the rifle went back inside the house."

A local sheriff's deputy arrived 45 minutes later and convinced the homeowners to let us search the house. We came across several items that led us to believe that it was the bail fugitive who had run into the woods.

The deputy told us that there weren't enough resources to assist in searching the woods, but that we were free to take the risk of being shot by landowners if we wanted to continue the hunt. We declined but opted to question the homeowner, who by now had unloaded the rifle and removed the bolt. He stood with his arms crossed over his large belly and declared angrily, "I would have shot all your asses."

I looked at the deputy, who was nodding in approval at the man's words. I tried to explain the situation to the uncooperative man, but his listening devices were disconnected.

"I told that bondsman to go ahead and send you," the man boasted.

"Excuse me?" I responded.

"Yeah, the bondsman told me to turn in my brother-in-law or he would send bounty hunters here."

"When did this occur?" I asked.

"He called about three hours before you got here. He told me that you'd be here unless I told him where my brother-in-law was."

"Thank you for your time," I said concluding the field interview.

Are you wondering what happened here? Putting it succinctly, William had not only screwed my team and me financially, but had put our lives in danger. He tried to use us as intimidation to convince his bail fugitive to surrender without telling us. After all the time and money I had spent on the case,

William—who had never even paid me the $25 he promised on the first case—had actually called ahead and told the rifleman with the pack of dogs that we were coming, resulting in an ambush.

In an effort to avoid paying $1,000, William had created a situation where a firefight could have erupted between my team armed with handguns and the rifleman with canine backup.

I have not worked with William since.

As a new bail fugitive recovery person, you will probably be taken advantage of several times before you catch on, but at least now you have a heads-up on what to look out for.

CHAPTER THIRTEEN

Choosing Partners
or Individual Contractors

One of the most important things you will have to do in bail fugitive recovery work is choose a partner or individual contractors to work with. Some impetuous people never fully develop a fear of consequences, so they tend to make the same mistakes over and over. I will simply define these people as stupid. I don't want to offend anyone, but this manual deals with the trade of hunting humans. Are you really going to trust such serious business to a person who takes actions irrespective of their legal, moral, and ethical nature? Frankly, I will not work with people of low character, and you shouldn't either. Danger levels rise geometrically when you team up with hot dogs or cowboys with a penchant for trouble.

In choosing a partner, I am of course looking for someone who is in compliance with all applicable laws of my state and has some sort of training when it comes to confronting people. In this trade, there is no way to avoid confrontation, and if someone cannot deal with confrontation, then I can't use him because of liability concerns.

My partner of 12 years had prior military experience and nothing else when he first started working for me. I trained him to function on the streets just as I do, and we have remained good friends to this day. We each came to know what the other was going to do without saying anything. I always knew that he would back me, and he knew that I would back him. This example is proof that you can take someone not specifically trained in this business and develop their skills, as well as a good relationship. The problem is that you won't know what to expect until you're out there doing the job, and you had better hope that you read your new partner correctly.

In preparing for this book, I reviewed a number of videotapes and photographs from the past decade or so. They reminded me of the number of would-be bail fugitive recovery persons who, for whatever reason, had jumped into this work with both feet, only to jump back out twice as fast.

Bail fugitive recovery work is not for the *Nintendowave* generation (a term for those raised on video games and microwave food) who expect instant gratification. An aspiring recovery agent could very well find himself out there on the cold, unforgiving streets night after night with no results, which makes this work too difficult for people who expect instant results. There is a lot of turnover in this trade, and quite a few prospective bounty hunters have washed out with me as well.

One example that comes to mind is the guy who used his soon-to-be ex-girlfriend's credit card to purchase $2,200 worth of equipment for this job and then gave up and disappeared after only two long nights on the job. Another guy failed to mention his heart condition to me when he applied, while another was arrested for allegedly striking his wife, which made it illegal for him to possess a firearm and also demonstrated certain personality traits that made him unsuitable for this type of work.

Indeed, there always seems to be a ready supply of wannabes, but good help is nearly impossible to find. That is why you must scrutinize anyone wishing to work with you in the bail fugitive recovery trade before putting both of you in harm's way.

Your partners must be qualified for the job, as described in Chapter 1, and it is your responsibility to make sure that your help is in compliance with all applicable laws.

Where should you look for partners or part-time help? The obvious answer is law enforcement because of the similarities in duties between police officers and recovery agents. In fact, some people argue that bail enforcement is not just the enforcement of a private contract between private parties, but that it is a quasi form of law enforcement. For example, I can arrest a bail bond client by means of a bail surrender before he fails to appear on good cause (e.g., failing to notify me of any change in address or employment information, failing to check in, or leaving the state, or if a co-signer gets nervous and wants off the bond). However, once the bail bond client fails to appear and the court holding jurisdiction over the bond issues a warrant, the sheriff in that area won't accept the bail bond client as a "bail surrender"; he will

only accept the bail bond client as a wanted fugitive under a citizen's arrest. So, in essence, the law only allows me to book the bail client as a fugitive subsequent to the issuance of a warrant, which is largely in the realm of a law enforcement officer's duties.

Law enforcement is very tricky to get into. Some people get hired their first attempt, while others try for years yet can't get through the hiring process or just don't score high enough to make the hiring list. From these ranks of would-be cops, you find people who are drawn to bail enforcement. In fact, the partner I described earlier attempted for 12 years to get a job in law enforcement while he was becoming an established bail enforcement agent and bail bond company owner. Then one day he got a call for an interview, and now he is a federal agent. He credits his training and experience in bail enforcement for ultimately giving him the tools to steamroll the competition and get the nod for his current job.

People who have retired or been fired from law enforcement also look into bail enforcement work. The former are the people who have spent most of their lives wearing a badge and miss the excitement of interacting in the justice field. Then there are the ex-cops who are exes for many reasons. These are the people who spent their whole life trying to become a cop and have no other marketable skills. Getting fired from a law enforcement job isn't that uncommon, despite union and civil service safeguards. It is the thirty-something person who unwillingly found his way out of law enforcement with no marketable skills who seeks out bail enforcement or other security jobs.

An added incentive to hiring retired law enforcement officers is their ability to carry concealed weapons in all 50 states as mandated in the Law Enforcement Officer's Safety Act (described in more detail in Chapter 5).

People just getting out of the military are also on the hunt for jobs in the civilian sector. Unfortunately, there aren't too many jobs—aside from the adventure trades—that would favor people with infantry or Special Forces training over experienced or college-educated applicants vying for the same positions. To make matters worse, people who have taken the warrior path and lived the warrior life will most likely be bored stiff in an office job, where they have to punch in and out while being micromanaged by a nonwarrior.

From time to time I get queries from people with no military or law enforcement background but who have an extensive martial arts background and are looking for ways to put their training to use. So far, I haven't worked with anyone who started with a purely martial arts background.

There is a common thread among the individuals who want to be a cop, were a cop, are just out of the military, or are tired of sparring in a martial arts environment. In most cases these are the people who know, or think they know, whether or not they can handle a confrontation with a felony fugitive.

As I have stressed, good people for this job are very hard to find. I've encountered many people who couldn't do the work, although they thought they could at first. I'm always on the lookout for prospective team members who can stick it out and keep going. My mentor took a chance on me, and I have given that same opportunity to many prospects, with most of them giving up very quickly.

There is one aspect of being an employer that still perplexes and infuriates me. I use my reputation, which in itself is highly valuable and deserving of strenuous protection, to win a bail fugitive recovery contract from a well-established client. I spend my time, money, and effort tracking a bail fugitive, and in the process placing wear and tear on my personal equipment. I get chased by pit bulls to confirm an address. Finally, I use years of experience to lead a team—that I recruited and trained—into a hostile environment where a felony fugitive is arrested. After all this, I have had new guys, who stepped in for a couple of hours' work, demand a lion's share of the commission—up to 50 percent!

Whenever you take on a partner or independent contractor, you should make it very clear that *you* will decide what their time is worth. It makes no sense economically to split your commission in such a way that you are not being covered for something that your help would never have even been a part of without you.

All my guys sign the following documents before coming to work for me:

- Independent contractor agreement—spells out what is expected of each bail fugitive recovery person, what laws they agree to follow, what procedures they must adhere to, what their pay structure is, and so forth (see Appendix E)
- Intellectual property agreement—ensures that my methods and polices remain confidential
- Hold-harmless waiver of liability agreement—forces the signer to acknowledge the danger of the work and protects me and my business from any claims of injury or harm
- Noncompete agreement—requires the signer to agree not to advertise a similar business within my area of operation
- IRS Form W-9—required before you can deduct payments to employees from your taxes

Do not hire people to work with you who won't sign any of these documents no matter how desperate you are. You'll be thankful for holding firm in the long run.

LESSON FROM THE STREET

I had received multiple, time-sensitive contracts from a large bail bond corporation, with the promise of continued contracts for as long as the business relationship remained productive. To complete these contracts, my team had gotten spread out all over California, so I was in a bind for more help.

I contacted a 1299-qualified gentleman who had approached me earlier and who appeared to have impressive credentials and an attitude to match. He was experiencing a slowdown in his current job, so he jumped at the chance to learn bail fugitive recovery work.

I provided him with the documents listed above, as I do all new independent contractors. It didn't occur to me at the time, but he kept making excuses for his failure to produce the signed documents.

The two of us spent approximately 48 hours in a distant city, with me fronting all the expenses. The initial results were disappointing at best. As so often happens, by the time I got the contracts the bail agent's incompetent, in-house recovery people had beaten them beyond any semblance of workable cases. Although some of the cases were eventually closed, a few were terminal because of the time available to work them.

The new guy had quickly learned the lessons I showed him on the job and had done good work. I hoped to bring him onto the team full time. Unfortunately, I soon learned that he had gone behind my back and tried to scoop my contracts from the corporation I was romancing. To make matters worse, he claimed to be a master bounty hunter and penned a quick manual using my techniques and marketed it. The manual flopped. Although he may have learned some of my techniques, he didn't really know the business. As far as I know, he isn't doing any bail fugitive recovery work in California.

You can learn a valuable lesson from my experience. Protect yourself from any scheming independent contractors by making certain that they have signed the contracts up front, outlining what they can and cannot do.

AVOIDING SUBSTANCE USERS

Never team up with a drug user—it's just that simple. As a matter of fact, I advise reporting any drug-using bounty hunters to the authorities to help clean up the industry. I hear some grumbling out there, so let me illustrate my position on this.

You and your new partner encounter a bail skip hiding in the closet of a dimly lit room (this is pretty common). You open the closet door to find a shotgun rising toward your chest. You dive out of the way, and your new partner shoots the bail skip, who dies from the gunshot. What can you expect after such an incident?

You and your partner are detained on suspicion of murder (remember, most cops and lawyers are ignorant of bail law and the rights of depositors of bail). You are both hauled to the station for extensive questioning. Your partner, who does not exercise his right to remain silent, rattles off like there is no tomorrow. In fact, he submits to a drug test. The authorities find out that your new partner has alcohol, doctor-prescribed tranquilizers, marijuana, and even a little speed in his system.

All of a sudden, his clean shoot is considered involuntary manslaughter because of his probable clouded judgment. At any rate, a district or prosecuting attorney (or in rare cases a grand jury) will evaluate the evidence to determine whether the shooting was justified. His being under the influence is not going to help him make a case for a justified shoot. Additionally, you had better hope that your partner's gun is legal; that he used "defensive" rounds instead of ammo that might look excessive to a district attorney or, worse, to a jury; that all your documents are in order; or that the bail skip hadn't appeared in court earlier that day and cleared up his warrant, because an error in any of these situations would really cause both of you serious problems.

You are both tried. You are acquitted, but your former partner is convicted of burglary and being under the influence. So you go home, where a process server hands you notice of the civil suit brought by the family of the dead bail skip. You are about to spend the next five or so years defending yourself in court.

Long-lost relatives will suddenly come out of the woodwork seeking justice for their "loved ones" under these circumstances. Civil suits may not always be avoidable, but staying out of jail is completely up to you. Your best bet for avoiding jail following the advice in this book.

How exactly does the foregoing scenario justify ratting out a drug-using bounty hunter? You don't want politicians jumping on incidents like this to enact new laws designed to regulate or even abolish the fugitive-recovery trade. In fact, some states already ban bounty hunters. So far, the new laws in California have been for the greater good—in my opinion. However, I can see how a series of controversial incidents could eventually lead to laws that make bail fugitive recovery much more difficult, if not impossible. For example, in Arizona there was a shootout involving men posing as bounty hunters as a cover for a drug rip-off. People died in the shootout, and the story made national news. The initial news stories erroneously reported that bounty hunters had initiated the shootout, and by the time subsequent stories corrected this misinformation, the damage had already been done—by then there was pressure in about a dozen states to enact legislation to regulate the trade.

Right now there are bounty hunters on various reality shows, and if one of them does something wrong, or if other real-life bounty hunters do something that ends up on the nightly news, history tells us that changes could follow. These changes may not be in the best interests of the trade, far as I'm concerned. It is in your best interest to see that this doesn't happen. One way is to weed out the bad recovery agents.

LESSON FROM THE STREET

Before going out solo to apprehend a bail skip suspected of hiding out in a motel in South Hampton, Henry, who was on my team, had a few drinks. Henry, who was rather aggressive when he drank, approached the motel clerk and made various loud demands. In fact, Henry was so aggressive that the motel clerk called the local police.

The police arrived just after Henry had arrested his bail fugitive. The smell of alcohol on Henry prompted the police officers to investigate further, and they found that Henry did not possess the "authority to arrest defendant on bail bond form." One of the police officers knew that the arrest was not legal, and, therefore, carrying the gun was not legal. Under California law, a private citizen may carry a weapon when making or attempting to make a *legal* arrest. But Henry did not have the authority-to-arrest form, so the arrest was not legal; hence the carrying of the weapon did not fall under legal guidelines.

Henry was arrested and charged with violating various laws: false imprisonment, kidnapping, brandishing of a weapon, possession of concealed weapon, and public intoxication.

Henry never worked in the bail bond industry again.

I attribute all this to Henry's drinking. If he hadn't been drinking, I believe he would have approached the motel clerk calmly and rationally, so the police wouldn't have been called, and he wouldn't have been asked to produce the authority-to-arrest form, which he probably wouldn't have forgotten to carry in the first place if his judgment hadn't been clouded by alcohol.

CHAPTER FOURTEEN

The Pros and Cons of Wanted Posters

During your investigations, you'll likely visit shopping centers, subdivisions, apartment complexes, and other sites frequented by lots of people. You'll meet more people than you can approach individually and tell the same long story over and over about the persons you're trying to find. A much easier and more efficient way to reach a lot people is with wanted posters that include your dedicated phone number and any other contact information you think is relevant.

Let's say that you have reports that your bail fugitive is known to frequent a certain shopping center and nothing else. If prudent, visit every shop owner in the mall to gather leads. A poster enables you to make quick contact and leave the people you talk to with a photo and all relevant information.

Before producing and distributing any poster, you have to be absolutely certain that the information is accurately drawn from public record (e.g., court files, newspapers, city records). Observe the following rules:

- Do not misrepresent the bail fugitive's record to make him appear scarier, such as calling someone who jumped bail on a minor offense a serial killer or rapist.
- Do not include persons not directly related to the bail fugitive's unlawful flight from prosecution. In other words, do not put his wife, kids, or other relatives on the wanted poster to encourage contact by the bail fugitive.
- Do not represent yourself, as the creator of the poster, as being directly affiliated with any law enforcement agency.
- Make sure that you put the right photo on the poster. You may recall that earlier I cautioned you against using photos from the bail agent. Bail agents have mistakenly given me photos of brothers, aunts, and unrelated fugitives to use on wanted posters.

- In some cases you'll want to limit the use of wanted posters to avoid tipping off the bail fugitive and causing him to run or be wary. On the other hand, smart use of wanted posters can be very embarrassing and cause the bail fugitive to surrender. Only you can judge whether and when to use wanted posters on your various cases.

I started printing the fugitive information and photo on a standard business card and distributing that as a wanted poster after seeing my legal-size wanted posters being used as floor mats by various cops. Full-sized posters are still used for street contacts and posting in areas where the bail fugitive is believed to frequent. (Examples of a business card poster and full-sized poster are located in Appendix C.)

LESSON FROM THE STREET

I put the file in my carry bag and ignored it for three days. Then I pulled it out to see if anything would jump out at me, but nothing did. I even passed it to a team member for a fresh perspective, but he also drew a blank.

The bail fugitive knew I was looking for him, and he proved a worthy opponent. As it turned out, he had 23 separate places where he could stay with assorted relatives and friends. I had been to 10 of the locations, and in each place everyone had played dumb about the fugitive's location.

Finally, I created a wanted poster with all the details, including the information that the bail fugitive would be the subject of a massive sweep during a given week. I mailed the poster to 22 of the locations but purposefully did not send it to the 23rd location, which hadn't yet been inspected.

The bail fugitive was wearing on my nerves, so on Monday afternoon I drove by location 23, a single-story structure on a street with oversized lots. The backyard abutted a large field being prepped for planting.

My team and I assembled at 0200 hours the following morning. I wasn't sure if the fugitive would be at this final unsearched house, but I was certain he wouldn't be at any of the other 22 locations. I grabbed the grease board from my car trunk and drew up a plan. We would pay the bail fugitive a visit at 0330 hours. I approached the front door and waited until I was informed by bone transducer mic that all team members were in position. I then knocked on the door, waited, and used my flashlight to knock louder.

A beautiful woman peeked through the curtains near the front door. I keyed my mic, "Contact, one female front door." I shined my flashlight on my uniform to show her that I was not a home invader standing in the dark. Seriously, a bad guy is not going to shine a flashlight on himself, and my action implied that I had a right to be there. So she opened the door.

"Yes?" she asked.

"Good morning, ma'am, we're looking for a felony fugitive, and we have information that he is staying at this location. Are you alone?"

Her sleepy face grew concerned. "Oh my God, there's nobody here but my kids and my husband."

I smiled and maintained a polite tone. "Again, ma'am, I must apologize for disturbing you at this hour, but we really have to be sure." I pulled a picture of a bail fugitive. "We're looking for this guy. He's a bad one."

"I've never seen him before," she insisted.

"Ma'am," I said reassuringly, "it'll take us two minutes to check, and then we'll be gone. I'll take your telephone number so as not to disturb you like this again."

She looked at me and my cruiser and then said, "Come in, but please don't wake the kids."

"Agreed," I said. I keyed my mic, "Search team in."

"Ma'am, do you have any weapons or anything else that we should be aware of in the house?"

"No," she said firmly.

On the living room sofa a man slept soundly. "Who is this?" I asked.

The woman walked to the back of the sofa. "That's my husband."

"What's his name?" I whispered playfully to put her at ease so she would identify the sleeping man.

She confirmed that sleeping beauty was my bail fugitive—almost.

"Does he have any ID?"

She turned around and removed a wallet from the kitchen counter. She tried to hand it to me. "Could you please remove his ID for me?" I requested.

"Oh sure." She took the man's driver's license out and handed it to me. "See, he's not the man you showed me."

"I don't know." I keyed my mic, "10-87 code 2 10-15, 1."

"What does that mean?" she asked.

"That means I'll have to speak with this man momentarily."

My team entered the living room. At the same time a child appeared. One of the team members withdrew a stuffed toy from his gear and got Mom's permission to give it to the child, who was then sent back to bed.

I nudged the bail fugitive, but he didn't wake. I envied his ability to sleep the way he did, but at the same time our arrival in the living room at this hour was no accident: most people are in their deepest sleep at around 0400 hours. This little-known fact decreases the danger factor somewhat when entering a strange house. With some prodding, the man finally woke up.

"Excuse me, sir, I'm going to place these handcuffs on you. It's just procedure until we figure everything out."

The bail fugitive looked very confused, but his wife was a big help. "It's okay, sugar; just do what he says."

I handcuffed the bail fugitive and confirmed his identity.

"Well, ma'am, the good news is that creep isn't here; however, your husband is wanted as well."

"What!"

"Sorry about that."

"You tricked me!"

"He's going to the county jail."

My team and I left the area with due haste while being screamed at the whole time by the angry wife.

My tactic had been a long shot, but it worked. I didn't know the bail fugitive was married (I later found out that he wasn't legally) or had kids, but the wanted posters flushed him to the one location he thought was safe, as evidenced by his deep slumber.

CHAPTER FIFTEEN

Getting Paid for All Your Hard Work

For the most part, I haven't experienced many instances where payment has been a problem. Some bail agents, after their liability has been taken care of, have tried to nitpick verbal agreements to renege on paying me, but I have managed to get paid on *nearly* all my work.

The biggest problem you'll probably have is slow payment. Usually, a series of telephone calls and perhaps a letter or two will do the trick. You may have to make a personal appearance at the bail agent's office or knock on the door of his residence in the middle of the night, but this is very rare. You'll likely get your money eventually.

If push comes to shove, you may have to take the bail agent to small-claims court or even superior court to press your rights. I've never done either, but I am capable of running through the court system with relative ease because of my experiences with the legal system garnered from this job.

LESSON FROM THE STREET

My team and I hoped to get some information on Rick from his brother Ray, whom my team and I had mistaken for Rick earlier in Chapter 6 and almost arrested.

The team member who accompanied me into Ray's apartment this night had not been with me the time I had almost arrested Ray. Upon seeing Ray, my partner immediately pulled him off the couch and handcuffed him even though I kept insisting that he leave Ray alone. We cleared up this misunderstanding fairly quickly, and I started my questioning.

"Ray, have you seen your brother?" I began.

Ray lay back onto his ratty sofa and twisted around to get comfortable. "Nah, man."

This went on for a few minutes until I decided to interject a new dynamic into the conversation. "It's too bad you haven't seen him, Ray. There's a $500 reward for his arrest." I turned my back and started out of Ray's smelly apartment. I hadn't traveled 20 feet when Ray hissed at me. I turned around to find that he had followed me out.

"Are you serious about the money?"

I had him. "Absolutely."

He perked up and whispered, "That motherfucker came over here trying to act all bad 'n' shit. He called me a punk and said he was going to kick my ass."

I realized that Ray was trying to justify what he was about to do. I also realized that $500 was about to cut family ties. "So where is he?"

Ray hesitated for show and then said, "You remember the room you guys got me in?"

"Yes," I replied.

"He's there. Right now." Ray looked around to make sure no one was listening. "You're sure about the money?"

"You write down how you want the money order made out and where you want it sent, and you'll get it," I promised.

"Right on," Ray said, nodding in approval.

The bail fugitive was right where Ray said he would be. The team and I hooked him up and loaded him into my sedan, and I headed three counties away to book him.

This particular contract involved a bail agent who had a slow payment history. It would take this guy 90 days or longer to make good on his debts, so I decided to get paid that very night.

I called the bail agent and told him that I was en route to book his bail jumper. Naturally, he was ecstatic since the summary judgment date was just two short weeks away and his bounty hunter hadn't been able to find the bail fugitive for the past 12 months.

"You know that gas station just off the freeway by your house?" I asked.

The bail agent hesitated for a moment. "Yeah, how do you know where I live?"

"That's what I do," I said. "Anyway, meet me there with the commission check."

"It's 4:15 in the morning! I'll mail you a check later on today. I'm going back to sleep."

I wasn't going to play this game again. "Well, that's not going to work for me."

"Dude, if he's going to fuck you over, you may as well just drop my ass off," piped up Ray, who had no idea how much he helped me by saying that loud enough for the bail agent to hear.

After ordering Ray to be quiet, I said to the bail agent, "You still owe me money for the work I did last year. I fully expect to get paid on that work and this arrest in 15 minutes."

"Sorry, I can't do that," the bail agent responded.

"Okay," I began, "I'll cut this guy loose right here, and good luck finding him now that he knows he's hot."

My bluff worked. The bail agent met me with two checks at the gas station.

Would it have been right to cut the bail fugitive loose? No way.

Did I keep my promise to Ray? Yes.

As a bail fugitive recovery person, you will have to take measure of your resources and act in your best interests because the bail agent isn't going to worry about whether or not your bills get paid.

GETTING STIFFED

Running a bail bond company means that the bail agent is running a highly complex organization, complete with paying bills, billing accounts receivable, making court appearances, posting bonds all hours of every day, and incurring horrendous advertising and telephone costs. There are a lot of factors that can prevent you from getting the hard-earned money you should, besides greed on the part of the bail agent.

A bail bond company must advertise to even think of surviving. Take a look at most telephone book directories and you'll see various advertisements. Each ad, depending on the size and color, is very expensive. In addition, a bail bond company will most likely have to advertise in numerous geographic areas to make a profit. In short, advertising costs can eat up a bail bond company's profits rather swiftly. And if he pays all his money for ads, the bail agent may not have enough left to pay you.

Another factor that can prevent you from being paid is if the bail company goes out of business. The much-feared summary judgment can literally do this. The summary judgment, as you may recall, is what happens just before the court loses jurisdiction of a forfeited bond. This means that the bail agent or the bail agent's surety company has to pay the summary judgment or the county where the bond was posted can refuse to take any further bonds from the bail agent and all of the bail agents using the surety's bonds.

If an agent's company has a series of slow months, he cannot pay his bills—including the debts owed to bail fugitive recovery people (that means you) who have, well, bailed him out from having to pay summary judgments.

You can tell that a bail bond company is in financial trouble by the type of bonds the company is writing. Sole proprietorships responsible for writing loose-bail (bail-speak for posting bonds with little or no money down, unreliable cosigners, and no collateral) are generally in trouble and are trying to stay afloat by bonding out anyone with a beating heart and a little cash.

This is normally when a recovery person gets the call to clean up a bunch of fast-approaching summary judgment dates. Be wary of these because it could mean that all your hard work is for naught. Also pay attention to the talk among others in the bail business. News of financial reversals has a way of leaking out.

LESSON FROM THE STREET

I received a frantic call from Fast Freddy, a bail agent who had been pleased with work I had done for him about eight or nine years ago and decided to do me "a favor" by sending me 19 contracts by overnight delivery.

The package arrived the next morning, and I wasn't altogether impressed with the underwriting: sparsely filled out bail applications, no collateral, little to no money down, no co-signers, no proof of employment, no indication of U.S. citizenship, etc. I could tell right away that these contracts weren't going to be easy, but I dispersed the contracts to my team.

Within a week, we had closed five of the contracts, and I took the completed paperwork to Fast Eddy's office, only to be greeted by an eviction notice prominently displayed on the front door. I called Fast Freddy on his cell phone, but the service had been shut off. Next, I had one of my team members do a computer search for Fast Freddy's home address. When I arrived at his house, I saw that he was setting up business in his garage.

"Rex!" Fast Freddy screamed. "Tell me you took care of those contracts for me."

"Well," I said while handing Fast Freddy five booking sheets, "we're moving right along." I surveyed his garage. He had moved his entire office to his home. "I'll take a check or credit card on these."

Fast Freddy pointed to his work in progress and shrugged his shoulders. "My checkbook is in there. I'll mail you a check."

"No problem." I drove away knowing that my guys had just spun their wheels and made five arrests for no compensation whatsoever.

Things happen that aren't necessarily in the control of the person holding your commission. It's a rarity in my experience, but you may find that it happens from time to time.

Fast Freddy probably knew that his ship was sinking when he contacted me. I just wish he hadn't wasted my time and the time of my team when we could have been taking care of paying jobs.

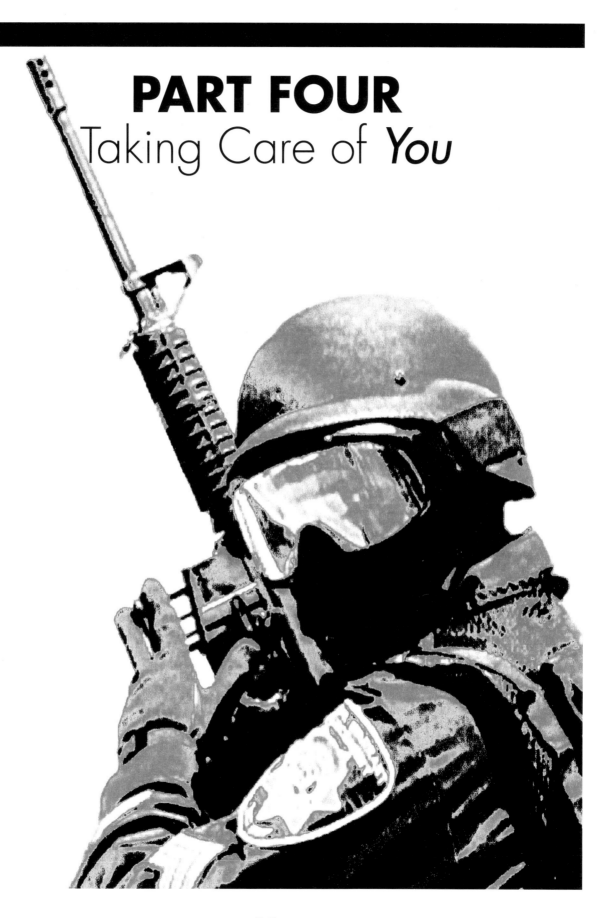

PART FOUR
Taking Care of *You*

CHAPTER SIXTEEN

Preserving Your Anonymity

In the last part you learned how to take care of your business; in this part you will learn how to take care of you by ensuring your personal security. You will find out that by establishing good safety habits at the very start of your career, doing things properly on all your cases and not taking shortcuts, and using a little common sense, you will have gone a long way toward making sure that you and your family are safe and secure.

By now you should realize that there is more to bail fugitive recovery than what is portrayed by the entertainment industry. But there is one emotion common to real-life bail fugitive recovery agents and fictional characters alike: fear. Settle down—I know what some of you are thinking, that you aren't afraid of anyone because you're one bad hombre. That may very well be true; however, you aren't invincible—and neither is your family.

If you decide to pursue bounty hunting, then one thing is inevitable: you are going to upset some unstable, unpredictable, and, possibly, homicidal people—no matter how well you treat people or how thoroughly you do your investigations.

The only real way to protect yourself and your family from vengeful people is to preserve your anonymity. You must be able to fade away when the job is done, which is very difficult in our present-day world where more and more of our moves are recorded and stored electronically. And you aren't the only one who knows how to track down people.

There you are with your family enjoying the latest reality television show (don't pretend that you don't watch them) when the doorbell sounds. You nonchalantly open the door to find the felon you arrested standing there with bad intentions in his eyes. BOOM! You've just become another assassinated bail fugitive recovery person because the local telephone book led the shooter straight to your front door.

Another scenario goes like this: you're hot on the trail of some punk whose mother put up her home as collateral for the bond. The punk isn't going to blame himself for putting Mom's house on the chopping block—no way! He is going to see you and the bail agent as the immediate threats to her house. Pretty soon there are a couple of gorillas looking to break your legs. I know this sounds far-fetched, but it has happened to me.

"That's easy to prevent," you say. "I'll just get an unlisted phone and a post office box for my mail."

Simply getting an unlisted telephone number and post office box is what I call an illusion of anonymity. Give me, a private citizen, this basic information, and I can find you in minutes. I understand that your typical hood probably isn't sophisticated enough to track down people as easily as a trained investigator can, but not all bail jumpers are unsophisticated. Fugitives with access to resources can be a significant pain in your ass.

So what do you do to preserve your anonymity? At first it may seem that there isn't really much you can do without a lot of cash, but here are some avenues worth considering:

- Open a mail drop in the next town, using a dummy address.
- Get a dedicated cellular phone billed to the mail drop address—and never use the phone to call home or any family members or for anything unrelated to your work.
- Use the fax machine at the mail drop for any unsecured incoming or outgoing faxes.
- If it is legal in your state, change your driver's license so that your home address is not used.
- Use your mail drop for your personal and business checking accounts.
- Dedicate a vehicle just for recovery work.
- Do not give any retail operation your actual home address.
- Never use your home telephone number or actual address to apply for credit.
- Do not use your home address to register to vote.
- Keep your home address out of court files.
- Avoid discernable patterns in your everyday

activities (e.g., picking up your mail at the same time every day, traveling the same route to and from your office, going to the gym at the same time every day).

I know this sounds like a pain, but I told you at the very beginning that this work is dangerous, so be careful to leave no trails for the bad guys to follow to your door.

LESSON FROM THE STREET

The team and I had tromped all over the moonless San Francisco East Bay looking for our bail fugitive, a bona fide survivor of street gunfights, according to the local cops. He was so notorious that a string of eight police vehicles trailed our five cruisers all over Oakhurst looking for the six-foot-three, 350-pound drug dealer with bullet scars.

We took the whole troupe on over to the bail fugitive's mother's house, looking to close this $150,000 case without anyone getting hurt. I knocked and led the first wave on the interior search, while the cops surrounded the large, two-story Victorian-style house. The interior was unbelievable. The floor-to-ceiling junk that lined the passageway from the front door to the kitchen created the sensation of walking through a damp cave. In addition to the trash everywhere, people were lying around in crevices. We searched everywhere we could in the trash-filled house, but our bail fugitive was not there.

I found my way outside and walked around to the backyard. Stepping through a maze of junk, I noticed a half-sized door at the base of the house. One of my team members joined me, and we slowly entered what appeared to be a sort of basement. Junk was stacked floor to ceiling here as well, save for a single walkway.

The basement was dark, with spiders dangling about the rafters and with half-curtains as backdrops. I heard a television playing inside and was fearful of being ambushed.

Inside the basement I found a convalescing man watching TV while lying on a torn-up, smelly couch in front of a coffee table strewn with rotten food. He told me that he was the bail fugitive's brother and that he was recovering from gunshot wounds received a week earlier.

"Where's your brother?" I asked politely.

"He gone," the bandaged man replied.

"Do you know where?"

"Nope."

I explained to the brother that his mother's house was in foreclosure and because his brother had skipped out on the bail. I asked him to relay a message to his brother to turn himself in so the house wouldn't be foreclosed on. I handed him a business card with my name and mail drop address.

That night on my way home I ended up posting a bail bond, which fattened my business accounts but drained my energy reserves, so I got a late start the next day on my yard work. I stared blankly at the grass while turning up the sound on my portable tape player. It was like walking through a dreamy haze cutting the lawn. I stopped the mower to turn the tape over, and, just then, someone tapped my shoulder. I thought it was lunch, so it was startling to find the gargantuan bail fugitive making some pretty deep impressions on my front lawn. I took off my headset and pretended that this giant of a drug dealer was just what I expected to see at my house.

"Can I help you?" I asked.

"Yeah, bitch," he said as he stepped closer. "You the motherfucker threatening to take my mamma's house?"

I looked off to the left and saw a running Cadillac filled with three less-than-casual observers and then up at the bail fugitive. "I'm sorry, sir, but you seem to be confusing me with someone else."

The bail fugitive kept his eye on me and yelled to his backup, "Is this the place?"

I was shocked by what happened next. The backseat passenger held up what looked like a business card and compared it to a telephone book. He then nodded.

"My boy says this is the place."

"Who am I to argue?"

"Now lookie here. You tell that motherfucker that he be dead if he fucks with my mamma's house." The bail fugitive sauntered over to his ride, got in, flashed me a dirty look, and rode off.

I darted inside the house, located my local telephone book, and found that my unlisted name and address had been published there.

I immediately began searching for a new house in another county, and in record time I had moved my family into a new unlisted residence. The day after the move, I resumed the hunt for the fugitive who had threatened me at my own house. It took another two weeks to find that prick in Texas, but we got him.

I did everything right to maintain my residential anonymity, but an error out of my control led a potential assassin right to my front door. That is the nature of this business. Can you handle it?

CHAPTER SEVENTEEN

Taking Universal Precautions

In this business, you will find yourself rubbing elbows with the very bottom of our society, and these bail fugitives may not place the same kind of priority on hygiene and health as you. Believe me, you do not want to catch some disease from one of these scumbags. Besides your own health, this could endanger your whole family.

Under no circumstances are you to assume that a bail fugitive is free from such communicable diseases as hepatitis, HIV, tuberculosis, or an assortment of other infectious illnesses or infestations. As the saying goes, an ounce of prevention is worth a pound of cure, so you should always wear gloves and ask a bail fugitive to reveal the presence of any sharp objects before patting down his clothes and body. You don't want to discover too late that there is a used needle hidden somewhere on his body. Also, you might consider loading your first aid kit with (at a minimum) small squeeze bottles of iodine syrup (e.g., Betadine) and Clorox, strongly disinfectant baby wipes, hand cleaner, and other sterilizing and disinfecting aids.

Hepatitis, usually transmitted through bodily fluids, is 40 times more contagious than the HIV virus. You can contract tuberculosis by having a contagious bail fugitive cough in your closed cab during a long trip to the jail. I'm convinced that you can get scabies by rubbing your sweaty skin against the critter-invested skin of a sweaty bail fugitive. And unless you have ultrashort hair, head lice are another occupational hazard you have to watch out for.

At the very least I wear my pants tucked into my boots, long-sleeve shirts, gloves, and eye protection when making arrests. All of this stuff gets disinfected well when I get home.

I recommend that you take a community college course on universal health precautions designed for emergency medical personnel and police officers, for more information.

LESSON FROM THE STREET

The case file perplexed me. By all accounts, the bail agent had given me a simple pick-up with full commission. Although I was suspicious, I had bills that needed to be paid.

The bail fugitive, Tony, reportedly lived in a rather swank neighborhood. As we drove into the neighborhood, every property had professionally groomed landscaping, and the house belonging to Tony's mom appeared to be the nicest one on the street. We decided to visit her because Tony had failed to appear on drug-related charges and she had cosigned on the bond, using her home address.

I knocked on the cherrywood front door, and an older lady with a Victorian look about her answered the door. "Can I help you?" she asked eloquently.

"Good day. Are you Mrs. Smith?"

She nodded and replied, "And you are?"

"Ma'am, we're from the bail bond company, and our visit is in regard to your son." I showed her the booking photo of her son. "Your son failed to appear in court, and he has a warrant out for his arrest."

Mrs. Smith chewed her lip for a moment, turned to look inside her house, and then turned back to me. "Tony isn't here."

"May we come inside and see for ourselves?" I asked.

After hesitating for a moment, she blurted out, "He's at the hospital," and then gave us the name of the hospital and shut the door firmly in our faces.

At the hospital, I told the receptionist that I was Tony's cousin so that I could visit him. He was in a locked isolation room with evacuation air filtering. Except for the hand-sized pustules on his upper torso and his underfed frame, he didn't look sick as he quietly paced back and forth like a restless tiger at a zoo.

The nurse left the room, and I snuck a peek at his chart. Tony was suffering from AIDS, hepatitis, tuberculosis, and a nasty temper. A note on the bottom of the chart read "will fight."

It was obvious that Tony was being kept locked up in that room to avoid contaminating other people. The bail agent had a clear-cut case to petition the court to vacate the forfeiture and exonerate the bond because of Tony's condition. I was damn glad that I wouldn't have to wrestle with this unhealthy lad.

I later learned that the bail agent had known of Tony's health status but not of his involuntary quarantine. I billed the bail agent for my time and told her off for sending me after this guy with no warning about his communicable diseases. She reluctantly paid me and still calls me to do work for her.

As I've maintained all along, bail agents don't have your best interests at heart. You are responsible for doing your homework and taking every precaution to protect your own personal security and health. Be careful out there.

CHAPTER EIGHTEEN

Dealing with Bail Fugitives Under the Influence

As you will learn, I am not in the practice of hunting down fugitives on the weekends, for a variety of reasons ranging from practical to personal. First of all, I did not become self-employed to have my weekends taken up by work. Most important, I have found that the use of controlled substances by bail fugitives is far greater on weekends, and dealing with intoxicated people can be very dangerous.

Back when I was in law enforcement, I was present in a large county booking area during a study designed to determine what percentage of people booked were under the influence of a controlled substance. The study found that 80 percent of new arrestees were under the influence. Moreover, it was my observation that the number of people brought in under the influence of controlled substances was higher on the weekends than in the middle of week. So remember that when you're looking for fugitives and try to avoid weekends if you can. Of course, this may not be practical in this line of work, especially when you are just getting started. If a hot lead comes in on a difficult case on Saturday night, you sometimes have to respond. Just know that weekends tend to be more dangerous for those in this line of work.

Let's go over the more common drugs you will encounter and some of the types of behaviors you can expect when the bail fugitive is under their influence.

ALCOHOL

Depending on the amount and type of alcohol ingested by the bail fugitive, you can get a happy drunk, a hostile drunk, an unpredictable drunk, or a drunk who smells very bad and has little concern for your automobile upholstery. In any event, you're going to have to play this one by ear and respond according to the subject's behavior.

You may run into a bail fugitive with delirium tremens (DTs), who will shake and generally be extremely sick. If your detainee has such symptoms, you should have emergency medical services check him out before taking a long trip. The last thing you need is a dead bail fugitive in your car.

If you have to arrest an intoxicated fugitive, then you should be prepared to fight him into handcuffs and even all the way to the jail. If it will calm him down, you can tell the bail fugitive that you're taking him to a bar for more drinks.

Finally, don't waste time trying to reason with a person who is highly intoxicated. Your best bet is to humor him into handcuffs, into your car, and all the way to jail.

METHAMPHETAMINE

Based on my law enforcement, bail bond, and bail fugitive recovery experience, you are most likely to be contracted to bring in a bail fugitive who is either under the influence of methamphetamine (also called "meth," "crystal," "crank," or "ice") or is involved in the highly volatile production of the drug than with any other illegal substance.

I've seen bail fugitives act absolutely insane with paranoia after prolonged use of methamphetamine. My advice is to take every measure to involve the police when a freaked-out meth user is the focus of your hunt. Meth users are extremely dangerous.

A very serious aspect of hunting a meth user is the possibility of coming into contact with a meth lab. Involvement in a meth lab is a very common reason why people get busted and end up as bail fugitives. These labs can be stationary or mobile. They can give off the strong odor of ether or none at all. If you come up on a drug lab, you should take care not to cause any sparks or contaminate your clothes and gear. And you should call 911 immediately. The chemicals there are hazardous and need to be disposed of properly.

This is one of those rare circumstances where you can order every person in the room of a drug lab to get down on the ground and arrest them all. Why? Because every person in a room where a drug lab is in production is committing a felony, and, if a felony is being committed in your presence, then you have the lawful right to make a citizen's arrest, according to the laws of most states. Moreover, arresting all the perpetrators ensures your personal safety. Indeed, you cannot get distracted with arresting the bail fugitive while multiple felons are milling about—it just isn't safe! The key here is being completely sure the activity you are witnessing is in fact felonious so that you don't encounter any civil or criminal penalties.

PCP

Use of PCP (phencyclidine, also know as "angel dust," "blast," or "dust") by a bail fugitive can cause a lot of problems for anyone who tries to arrest him. Symptoms of PCP use include blurred vision, inability to think or speak coherently, exaggerated gait, violent behavior, and superhuman strength.

If you absolutely must make the arrest, the number-one rule is to not shock the fugitive's senses. Quick jerky movements, yelling, bright lights, talking too fast, or suddenly touching the skin can set off the arrestee. Talk to the bail fugitive slowly in a monotone voice. Do not shine bright lights into his eyes or get too pushy. Finally, *never* try to arrest a PCP user by yourself. Aside from its staggering hallucinogenic effects, PCP is a painkiller. This means that your bail fugitive will feel no pain in a fight, including the tearing of tendons and muscles to overpower you. I have been in struggles with PCP users where it took seven or more officers to make the arrest.

Finally, do not use pepper spray, a stun gun, or a carotid restraint on a PCP user. Although the reasons are not completely understood, people under the influence of PCP have died after being subjected to a high volt, a less-than-lethal restraint system, or the largely disallowed choke hold or carotid restraint.

MARIJUANA

Frankly, I've never had any problems with bail fugitives under the influence of marijuana (also called "pot," "weed," "Mary Jane," or "cannabis"). At the very worst, I had to listen to philosophical ramblings on various topics on the way to the nearest jail with pot-smoking bail fugitives.

The danger with marijuana-related arrests is primarily with marijuana dealers or growers. For example, armed persons may guard clandestine marijuana fields or indoor-cultivation centers. Additionally, the fields may be booby-trapped.

• • •

All in all, I'd have to say that involving the local police or sheriff's personnel is your best way to stay safe and out of trouble irrespective of the type of illegal drugs associated with your bail fugitive.

LESSON FROM THE STREET

The bail fugitive in this case was Cooper, a meth user and cooker. Additionally, Cooper's girlfriend, who worked at a jewelry store, stole credit card numbers and expiration dates of store customers for her and Cooper's use, so some of Cooper's charges were for credit card fraud. And you guessed it: the bail agent took a credit card as payment to post the bond for Cooper. Consequently, the bail agent had to pay all the money back and lost his credit card machine in the process. Shortly thereafter, he called me to find Cooper and bring him in.

The team and I had been hopping from house to house in search of Cooper. In fact, the dozen or so police officers helping us had decided that the bail fugitive was such a danger to the community that they were willing to jump their jurisdiction and operate in the local sheriff's jurisdiction, where the on-shift deputies joined us as well.

Cooper had a history of setting up his three-day meth labs in motel rooms with complete disregard for the safety and welfare of the occupants. Confidential case contacts had provided us with the locations of several of Cooper's lab operations, but he was long gone by the time we got to each of them. The last location on our list was identified by nothing more than a street and city name.

On this night 12 police officers, 10 sheriff's deputies, and my team of five congregated behind a grocery store to put the game plan together. Everyone agreed that the information on the last location was sketchy at best and most likely undeserving of any serious effort, but, all things considered, we decided to move the whole troupe on to the street in question.

Incidentally, we didn't have our regular recovery sedans (my team and I were at an annual dinner *on the weekend* at the time the call came in), so we jury-rigged standard camcorders on tripods with bungee cords that didn't work very well.

The caliber and professionalism of the law enforcement officers working with us on this particular night were impressive. Ordinarily, in a group of cops this large, I can tell the experienced ones from the rookies, but there was no discernable difference in the skill levels of these peace officers; indeed, they were all top-shelf.

The train of police cruisers and team vehicles parked on both sides of the street in question. We then disgorged from our vehicles and walked the street from both directions. The street had two rows of tract homes laid out in typical fashion. The lighting in the area was very poor, but it didn't take long to zero in on the target location by just walking the neighborhood. The unmistakable stench of a drug lab permeated much of the neighborhood, so all we had to do was follow the odor to a house seriously overgrown with shrubs and in need of repair.

We decided that my team should handle the

door-knock because a bail fugitive recovery agent has a wider sphere of authority than the cops in certain instances. In this case, acting on an informant tip, we had led the whole party to the house in question. The cops didn't need a warrant to be there, and, if our presence revealed any type of criminal activity, the cops—who were providing a civil standby at our request—were right there to jump in and take over. It was beautiful.

The cops and my team quickly surrounded the house. I knocked on the door, and a shadowy figure rattled the blinds to get a peek at me. The equally shadowy figures of six or so cops standing behind me must have been unsettling because a tremendous series of crashes erupted from inside the house. Windows popped out, doors flew open, and people bolted from the house in all directions.

Several foot chases ended just as quickly as they began. The cops were having a ball until a batch of them ran headfirst into Cooper. Calls for assistance went out three yards to the north. Cooper had fought his way through three cops and was hopping fences. Jumping over a fence and into a sludgy swimming pool slowed him down. By the time he worked his way to the edge of the pool, six cops were waiting to fish him out. Cooper started fighting the instant he was on land.

It took a total of 14 cops to get that nut into handcuffs. It was also necessary to hog-tie him. The paramedics who responded characterized Cooper's condition as acute paranoia because he thought he would melt if touched by anyone.

A deputy in a filthy class A uniform signed my 1301 form (see Appendix D). With that, we thanked the cops, received thanks in return for multiple felony and warrant arrests, and were on our way.

No way could my team of five have dealt with this situation effectively or safely. The number of runners was too great, and our bail fugitive would certainly have melted away, so to speak.

CHAPTER NINETEEN

How Does the "Three-Strikes" Law Affect You?

The county jail where I was working at the time consisted of various facilities, with each specifically designed to house varying security levels for inmates: the maximum-security hardlocks, the medium-security direct supervision modules, and the minimum-security camp. At this time, PCP was very popular, and regular users might suddenly be unable to come down off the debilitating high. The jail had what they called the "space shuttle," an isolation cell for "moon walkers" (so-called because one of PCP's effects was to distort senses, so a crack on the sidewalk might appear much larger to a PCP user, thus causing an exaggerated gait) who had been arrested for being under the influence of PCP at the minimum-security camp.

One day I was working with a deputy the inmates called "Dracula" because he had ordered blood to be drawn by medical staff as evidence hundreds of times from inmates suspected of being under the influence of PCP. Dracula and I discovered a gram of methamphetamine on an inmate and properly arrested him for possession of a controlled substance on jail property—a felony. I later learned that this inmate, arrested for what would have been a misdemeanor on the street, had been sentenced to 25 years under California's three-strikes law. This incident occurred shortly after the three-strikes concept had been enacted in California, the first state do so. Hearing of this inmate's sentence, it dawned on me that some people, knowing that they were looking at 25 years to life for otherwise minor offenses, might react violently when they were facing arrest.

Today, you, as a new bail fugitive recovery person, must consider how three-strike laws or other laws that require mandatory sentences for repeat felony offenders will affect your method of operations. You could very well get a contract that seems run-of-the-mill, when in fact things are much more serious. Again, this is why it is crucial for you to do a preliminary investigation before attempting to arrest a bail fugitive.

As a bail agent, I would receive calls from people who were desperate to get their family or friends out of jail as quickly as possible. The expressed urgency from these callers served as a cautionary signal to find out what the hurry was. Usually the hurry had to do with as-yet undiscovered probation or parole issues or the possibility that the arrestee was a three-strikes candidate. Not all bail agents will react negatively to this type of bail risk and in fact will write the bond out of shortsightedness brought on by greed. Naturally, the bail agent's new client will jump bail and disappear. Weeks will turn into months, and then you, as a bail fugitive recovery agent, will get the call to bring in this repeat offender.

Arresting a professional businessman for failing to appear on a suspended license charge is one thing, but going after a bail fugitive who is looking at 25 years to life is a whole different set of risks. You need to be aware of the risks and plan for them before you attempt an arrest.

LESSON FROM THE STREET

The bail fugitive I was hired to find was looking at his third conviction, which made his apprehension more unpredictable and dangerous. Compounding the problem was the fact that he was living in a house filled with children and elderly relatives. The bail fugitive wouldn't leave the house, so we had no choice but to take the bail fugitive there.

To make this situation even trickier, preliminary investigation had revealed that his immigrant family had a long track record of filing civil suits ranging from disputes with neighbors to racial discrimination against the city, which is how we found the bail fugitive. It was my fear that we could do everything by the letter of the law and still find ourselves the focus of a frivolous civil action. In fact, my attempts to involve the local cops had proved futile because one of the family members had a pending civil suit against the department and the city alleging civil rights abuses.

On the night of the operation one team member had the flu and couldn't make it. We wired the other team members (four, counting myself) with audio transmitters fed back to a recorder in my sedan, and dash-mounted video cameras would capture everything in the front of the house. I assigned one of the team members to video camera duty, and he was to follow me with no breaks in the tape.

The factory-installed spotlights on our sedans lit up the front of the target house. I walked to the front door, with my every move being recorded on video, and knocked on the front door. The woman who answered was dumfounded by all of the lights and the camera-laden team member just behind me.

"What did I win?" she asked curtly.

I got permission to enter the house and found the bail fugitive asleep on the living room sofa. By now a dozen or so family members had gathered and were watching our every move, but so was the video camera.

I nudged the bail fugitive, who jumped to his feet, pulled a knife from his waistband, and brandished it at me. Various family members began screaming lawsuit this and lawsuit that, but I ignored them.

I had just purchased a brand-new Level III holster and had practiced drawing my firearm until it came out smoothly, but I was under stress. For some reason I couldn't draw my weapon—it was locked into the holster for keeps. To make matters worse, the bail fugitive rushed me with his knife.

By now my team was all spread out: one was at the back, one was at the front near the sedans, and one was holding the video camera. But luck was on my side.

As it turns out, the bail fugitive had been awakened out of a very deep sleep, enhanced by the use of some unidentified chemical substance, so his attack was sloppy, ill timed, and reasonably easy to defend against. I took his blade away, whipped him around, and used pain and compliance to control him so that I could handcuff him. The bail fugitive was taken to the sedans outside, where he was relieved of crack cocaine, a crack pipe, and another edged weapon.

During all this, the family never made a peep. One has to wonder whether or not the camera made a difference.

The bail fugitive had jumped up out of deep sleep acting as if he had nothing to lose because, in my opinion, he was looking at 25 years to life under the three-strikes law. Sticking me with a blade wasn't going to make his situation any worse. Moreover, he was on drugs and willing to kill.

The three-strikes law has changed the playing field, and this is something you will have to deal with at some point.

CHAPTER TWENTY

Just Say No

Preliminary investigation on a $1,500 contract from an East Coast surety revealed a number of disturbing things. First, the commission on this case split five ways left me with a grand total of $50. Second, the bail fugitive, an old guy, had an extensive history of resisting arrest. Third, he had once been arrested for murder but had been acquitted. Last, my case contacts told me that he was spouting off about killing bounty hunters the first chance he got.

To me the case wasn't worth the potential trouble or even my time. I called the surety and explained the situation. He agreed and decided to pay the summary judgment, which surprised me.

At some point, you will be offered a case where the risks far outweigh the benefits. This will probably be a difficult decision for you, since turning down a case may mean that the bail agent won't offer you any future work worth taking. You'll have to decide for yourself how to handle this inevitable part of the business, but you need to know when you should just say no. Some factors that might cause you to decline a case are as follows:

- The commission isn't worth the amount of time and effort that you would have to put into finding and apprehending the fugitive.
- The fugitive has a violent record, and the dangers to yourself or your teammates far outweigh the rewards.
- The bail agent who offers you the contract has a reputation in the field as someone who will try to cheat you out of commissions.
- There isn't enough time to find the fugitive before summary judgment.
- The bail agent or his in-house staff have worked the case exhaustively and have alienated every potential lead and put the fugitive on notice.
- The fugitive is probably hiding in a jurisdiction where the police are uncooperative at best or

maybe even obstructionist toward recovery agents, and the hassle or fear of legal liability outweighs the reward.

- To apprehend the fugitive you would have to travel across state lines, which would require travel expenses and that you be in compliance with the bounty hunting laws of other jurisdictions.
- The fugitive has fled across an international border (e.g., to Mexico or Canada), where you have no legal authority to arrest anyone and return him to the States.

LESSON FROM THE STREET

John and I had worked together many times before; I had complete faith in him, so I agreed to go along with him as backup on this particular arrest.

I had never seen a classier setup on a car than what John was driving when he picked me up that day. He definitely knew how to mix up aftermarket parts to come up with impressive lines; moreover, the car had a flawless black paint job. I offered to buy the car at first sight, but John turned me down.

We drove into a neighborhood stacked with double-story apartments on both sides of the street. The mature trees lining the sidewalks indicated that the neighborhood had been in existence for some time. Large kids played all around with miscellaneous toys, and nobody seemed to pay too much attention to us.

We pulled up to the target apartment building, got inside the apartment with permission, and handcuffed the huge bail fugitive without too much trouble, except for the bail fugitive's mother and wife screaming their heads off.

Stepping outside was like stepping into a nightmare. The whole front yard was covered with gigantic men, women, and kids demanding that we release their relative. We started to move toward John's gorgeous car, but the mob of jumbo-sized relatives rushed us, pushing and shoving us until they wrenched the bail fugitive from our custody.

John and I ran to his car and got inside. About a dozen or so of the family members turned John's car into a trampoline, causing considerable damage. John couldn't move his car or he could have been charged with assault with a deadly weapon, so we had to pull our weapons. Seeing this, one of them yelled, "Gun!" and the crowd dispersed. We drove away.

Later after regrouping, John and I put a plan together to rush in, grab the bail fugitive, and rush out. On the night of the new operation, John and I, along with my team, waited in the parking lot of a local department store for officers from the local police department. A patrol supervisor called Sergeant and eight police officers arrived to assist us. I let John do the talking.

"This is what we got," John told Sergeant. John passed around posters on the bail fugitive and explained everything: who we were, who the bail fugitive was, and where we expected to find the bail fugitive.

"Excuse me," Sergeant said to John. "Can I talk to you over here in private?"

John looked puzzled but replied, "Sure."

John and Sergeant conversed in private while the team and I passed the time socializing with the crew of young-looking police officers. After a while, John and Sergeant returned.

"Let's roll!" Sergeant yelled out to his fellow officers. With that order, our police assistance drove out of sight. "What's the story?" I asked John.

John smiled patiently. "Well," he started, "they don't want to go in."

"What?"

"Evidently, that cluster of apartments is a gang stronghold, and a bunch of cops have been hurt there." John continued while putting his gear into the trunk of his banged-up car. "The supervisor didn't want to go in with a new batch of rookies. He said that they'll grab the guy with veteran officers when the bail fugitive leaves the stronghold." With that, we shut down the whole operation.

True to his word, Sergeant arrested the bail fugitive three days later at a convenience store one mile away from the gang stronghold, and John paid my team for our time.

Standard preliminary investigation would not have revealed the dangers associated with the gang stronghold. The only way to realize the danger was to go in firsthand and get attacked in an area that the police officers declined to go into.

There is nothing that says a bail fugitive recovery person must make an arrest. You can back off anytime you want—and sometimes it's the best move.

PART FIVE
Tracking Down, Arresting, Transporting, and Booking Fugitives

CHAPTER TWENTY-ONE

Where to Start?

You have now started your own business, done your research, advertised, and got your first case. What's next? Apprehending fugitives and bringing them in so you can get paid. This section will teach you to remain safe as you arrest bail fugitives.

Before getting into this chapter, a note is in order about why I chose not to include a chapter specifically about investigations. It would take a book to cover this topic in the depth it should be, and that was just not in the scope of this book. In fact, there are many books just about investigations, and rather than cover the subject inadequately I recommend that you pick out a few of them and find out the tricks of the trade from the investigators themselves. I have included some titles in the back of the book that you might want to consider, or you can go to the library and online and find other sources on your own.

Assuming that you have acquired all of the documents listed previously (Chapter 3), go to your home or office, spread everything out, and get your file folder ready. You'll carry this folder with you at all times: don't leave home without it. It contains everything you need to make a lawful arrest.

On the file folder tab, I suggest that you write the bail fugitive's last name followed by the last two digits of the year, and a two-digit code for the bail agent and summary judgment date, which is normally about 180 days from the date the clerk mailed the notice of forfeiture but varies from state to state (see Appendix K). This way you'll know at a glance to whom the file pertains, which client the case belongs to, and how long you have to work it.

Next, place all of the stapled documents on the left side of the folder and everything else on the right side so that when you need to mobilize you won't be scrambling to put everything together.

Thoroughly study every square inch of every document in the folder and make your own notes. Bail agents tend to write important information on napkins, paper place mats, and business cards. To make matters worse, you'll find odd notes written in weird angles. I don't exactly know why, but that's just how it happens. One of the documents you should have from the bond is the bail bond application itself (see Appendix I). It contains a treasure chest of leads about the fugitive and the person putting up the money for the bail, including past and current addresses, phone numbers, employers; Social Security numbers, spouses; and any property owned and its value. Of course, as noted previously, bail applicants and their relatives have been known to lie on this application, so keep that in mind.

You may want to conduct Internet searches, call nearby jails for in-custody checks, and visit the courthouse holding jurisdiction over the bond. Once at the courthouse, which could be several counties or even states away, you should check criminal, civil, and small claims courts, as well as any other public information sources available to you. Make copies of everything you find even if it seems irrelevant at the time.

You should then go to your home or office, sort all the documents, and make a list of possible addresses based on the information uncovered.

In the interest of moving quickly, it is very important to plot directions from each address to the other with stops at police jurisdictions if the addresses jump from one jurisdiction to another.

Whether or not you decide to use the telephone for pretext investigation is up to you. I send my entire intelligence dump over to my pretext guy because I cannot lie well, even over the telephone. My idea of a phone pretext consists of demanding to know the bail fugitive's whereabouts, and this would not be effective at all.

If possible, do a cursory drive-by of probable locations—after notifying the local cops and making sure all your documents are in order (just in case)—and record potential hazards (e.g., dogs, gangs, bad approaches, security systems, fences).

For the actual apprehensions, I usually pick a Monday or Tuesday to meet with my team at 2200 hours; I avoid Friday, Saturday, and Sunday because traditionally these days have not worked well for me, as explained previously. This initial meet is ordinarily at a 24-hour copy place so that all team members can get copies of the documents that I'll be carrying. From there

we systematically inspect every location on the list where we might find the bail fugitive or any new information leading us to him.

Make no mistake, it takes more time to do things this way, but it is more effective and much safer. Of course, you could simply take an address off the bail application and go sit for days at a surveillance post, waiting for your bail to show up, or you can make things happen. The choice is yours.

LESSON FROM THE STREET

After being split six ways, my commission on Jay would cover my house payment. Therefore, even though I didn't like working for the bail bond company on the hook, I decided to help out Tim, a fellow bail fugitive recovery agent. Tim's preferred methodology consisted of long hours of nothing but static surveillance, usually at just one location.

"Rex, I really do think the guy's there."

I had the feeling that Tim was simply working off a hunch. "Why do you think that?" I asked.

Tim didn't answer for some reason.

"Have you actually checked the house?" I persisted.

"Well, no, but I think the guy's there."

Tim had one eye that shifted back and forth horizontally in such a way that it was terribly distracting when searching a house with him. You'd keep wondering what he saw when he hadn't seen anything. It was very unnerving around closets and just before entering a room. "Okay, Tim, saddle up," I said with a smile, while avoiding eye contact.

It went like clockwork. It took about five minutes to discover that the house Tim had sat on for three days had gotten a new set of tenants a month ago, but the new occupants did provide us with a new address for the bail fugitive.

This bail fugitive, had an extensive history of beating up people, including a police officer in the town where our fugitive's old address was. We called dispatch and relayed all the pertinent information, including the identity of the bail fugitive, and shortly thereafter, 10 police cruisers with two officers in each showed up at the gas station where we were holed up. Some of these cops really made me feel old, because they looked about junior-high-school age. (One of the key advantages of doing your work at night is that you generally work with newer, more aggressive cops since the older cops with more seniority—and less time to go before their retirement—opt for the day shift.) One of the older-looking police officers approached me and asked, "Where is this guy? Let's go tune him up."

"Excuse me?" I asked.

"This is the guy who fucked up my partner."

"Oh," I said while trying to maintain my composure. I looked around at the 20 cops. "So which one of these fine officers will be coming with us?"

The motivated police officer smiled and said, "All of us. Let's roll."

Had I not been driving a decommissioned Crown Victoria Police Interceptor, I wouldn't have been able to keep up with the convoy. There were 15 cars all together, which provided quite a sight. These ultratrained young police officers demonstrated excellent skills as they assisted us in searching target locations two through nine for Jay, the bail fugitive.

"Dude, we're all getting off in five minutes," the brash young officer informed me. I was beginning to like him, knowing he meant well. Although he and his partners had done well

searching the eight houses, we had one more house to check.

"Do you have to?" I asked. "We only have one more house, five minutes from here."

"I'm sorry, man, we got to go. Good luck."

With that, the energetic young police officer shook my hand, and our 20-officer crew headed off duty at 0700 hours. It had been a good night with them along, and their presence would be sorely missed.

The team and I entered the last target house at 0710 hours. The occupants swore that they had no idea whom we were talking about. Then a door opened behind me, and I saw Jay. On this occasion, the fugitive did look like his booking photo.

According to his record, Jay had a violent streak, but, luckily, he had just awakened. I talked him into handcuffs, loaded him in the car, and had him standing in line to be booked into the county jail by 0720 hours. As I was about to leave the jail, Jay yawned and asked me, "Who are you guys again?"

I fanned his breath away, turned my head, and told him. Then he got mad and decided to fight, but by then he was the jail's problem—and I had just made my house payment.

My method of investigation is highly proactive and effective, but it's not for everyone. We searched 10 houses that night when only one was on Tim's original list—and his address was actually in the wrong city—but that's how he was taught.

You'll find many sources on how to skip trace, but remember that as a bail fugitive recovery agent you'll most likely get the cases that cannot be tracked conventionally. You have to be assertive and know what you are doing.

CHAPTER TWENTY-TWO

Working with Law Enforcement

As a bail fugitive recovery person, you'll have a solid strike against you before you even meet the law enforcement personnel from whom you request assistance. Therefore, it is imperative that you step outside yourself and try to visualize what the hardworking cops will see when you make contact with them.

I can recall my first sight of a bounty hunter. I was a 22-year-old corrections officer when a large, bearded man climbed onto the booking intake ramp of the county jail. He wore a "great white hunter" style hat complete with leopard band. Two shotgun bandoliers filled with shells criss-crossed his partially exposed, furry, barrel chest. He casually sauntered over to the gun lockers, where he relieved himself of at least six separate handguns in addition to his shotgun.

Would you have put your life in the hands of the man described? I wouldn't, and most cops would be reluctant to as well. In fact, at the time I could never have imagined myself in the same profession as this caricature of a bounty hunter!

Always remember that cops think in terms of liability first and foremost. Ask a cop what he is going to have for lunch and he will undoubtedly weigh a multitude of factors into the decision. Is the eatery in a gang neighborhood? Will the waitress make some unfounded allegation? Will the patrol vehicle be vandalized in that particular parking lot? Will the food take too long and cause him to be late on a call? A police officer's first reaction to every situation is to evaluate it based on the risk involved to himself and to others. And it is on that basis that he will judge you when you request police assistance.

You should project an image of competence and professionalism to allay the police officers' concerns and secure their help. My team and I are clean-shaven with crew-cut hairstyles and professional uniforms. We all appear to be in excellent physical health. Any one of us can present a well-articulated notice of intent to arrest or request for police assistance based on rule of law and common sense. As a result, when we request police assistance, we get it about 80 percent of the time; the 20 percent of the time that we don't get the requested assistance is usually because of police policy restrictions or limited personnel.

That brings up the issue of whether or not you should request police assistance. The answer is contingent on your bail fugitive and the laws of the jurisdiction you're in. For example, you should request police assistance if your bail fugitive has a history of violence or you have reliable information that he is armed and dangerous. On the other hand, sometimes you're better off not directly involving the local cops and doing things your way. For example, sometimes to get help from a police department you will have to work on its schedule, which could result in long delays and perhaps in your suspect getting away.

In many cases the nature of the charges your bail fugitive is charged with could determine whether or not you get police assistance. In some jurisdictions your bail fugitive may be well known, and the department will practically throw help at you. At the same time, larger jurisdictions tend to have unofficial policies against helping bail fugitive recovery people.

Of course, there is one circumstance where involving law enforcement is the only option you have, and that's when the police officers are there with the fugitive and you cannot be because of distance, time restraints, an accident, or some other reason. It is going to happen to you, of that you can be sure. This is where the National Crime Information Center (NCIC) comes in. Bail fugitives who fail to appear on felony charges are placed on the NCIC, so that out-of-county cops will know that the person being stopped is wanted in another jurisdiction. However, this isn't always the case; sometimes someone fails to enter the bail fugitive's warrant into the national computer, so he won't show up when the police officer checks NCIC. This has happened more than once; it could form the basis for a legal motion to have the bond exonerated.

Peace officers will routinely run your bail fugitive's information as soon as you make contact with a police agency. Bail fugitives who

are on the NCIC are fair game. Conversely, bail fugitives who are not on the NCIC may not draw law enforcement attention or resources to your aid.

Having a fugitive listed on NCIC helped me solve the case of a female fugitive that I had been working on for 30 days straight with zero results. Suzy had friends all over three counties, but none of the dozens of contacts I made could tell me where she was. I was at an impasse since the cost of the case had surpassed any commission I would receive upon her capture.

I finally came across credible information leading me to believe that she and her methamphetamine-dealing boyfriend were planning to abduct her minor daughter from the custodial parent. Suzy's plan called for them to detour (while transporting a new batch of meth) into another state, where the abduction would take place.

Armed with this information, I called the custodial parent and warned him of the plot so he could protect the child. He was happy to give me Suzy's address in Oklahoma, but by now it had become cost prohibitive for me to travel to Oklahoma to make the arrest myself. I decided to contact the law enforcement agency holding jurisdiction over Suzy's hideout, and after a couple of dozen faxes and phone calls, the local heat picked her up. The deputy I was working with in Oklahoma faxed me Suzy's booking sheet, which I dutifully used to collect the commission. The Oklahoma cops helped me because Suzy was on the NCIC.

Although this case cost me more than I collected, it led to more work from the same bail agent.

LESSON FROM THE STREET

The team and I presented ourselves at the police station, waited for about 90 minutes, and then drove across town with a dozen police officers, a K-9 unit, and a police chopper to arrest a bail fugitive hiding on a $3,000 misdemeanor bail from another county.

I chose to involve the police on this case because this agency had an excellent reputation for solid community policing and professionalism, and my past experiences with it had always borne this out.

The operation was successful, and we arrested the first bail fugitive. Since the first operation had gone so smoothly, the team and I decided to drift on over to another county where a second bail fugitive had also been cooperative with my pretext guy.

After arriving at the new staging area, I pulled the next file to be worked to take one last look for anything that we may have missed. As a result of working for some time in a county jail, I had become gifted, if you will, at being able to look at a booking photo and predict the behavior of the subject. So, as is customary, I reviewed the file before determining our course of action and in this case judged the bail fugitive to be a runner. Therefore, we requested police assistance for this case as well.

While waiting for the police help to arrive, I decided to stretch my hamstrings and quadriceps since I thought we would have a runner on our hands. Within minutes eight police units arrived to coordinate our plan of attack.

"Why are you stretching?" a police officer named Steve asked me.

I stood upright and said, "This guy's going to run."

Steve looked puzzled and asked, "How'd you arrive at that?"

"Look at his booking photo," I responded.

Steve used a small flashlight to study the bail fugitive's face. "You know he's going to run by looking at his mug shot?"

By now, Steve's fellow officers were gathering around and looking skeptical. One of my team members offered, "He hasn't been wrong in more than 200 felony arrests."

Two of the officers joined me in stretching.

It is convenient to have local cops around to lead you to a specific location. They usually are familiar with the area and can give you important safety tips, but this time we were giving the tips.

The train of vehicles pulled behind the square, two-story apartment complex. The police officers began to slam their car doors while the team and I gently shut our doors. It was a semi-warm evening in a generally cool part of the San Francisco Bay Area, so I wasn't surprised to notice that many of the apartment windows were open. Suddenly, a well-intentioned police officer yelled, "Hey! What's this guy's name again?"

"Charlie Logan!" another police officer yelled back.

I flagged down Steve. "With all due respect," I said while pointing to the vast array of open windows, "can your guys not yell out the fugitive's name?"

Steve quickly advised his partners to keep it down in a hushed tone.

At this point, I quickly made my way to the apartment courtyard, where I saw Charlie suffering from a split second of indecision concerning which way to run. Although the assisting officers were very loud, they had effectively surrounded the apartment complex except for one corner.

"Excuse me, sir," I called out, "I was wondering if . . ."

Suddenly, Charlie bolted through the one unsecured part of the perimeter, and I sprinted with my freshly stretched legs to catch him. The bail fugitive was wanted for narcotics distribution with weapon and gang enhancements, so, as a part of the house inspection team, I had suited up with a tactical vest with ceramic plates, Kevlar helmet, and assorted gear, all of which weighed about 70 pounds.

I was about 100 yards into the chase when one of my team members whose equipment weighed less than mine caught up with me. At about 300 yards into the sprint, Charlie started to pull away significantly from us. Just then, Steve darted by like we were standing still. It was a good thing too because my batteries were starting to give out. I lost sight of the bail fugitive and Steve.

Out of breath, my team member and I rounded a corner. I started to go one way, but Steve emerged from the shadows convinced that Charlie had run into a cluster of houses in the opposite direction. Steve told me to have my team set up a perimeter around the northwest portion of the block, which we did.

Meanwhile, I could hear a police chopper and K-9 dogs doing what they do. It took the cops and their dogs about 25 minutes to find the bail fugitive, who had actually run to his meth lab, where a number of his buddies were cooking up a batch of drugs.

Before long, a hazmat team arrived and hosed off our bail fugitive. The cops gave him a paper jumpsuit to wear and turned him over to us since none of them wanted to take him to county jail, which was fine.

I seriously doubt that the overweight "great white hunter" would have fared any better chasing the rabbit of the man who easily outran me, and I am certain that he would not have gained the type of cooperation we had on this night of hunting.

You must represent yourself as a professional who knows how to do his job so that you can put the concerns of liability-fearing peace officers at rest. It has worked for me, and it will work for you.

CHAPTER TWENTY-THREE

Working Solo

Working solo can be very lonely. You'll be hard-pressed to find someone with a common frame of reference, including your spouse or other love interest. This can result in some bumpy relationships.

For example, I can recall an incident where my girlfriend at the time, who didn't believe I was acting on a tip that my bail fugitive was serving drinks at an out-of-county bar, used her car to block my garage door. All she knew was that I was keeping weird hours and, therefore, deduced that I must be having an affair, which was not the case. It took about three hours to convince her to move her car. During this time, the informant had started to feel guilty and warned my bail fugitive away. Since I was working solo at the time, there was no one to call to come get me or to check on the fugitive, so he got away.

My girlfriend and I didn't last too much past this incident, but this example illustrates how recovery work can interfere with your private life—and how your private life can interfere with your work.

Should you decide to work solo, you should have a nice suit to wear while working. Because you will be alone, you shouldn't look anything less than professional. When I wear a suit while working a case, I am quick to notice that people treat me differently; by that I mean with more respect. Also, it is curious that people in normal settings seem to notice me more when I wear a suit versus when I wear ordinary street clothes. If you are wearing a suit and tie, I strongly recommend a breakaway tie to combat any attempts at a tie grab. Working with a partner offsets the need for a suit for most occasions; the presence of two people working together appears more official to most people. Don't ask me why. Of course, as discussed previously, you have to match the clothes to the circumstances. On some cases, blending in or staying safe is more critical than looking professional.

You may find that a small tape recorder is very handy when reviewing criminal records or taking verbal notes while driving. Believe me, you'll come up with all kinds of ideas while you're stuck in traffic. At one point, I use to call home and leave memos to myself on my answering machine. Hey, it works.

When you work solo, you must be available at all times. Again, you should use a cell phone that is 100-percent dedicated to your bail fugitive recovery work for security reasons.

Even if you choose to do your investigative work solo, when you are ready to arrest the fugitive try to get some qualified help to accompany you, such as the bail agent who hired you for this case or a police officer. If you must make an arrest alone, do what is necessary to get the drop on your bail fugitive because you have no one to watch the back door. This is where you may be tempted to enter a house surreptitiously, but you had better be ready to explain to the cops why you did it and under what authority you acted as you're being hauled off to jail. If your state laws allow you to enter a residence to wait for your bail fugitive, it is important that you notify the local law enforcement agency holding jurisdiction over that location to explain what you plan to do. If the officer says no, then don't do it.

Many bail fugitives take refuge in some pretty tough neighborhoods, and working in these areas alone can be extremely dangerous. You should always use common sense when you work, but it is especially crucial when you work alone. Don't cut corners or take any unnecessary chances whatsoever. Leave your itinerary with someone you know and trust before leaving your office, just in case you turn up missing. That way, your absence will be noted, and your friend can alert the proper authorities—hopefully in time to save you.

Above all, be prepared to run like hell.

LESSON FROM THE STREET

When I received the following case my team members were all tied up on other cases, so I had to work it alone. The booking photo of the bail fugitive, who was wanted for jumping bail

on a $3,000 bond for battery, made him look pretty scary.

My initial investigation resulted in the acquisition of the bail fugitive's address book, which yielded a telephone number. When I called the number, the bail fugitive answered. A cross-directory check provided an address for this phone number, but the information, *like all unverified information*, had to be confirmed firsthand before I took any action.

It was impossible to cruise the neighborhood where the target house was located, even in my T-Bird, without drawing unwanted attention, so I broke out my recently purchased oversized BMX bicycle for a the preliminary mobile surveillance. In fact, the bicycle and my trim 160 pounds (that was a long time ago) made me look like a typical teenager, so I blended in to the streetscape.

All the houses in the neighborhood were dilapidated, and most were missing some or all their house numbers, which made it impossible to figure out which one was the target of my investigation. I made an educated guess and rode my bike to an oversized lot bearing a tiny house at the very back of the lot. I estimated the distance from the front door to the street to be about 200 feet.

A disheveled-looking man stood on the front porch of the house with a large, powerful-looking pit bull at his side. The man had either consciously made a decision not to bathe, was mentally impaired, or was in competition with his companion to see who could be more aromatic. In any case, I quickly surmised him to be a sentry, though the need for such duty was unclear. It was possible that I had the wrong address or the wrong house and the sentry was there for another reason that had nothing to do with me, but I had to check.

The rectangular front yard was so strewn with debris that it was actually precarious to walk across. I picked a path that took me past a wrecked sedan in case cover was needed. Only after I was well into the yard did I notice another pit bull curled up near the front porch. As best as I could see, a collar and a line that ran behind some tree branches above the dog restrained the animal, so I guessed it to be of little consequence. But I had seen what damage a dog bite can produce and therefore retained great respect for man's best friend.

"Hello," I shouted to the soiled sentry, while keeping well out of reach of the tied-up pit bull. "I'm looking for Rebecca."

"There ain't no Rebecca here," the sentry countered.

"Really?" I reached into my pants pocket and drew out a piece of paper. "Is this 1243 Henry Street?"

"No," the sentry replied. "This is 1234 Henry Street."

I had the right house. Just then, the curled-up pit bull jumped to his paws and charged toward me. It quickly became clear that the line attached to the dog ran to a trolley line and that the fast-approaching pit bull had full access to the entire yard. In a matter of a second, the pit bull's teeth were within range on my lower half.

Now, I cannot explain what happened at this point, but somehow I was literally pulled off my feet and thrown back-first onto the hood of the junked car behind me. The object of my new friend's desires—my lower legs—quickly followed me. I ultimately landed feet first on the opposite side of the car, nearer the

crumbling fence—breathing real heavy.

I looked at the creep on the front porch but didn't see the other pit bull. Instinctively, I jumped onto the roof of the old car just in time to learn that the sentry had loosed the second pit bull.

With the superior vantage point gained from standing on the roof of the car, I could see another car of equal height just on the other side of the fence. With one dog scratching at the driver's side and the other about to join me, I took a leap of faith right over the fence and onto the roof of the other car.

I could hear someone yelling to unleash Killer or Man-Eater or whatever the tied-up dog's name was. It was fair to assume that the dog owners were ordering their dogs to run me down, so I ran and hopped fences. I made it to my car and got inside without any serious injury.

I'm not going mince words here. I cannot recall ever experiencing as much fear as I did on that day. I was alone, albeit by choice. This first probe was supposed to be nothing more than a fact-finding mission, but it turned into something else.

It was early enough in the day to let slip my own dogs of war. Within hours, my team had assembled an impressive intelligence dump on the bail fugitive, who had probably been the one yelling for the second pit bull to be untied.

I'm sure the dogs lived to attack another day, but in the hours following their attack on me, they were not a problem when my team swooped in and arrested the bail fugitive and retrieved my bike. (The subsequent raid resulted in the arrest is described in Chapter 8.) You may occasionally find yourself working solo as a last resort, but avoid it if at all possible.

CHAPTER TWENTY-FOUR

Team Operations

Everyone has got be on the same page for team operations to go smoothly. There can be no tolerance for maverick behavior because one idiotic mistake can bring the whole team in for questioning—literally.

A team must act in concert to protect each other from harm, to guard against liability, and to close cases consistently. Moreover, finger pointing and an inability to accept personal responsibility for failures are grounds for immediate dismissal from the team.

You have seen how my team operates throughout this manual, so I won't rehash information unless it is necessary. My team and I are regularly humbled at various paintball fields so we can stay sharp and cohesive in our field operations. It takes a good chunk of energy to spend the whole day in the bush running around with youthful paint slingers, and, in point of fact, my entire team has been taken out by 14-year-olds armed with pump paint markers and limitless energy.

Another training tool that we use to maintain our team skills is a "client house." The structure, which I have access to, is set up like a standard single-story family dwelling, but catwalks line all of the walls where the roof should be for videotaping our training. There are numerous pieces of wooden furniture laid out in typical living fashion since practicing on chalked-out tarmac isn't realistic and can lead to a false sense of abilities. The client house enables us to polish perishable skills when business slows down.

The single shortcoming to team operations is that a larger element full of different personalities requires constant and proper supervision. The team supervisor has to be well organized so that his subordinates can be at ease while he takes on most of the burden of coordinating tasks for the team. In other words, the team leader is the one who keeps things moving with the confidence that he himself has made all the arrangements: notified the local jurisdiction, mapped out all travel directions, seen that each member is properly equipped, and come up with a solid plan (within the team's limitations), whose successful execution he will ensure.

Times are changing rather quickly in terms of available technology at affordable prices, and this extends to what a team could acquire along the lines of radio equipment. Of particular interest is the use of walkie-talkie cell phones. I've never used them, so I can't speak intelligently as to the benefit of this technology, but I can state that the use of these units appears to be more problematic during arrest operations.

It might be fine to have one hand tied up with a handheld cell phone while cruising the streets, courts, or other areas where your bail fugitive is believed to be, but, believe me, you will want both hands free when getting ready to knock on a door or chase a bail fugitive over obstacles common to most housing areas. My team uses relatively inexpensive two-way radios with a one-mile radius in housing areas and a two-mile line-of-site radius out in the open. For longer distances we use cell phones.

We have the option of using shoulder mics, bone transducer mics, or ear mics. Shoulder mics are great for up-close work, because you have both hands free to do other things. However, confidential radio traffic is difficult because anyone standing nearby can hear what is being said. Bone transducer mics, which are very expensive ($500 a set on average), sit on your skull just in front of your ears. These mics use vibrations that your inner ear bones, instead of your eardrums, pick up to hear. The key benefit is that both your ears are fully clear to hear without obstruction from an ear mic. I don't care for ear mics because I lose an ear when radio traffic is being transmitted. I prefer to have both ears fully operational for safety reasons, including being able to hear and tell where a noise is coming from.

You should check your local laws before making any purchase of a radio since some radio models require FCC licensing, and a set of team radios should be checked for compatibility to ensure that you won't have problems with them in the field.

When it comes to radio communications,

you should decide whether to use Simplex or some form of code when communicating. Simplex is basically just talking over the radio as you would in normal conversation. While easy to do, this type of communication takes more time to get a message through, and it may not be understood the first time, thus requiring retransmittal. Moreover, your team's radio traffic may get picked up by scanners, and Simplex isn't hard to figure out.

My team and I use what is called Police 10-code, with 9-code and 11-code also available to adapt. The benefit is that the team can communicate ideas quickly, and, since the communication is standardized, each transmittal is easier to understand. Of course, your team can decide what kind of code you will use, if any at all.

As a general rule, you should know the range of your radios so that radio silence can be observed when getting near a target location. Again, we're encountering more and more problems with bail fugitives using scanners. A solution to this may be rather expensive digital radios that send each transmission over multiple channels in what is commonly called scrambled communications. The problems, aside from the approximately $1,500 price tag per unit, are that there is a one-second delay between the transmitting radio and the receiving radios, and the range of these radios is limited to about half a mile in urban areas. Despite the drawbacks, I intend to upgrade our team radios with scrambled radios for safety reasons, because safety trumps price.

Should you go with family radios, you may find that your cheaper radios have a problem with cross-talk from uninvolved persons. For example, one night I was about to knock on a door when loud traffic came over my shoulder mic that involved someone complaining about a toilet problem. We fixed that by readjusting the internal settings on each radio.

Once you've set up on a target location and are prepared to knock, everyone needs to keep radio traffic to a minimum. There are certain things that should be relayed in low whispers, such as the following:

- Advising the team that you are or are not in position
- Advising the team that you are about to knock on the door
- Advising the team that there is movement in your area of responsibility
- Advising the team of such problems as dogs, debris, or people living in the back of the target location
- Advising the team that you have made contact at the door
- Advising the team that you are entering the location
- Calling in the two-man search team
- Advising the team that someone just jumped out the back window

As a final note, radios are a part of your life-safety equipment and should be maintained as such. I recommend changing the batteries after every four to eight hours of use. I don't recommend rechargeable batteries because we've had numerous problems predicting how long the batteries will last. Goofing off on the radio should be discouraged since it detracts from your professionalism and ties up the radio when someone might be calling for help.

This book is replete with examples of how harmonious teamwork makes fugitive recovery work safer and more successful.

LESSON FROM THE STREET

Acting on credible information, my team and I had hit three target locations within blocks of each other over a two-week period, but the slippery bail fugitive had managed to evade us each time.

The bail fugitive's warrant was not set up for night service (a magistrate will indicate on the arrest warrant whether a peace officer can serve the warrant during the hours of darkness; see example in Appendix H), and the fact that we didn't know where the bail fugitive went during the day made any arrest efforts pointless.

While searching the third location, we discovered that each room in the house had a speaker wired to a central police scanner set for the local agency's frequency. We had known that the local police department was putting our information on the air by monitoring the scanners mounted in each of our vehicles just for this purpose, but nothing in the preliminary investigation pointed to this level of sophistication by the whole family of the bail fugitive.

On the third week, the team member responsible for the case had a break. The brother of the bail fugitive, who had put up his house for collateral, reported that the bail fugitive had been under the house the night we discovered their use of the scanner. He went on to report that the bail fugitive was now staying in a rundown studio, whose location he didn't know offhand. But he was able to obtain the address and get the information to us within hours. We mobilized for action.

Before we assembled at the target, we made a point of attending the beginning of the shift squad meeting at the police station, extracting a promise from the department not to broadcast our information over the radio and fulfilling our notification requirement to the beat officers.

The target location consisted of five apartments in a row approximately 50 yards in length. Assorted apartment complexes and single-family homes surrounded the row of apartments.

The bail fugitive's family had previously exhibited aggressive behavior toward the team by threatening us with clubs and knives during prior arrest attempts, so we approached the situation carefully. I took the lead as we advanced toward the rear of the target location in a single file. The approach consisted of a thin walkway, and the front door could only be approached from one direction. We converged at the caboose of the long house to find one door and three windows. The team quickly set up to cover each window and me at the door. I knocked on the front door and realized that the door was solid metal and, by the sound, had been reinforced.

"Let me see your hands!" I heard someone outside yell. I looked to my left where one of my team had drawn down on someone through the head-high window on the southwest elevation. I could hear a young woman responding to the verbal orders, with the exception of the order to open the door.

"I can't open the door," she claimed.

The team member who gave the first verbal order knew that he was pointman for all subsequent communication to avoid confusion. "Is there a backdoor?" he asked her.

"No," she replied.

"Are you alone?" he asked.

"No," she mumbled.

"Who else is in the apartment?"

She hesitated before answering. "Uh, my kids and uh . . . my boyfriend."

This dialogue went on for another minute or so.

I decided to breach the front door, or so I thought. The entrance was raised about four feet from ground level. A wooden porch limited the possibility of getting a running start for door-smashing momentum. I hoped that the solid metal door was cheaply installed, and, with that hope, I charged the door shoulder first. It hurt real bad.

One of my larger team members confidently motioned me aside. He thumped the door hard, but apparently union members must have installed it because it wasn't going to give.

"Breach tools!" I yelled, but there was no answer. I got on the radio. "R-4, R-1."

"R-4," the team member responsible for

carrying the crowbar, bolt cutters, and sledgehammer responded.

"952 on the breach tools." There was a moment of silence.

"Negative on the breach tools, R-1."

I later learned that R-4 had forgotten to put the breach tools back into his sedan after clearing his trunk for a trip to the grocery store. R-4 made a simple mistake that has not been repeated on my team because I now carry the breach tools myself.

I made my way to the open window where the young lady was talking to the team member who had initiated contact. I looked through the window. She looked to be about 22 to 25 years of age and was slight, about five-foot-three and 115 pounds. I deduced by her quick glances into the darkened portion of the studio that her boyfriend was our guy, since he wouldn't come to the window.

Under cover from the team communicator, I stepped onto the interlocked hands of two team members who braced their backs against the apartment wall just under the window. I was then catapulted through the open window headfirst. I tucked and rolled. The momentum of my roll continued until I was up on my feet and had my weapon in hand.

Pay dirt! There on the only bed in the studio apartment was the police radio fan wearing nothing but boxers.

"Let me see your hands!" I yelled as a thump on the kitchen floor behind me signaled the arrival of my backup.

The bail fugitive followed all my verbal orders. I handcuffed him as he lay face down on the floor.

"Status!" yelled a teammate from outside the window.

I got on the radio. "Code 4, 10-15 with one."

I attempted to open the front door, but it was bolted shut with a complex series of improvised locks and two-by-fours. Luckily, the bail fugitive weighed less than 145 pounds, so it was easy to pass him through the very window that served as my entrance into the studio apartment (and for my exit as well).

Just before leaving, I warned the woman that she would be lucky to escape a charge of aiding and abetting a fugitive. My statement carried absolutely no legal weight, but I hoped that she would consider herself fortunate and in the future avoid the kind of trouble her boyfriend had brought into her home.

This particular case presented a number of challenges that we as a team managed to work around by our strength in numbers. First, the bail fugitive's family was willing to use force to hamper our efforts. Second, the cops couldn't get directly involved because there was no night service on the arrest warrant. Last, one person could not have covered all the exits and been propelled through an open window simultaneously.

Could I have closed this case alone? I can't say for sure. Could you have closed this case alone? I don't have that answer either. Did a well-trained team of bail fugitive recovery persons all working in concert close this case safely and with no residual liability? Absolutely.

CHAPTER TWENTY-FIVE

Locating the Right Bail Fugitive

Occasionally bail fugitives look just like their booking photographs but not often. The emotional state of the person while going through the booking process tends to distort the way he looks in the photo. Some people are under the influence of a controlled substance and generally don't look their best. Other people may have taken a beating in the process of being arrested or on the way to jail. Still others may be freaked out about going back to jail—especially if the arrestee has just struck out in a state with a three-strike law, which carries a lengthy mandatory sentence (see Chapter 19).

This is why it is in your best interests to find out what kind of salient characteristics your bail fugitive has. The best features to look for are eye color, attached or detached ear lobes, missing extremities, and scars that are in plain sight. I don't rely a great deal on tattoos since body art can be altered or replicated, but tattoos have made positive identification of bail fugitives possible on many occasions. (However, recall from Chapter 7 that the man who had the same tattoos as my bail fugitive was not the man I was looking for, but rather his brother.)

You may have to use trickery to get a suspect to divulge his real identity. Normally, I will tell a person, "You know why we're here." You'd be surprised how many times a person will answer, "Yeah, because I failed to appear on that bail thing."

The plain and simple fact is that you can end up broke and in prison for grabbing a bystander you believed was your bail fugitive, so be sure before you act.

LESSON FROM THE STREET

It was a tough assignment. Acting on a tip, my partner and I had canvassed every strip joint in the city. We actually had to hang out in strip clubs for a solid week before finding the right one. At any rate, this gig had me in civilian clothes for a change.

On this night in the strip club, I was getting sleepy, the cigarette smoke was burning my eyes, and my waitress was pissed off because I wouldn't order anything with alcohol. I ignored my partner, who had come in five minutes after me, so that people would not know that we were together.

The stripper who came onto the dance floor looked like she could be my bail fugitive, but she didn't look exactly like the booking photograph. She swayed her hips, slid up and down the brass pole, and wiggled her well-shaped butt in my direction. I suppose this would have been helpful if the jailers had taken a photo of her butt. After five minutes or so, she finally finished disrobing, and that was when a distinguishing tattoo came into view. Bingo, she was our fugitive.

We couldn't arrest her on the spot because the bouncers, who had no idea who we were, outweighed my partner and me by about 800 pounds. So I went outside and called in the local cops to make the bust.

Make sure that you are arresting the bail fugitive being sought, not someone who closely resembles him or her.

CHAPTER TWENTY-SIX

Reconfirming Your Right to Arrest

So you are qualified as a bail fugitive recovery person, have secured a contract for a bail fugitive, and rigorously researched your right to make an arrest as a private citizen at your local law library, as outlined in Part I. But are you absolutely sure that you are within your rights as a bail fugitive recovery person to actually go out, put your hands on a designated person, handcuff him, place him in your car, and deliver him into the custody of the local sheriff?

To this very day, way back in the deepest recesses of my conscious mind, I still have a lingering worry about the power of the documents in my possession at the time of making every arrest. This is why I make every effort to practice strict due diligence when it comes to last-minute checks on the wanted status of any bail fugitive I intend to arrest.

Let's say, for example, that you arrest a person at 2200 hours as a bail fugitive, but he was reinstated to bail in court at 1600 hours that very day. Even if you contacted the court clerk, it is entirely possible that the clerk hadn't seen the memo yet and gave you less than up-to-the-minute information. In this situation you will still be okay. You will want to call the bail agent who requested the court to reinstate that bail bond in the first place and yell at him for not notifying you.

It's lucky for you that the defendant was reinstated to bail and that the case was not dismissed or in any way adjudicated. With the authority-to-arrest form, all you did was surrender the defendant, which is still legal (at least in California). However, if the case had actually been dismissed, then you just committed a whole truckload of felonies ripe for one hell of a civil action.

This is another reason to visit the law enforcement agencies in the area you intend to work. The officers you contact will check for warrants out on your bail fugitive, in all likelihood. If nothing comes back on a bail fugitive who was on the NCIC, then step back and double-check your information before taking any action to arrest a bail fugitive. This can be very frustrating after all the time and effort you have put into the case, but it is far better to back off than to act hastily.

You will frequently encounter incredibly convincing bail fugitives who will show you "court minutes" (usually a single page of barely legible writing filled out at the time of a hearing and handed to a defendant) as documented proof that their failure to appear has been taken care of and you are about to make a terrible mistake. This is unnerving for many reasons. First, if you pass on the arrest, then you run the risk of wasting time and money if the bail fugitive's claims are bogus. I wouldn't recommend relying solely on the bail agent for confirmation. Think about it. The bail agent may have taken the case personally and may want the fugitive arrested because of personal reasons. Or he could tell you to let the bail fugitive go, after asking where you found the bail fugitive, and then he will simply go over and pick up the bail fugitive so he doesn't have to pay you a commission.

In my experience, not all bail agents stay on top of their cases; after all, they are running a 24-7 business with dozens if not hundreds of clients. Chances are the bail agent doesn't know if the bail fugitive took care of his matter as claimed.

Your best defense against a wrongful arrest is to check with the court clerk the afternoon before you go out at night. Get a court-certified copy of the arrest warrant to prove that you checked to see if the case was still active. Have the local cops run a warrant check to see if the bail fugitive has an active warrant on the same case you're working on.

If you have a date-stamped, court-certified copy of the warrant, confirmation that the warrant is still in the system, *and* assurance of the bail agent that the case is still hot, then you should make the arrest. But if you are missing any of these pieces and you're in doubt about the arrest, let him go.

Why? Should you arrest someone who is no longer out of jail on an a active bond or no longer has an active warrant pending, then you could be arrested and charged with multiple crimes, such as trespassing, burglary, false imprisonment, battery, kidnapping, and quite possibly for weapons charges. You must do everything possible to make certain that any arrest you make is lawful.

LESSON FROM THE STREET

I went back over all of the steps it took to get me there, standing in the cold rain and using the cover of darkness to avoid premature detection by the occupant of the target apartment. I had checked and double-checked the status of the outstanding warrant, which indicated that it was still in effect.

The bail fugitive, Joe, had hit a tough patch as of late: his wife of 10 years had run off with their boss, his brother had just been sentenced to life in prison, his car had been stolen, his house was in foreclosure, his apartment had been burglarized, he had been cut out of his father's will, and he was suffering from burning urination brought on by a recently discovered case of venereal disease that his new girlfriend had given him. On top of all this, he had not cleared up his failure to appear, probably out of acute depression. I would have given him a break had he not failed to fulfill the first promise he made to me when I showed up in the middle of the night. Joe had missed court three months earlier and had falsified his bail application.

I walked up the wooden stairs with team support and knocked on Joe's door. Joe opened the door, took a sip of his alcoholic beverage, sighed, and motioned for me to enter his apartment. I didn't consider Joe a hazardous arrest, so I hadn't changed out of the business suit I'd worn to the courthouse earlier in the day. Joe had never seen me in anything other than Dockers and a polo shirt. After noticing my suit, Joe smiled nervously and asked, "What are you all dressed up for?"

I sighed deeply. The last thing I wanted to do was make life any harder for him, but my presence in his apartment was business. "Joe, you promised to take care of your court matter, and you didn't."

"Yes, I did," Joe said, while straightening his shoulders and firming up his tone. "I went to court, and the judge said everything was fine."

"When did you go to court, Joe?"

He rubbed his chin while looking at the ceiling to his left. "Let me see, last Thursday, I think."

"A week ago?" I asked. I had just been to the courthouse earlier in the afternoon, so I knew there were problems with his story. "What did the judge say?"

"He said everything was fine."

"Did he say anything else?"

Joe shook his head slowly while maintaining eye contact with me.

I placed my hand on my duty belt and said, "Let's go, Joe."

"What you mean?"

Two of my team members flanked Joe while I stood in front of him. "Joe, we're going to have to make sure that you see the judge."

Joe attempted to close the distance between us but instead ended up in handcuffs within

seconds. "I went to fucking court, you asshole!" he yelled at me.

"You got proof?"

Joe thought for a moment and then said, "Yeah, right there on the kitchen counter with those bills."

I checked the stack and found documents from the court. All of the documents were either outdated or had no relevance to whether or not Joe had actually satisfied his failure to appear.

"Sorry, Joe." I motion for the team to move out.

Joe loudly proclaimed that he had taken care of his failure to appear all the way to jail. He seemed perfectly believable, and, had I not checked myself, I might have allowed myself to waver. Of course, Joe had not taken care of his failure to appear, and it was a good thing that I brought him in.

The only way for you to combat the indecision brought on by this type of conflict is to double-check everything before attempting any arrest. Be prepared for bail fugitives to swear that they have taken care of their bail problems, because it will happen to you.

CHAPTER TWENTY-SEVEN

Arresting and Controlling Bail Fugitives

You have probably seen television shows where a bounty hunter goes to a house, knocks on the door, goes in, and comes out a couple of minutes later with his subject handcuffed and cooperative. By now, you must have realized these situations either reflect situations where in-house recovery people immediately arrive at the address on the bail application the moment a notice of forfeiture comes in or they are totally made up. Unless a bail bond company hires you as an in-house bail fugitive recovery person, things do not typically go down that easily. You have to prepare yourself to deal with resistive subjects.

You need to think deeply about how to physically control a resistive or combative bail fugitive without causing any type of serious injury to anyone.

Someone once said, "The Romans do not wait for war to pick up a sword." Waiting until a bail fugitive puts up a fight isn't the time to discover whether or not you are physically up to the task of subduing him.

One night, as I arrested a young bail fugitive, I could sense that he was clearly struggling with himself whether to resist or not. He was teetering and could have gone either way very quickly, I figured. As the three deputies and I escorted him to an isolation cell, he stiffened his body in what was probably nothing more than defiance. In response, I secured his left arm and shifted it behind his back in a common rear wristlock technique. The fugitive looked me straight in the eyes—while his other arm was secured by one of the deputies—and powered his left arm out from behind his back and to his front, despite my resistance. As he bared his teeth at me, I noticed that he was sweating profusely and his pupils were dilated. He dropped into a lower, balanced stance, convincing me that he was going to fight. Before he could take action, I let go of his arm with my right hand and used my right elbow to force him down onto a bench, where he was subsequently handcuffed without further incident. As I walked away, my left biceps began to hurt and I felt a burning sensation there. A nurse later told me that I had a minor tear of the biceps.

I wasn't doing any fitness training at that time, but that biceps injury told me a lot; it is essential to achieve and maintain good physical conditioning not for what happens but for what could happen.

Today, I can complete an Olympic distance triathlon—1.5-kilometer (0.9-mile) swim, 40-kilometer (24-mile) bike ride, and a 10-kilometer 6.2-mile) run—though I'm way too slow to be competitive. I can lift weights that are way above what is considered average for someone of my age and weight, and I can spar or grapple for 30 to 60 minutes, depending on the intensity and skill of my opponent.

The bottom line is that I absolutely refuse to lose a fight for a lack of air or power. I may get hit with a lucky punch, taken down by a blade, outwrestled or outgunned, but I won't go down because I'm in poor shape.

The types of fitness training mentioned above do not keep "perishable skills" sharp. To me, perishable skills are those tasks that do not come naturally, such as shooting, handcuffing, and even team strategies for approaching suspected bail fugitive locations. My team and I get together twice a week to practice handcuffing, arrest and control techniques, weapon retention, jiujitsu, and aikido. I can confidently say that, as a team, we are pretty efficient in escorting even the most violent bail fugitive to see the judge.

LESSON FROM THE STREET

The following incident illustrates a variety of things, including team operations, involving law enforcement, and dealing with hazardous situations.

A bail agent and I were looking for a bail bond client who had recently failed to appear for court in Tuolumne County. One of our leads produced a contact who gave us a verbal description of certain markers leading to an off-road property where the skip was believed to be living in a dilapidated fifth-wheel trailer. Upon finally finding the wreck, we discovered that the skip was not there but his belongings were.

During our investigation of the site, we learned from a confidential case contact (CCC) that the skip was coming and going from the trailer. We also learned that if he was there, the loud, annoying generator would be running to warm the unit. The CCC also told us that "strange people" were coming and going at all hours of the night when the skip was there. This information, combined with the drug charges the skip was facing, suggested that drugs were being sold out of the trailer.

The inside of the trailer was dirty and smelly, and various articles of garbage were strewn about. A portable heater was hooked up to car batteries in the center of the mess, and the overall layout made movement very tight. Near the sleeping area, a large hunting knife and replica pellet pistol were in plain sight.

Before beginning our search, we had done a criminal check of public records about the fugitive. The skip had a history of violence, was a parolee looking at 25 to life under the three-strikes law, was believed to be associating with druggies, and was capable of using weapons. Based on his violent history, the evidence of drug dealing, and the presence of weapons in the trailer, we discussed our tactical options and settled on a plan. We opted to leave no trace of our presence in the trailer so the fugitive wouldn't know we were onto him, and to have the CCC contact us the moment he heard the generator.

The following evening, I had just sat down in front of my TV after downing a sizable dinner when the phone rang. The CCC had called to tell us that the generator was running. Immediately after hanging up I called the sheriff's department, but all personnel were busy on calls and couldn't respond for several hours. Waiting for their assistance wasn't an option since the CCC had told us that the skip didn't stay at the trailer for long periods.

I met with two other bail agents in Tuolumne County, where we donned our tactical gear and requested a civil stand-by. Again, the dispatcher told me that there would be a delay. I told him that we couldn't wait and would be attempting the arrest within 15 minutes. She told me to hold on. Several seconds later the dispatcher came back on and told me that several deputies were en route to my location. I told her that they would need a four-wheel drive to reach the trailer, and she confirmed that one of the deputies was driving a Ford Expedition.

Two deputies arrived 10 minutes later and stared suspiciously at us. I intentionally turned my back to check on the file, thus revealing my tactical vest back patch that reads "Allied Bail Agencies" with "Bail Agent" in big, bold letters beneath. This seemed to assuage the deputies' suspicions.

On the grease board I pulled from the trunk, I drew a rough layout of the location, and we all agreed on a plan to approach the target location.

The trailer was located approximately 300 yards off the road and was tucked from sight as the ground sloped sharply downward to a quarter-acre clearing where the trailer was parked. Thick foliage surrounded the clearing, and I didn't know what to expect past the clearing and down the hill. Several wrecked cars were parked haphazardly around the trailer, and a number of dirt bikes also rested near the trailer.

My two partners led the way down the hill in a Hummer H-1 to the right. The deputies rolled down the hill in the Expedition to the left. I parked my Ford Police Interceptor at the top and ran in.

I took a position near the overhang of the trailer, where the sleeping area was. The deputies took up positions near the hanging door of the trailer. My partners were off to my right, providing a sort of overall cover for our approach and to cut off escape routes into the thick brush.

Suddenly I heard one of the agents yell, "He's above you! I got him!"

I shot deeper under the overhang, where I felt trapped. I could only move in three directions, and a separate window overlooked each direction.

"I got him!" yelled out a bail agent standing on the running boards of his Hummer.

I ran from the overhang and darted around the trailer, where I took up a position behind one of the deputies. One of the deputies pulled on the door handle after demanding that the skip exit the trailer, with no response. The door fell off and was thrown aside.

We repeated demands for the skip to exit the trailer, with no response whatsoever. I pulled a retractable pole and mirror set out of a tactical vest pocket and used it to peek inside the trailer. I couldn't see anyone. Moving past the deputies, I entered the trailer, cleared the nonfunctional toilet area to the left, and then moved right with both deputies in tow. The path made by clutter on both sides of me dictated my course.

A woman poked her head from behind a partition separating the sleeping area from the living area. She looked directly at me, taking in my black battle dress uniform, Kevlar helmet, tactical goggles, tactical vest, and Glock, and shrieked, "Oh my God! Billy, they're going to kill you!" as she jumped out of sight.

"Billy!" I yelled out. "No one's going to kill you—don't be silly!"

"They're going to fucking kill you, Billy!" the woman screamed over and over again.

I lowered my tone and called out, "Billy, this is a simple thing to take care of." Scanning for any opening that might provide a shot if Billy had a real gun, I saw no such problem. I moved forward a step and lowered my body—just in case. "It's just a cite and release," I lied. "You'll be out in a couple of hours. Don't do anything silly."

The woman reappeared, and I spoke to her in a calm, reassuring voice: "What's your name?"

"Lisa," she answered in a less excited manner.

"Lisa," I began, "you both are going to be fine; this is a really easy thing to take care of." She appeared to be receptive. "Are there any weapons in the trailer?" I continued.

She looked over to where Billy must have been and then to me. "No," she answered.

The deputies who were at my back during all of this didn't say a word. During team arrests, it is imperative that only one arrest agent talk to an arrestee to avoid confusion, and the deputies were well trained in this tactical procedure.

"Keep your hands where I can see them and come toward me," I encouraged rather than ordered. "Everything's going to be fine, Lisa."

Lisa glanced off to her right and then stumbled over some debris to reach my position. Under the cover of the deputies, I did a cursory pat-down for weapons and passed her back to the deputies, where she was handcuffed and escorted out of the trailer.

"Billy," I called out, but he did not answer. I called out again with no response. Pulling my mirror back out and approaching the partition, I poked the mirror around the corner, but, just like before, I couldn't see anything except for a pile of blankets. I collapsed my mirror and placed it on a nearby surface. There was only one way to

get this thing done. I would have to commit my head to see what was going on.

Quickly, I shot my head around the corner and just as quickly mentally documented what was there while retracting my head from the danger area. Processing the information took a second. From there I decided that I would follow my Glock around the partition where I saw nothing but a pile of jumbled blankets. I looked closer and couldn't make out the lump of a person. Where had he gone?

"Let me see your hands," I ordered without being able to discern whether or not anyone was even there. From the wall of the trailer and the edge of the mattress two dirty hands slithered out from under the blankets palms down. "Keep 'em coming out, Billy," I said in a monotone.

I moved deeper into the cramped sleeping area to allow the deputies to join me, but there was only enough room for one. I crawled over the mattress and took one of Billy's wrists, after which he decided to get jumpy. The first deputy jumped on him, and the second crammed in to help hold him down. Billy made a halfhearted attempt to resist, but I could tell that he was only resisting out of principle—he needed to put on a show to save face.

My first attempt to handcuff Billy failed when my handcuffs snagged on a hand-knitted blanket, but, in short order, I got one wrist secured. When we pulled Billy all the way out we found that he was completely naked, and it fell to me to put his pants on.

Billy was mad and snapped, "You didn't have to come down like that."

The sleeping area was very small, and I wasn't happy about the pants thing. I pulled his pants up to his waist and looked to zip them up, but his penis was in the way. "Watch your dick," I warned.

"*You* watch my dick," he countered laughing.

I exited the trailer, where Lisa was babbling to Billy about something. At first I ignored her, but then her words caught my ear. At first, I thought she was talking about the trailer and all of Billy's personal belongings, but then I heard something else between the lines.

"Billy, what am I supposed to do with all the stuff?"

"I'll take care of it," he responded.

"No," she said suggestively. "I mean *the stuff*."

"Shut up, Lisa," Billy ordered under his breath. "Call my brother; he'll take care of it."

Lisa looked at me and said, "His brother was coming to move the trailer tomorrow."

Once Billy was in the Expedition and Lisa on her way up the hill in her car, I told the deputies that there were probably narcotics on the property, but they didn't seem interested at that time. Billy had become verbally abusive to one of them, and I think that they were more interested in getting him booked before he freaked out.

My fellow bail agents and I declared the job well done and headed for our respective homes. The forfeiture was vacated and the bond exonerated. Thus ended yet another part of the bail enforcement trade: the arrest and surrender.

FEMALE FUGITIVES

Let's face it. The feminist movement has effectively changed the way men and women interact to such an extent that male bail fugitive recovery persons must take extra steps to protect themselves from allegations, however frivolous, of sexual harassment or attack by female bail fugitives. On the flip side, there are legitimate instances where females have been abused by men, including by officers of the law. Your chief concern is to safeguard your reputation by being careful about how you arrest a female bail fugitive and how she is treated until turned over to the police.

The first thing a male recovery person should do is recruit a female—she doesn't necessarily have to be certified—with a credible reputation. You should avoid anyone—male or female—who has a history of drug abuse, psychiatric commitment, or other traits consistent with low character. Of course, finding a female to tag along on apprehensions isn't always easy.

Another option, whether you have a female team member or not, is to use a camera operator to record the arrest, with no breaks, during the entire time you are in contact with the female bail fugitive. This technique effectively keeps everyone honest and is recommended for male fugitives as well.

After arresting a female bail fugitive, you must take the most direct route to the jail; you must never detour or stop on short-distance rides, especially when you don't have a female witness. It is highly advisable to call the jail and report your starting time and mileage, and then call the jail upon arrival and report your ending time and mileage.

Installing a prisoner partition in your work car is also a good idea. Aside from the obvious safety advantages the partition provides, a female bail fugitive will be hard-pressed to prove that you rubbed her thigh on the way to the jail if steel and Plexiglas separate the two of you.

The whole subject of males arresting females is very sensitive, and you should have a game plan prior to attempting to arrest any female bail fugitive.

LESSON FROM THE STREET

Larry contacted me to assist in the arrest of a couple who hadn't yet jumped bail but who had made no effort to pay their bail bond premium. (The premium is regulated by each state, but for most bail agents it is 10 percent of the penal amount of the bond.) Larry had costs associated with every bond he wrote, and it was his position that he could not stay in business by paying to get people out of jail. (What is meant by this is that bail agents generally pay a percentage of each bond to a surety company and, if required, a second percentage to what is called a "build-up fund," to cover bad bonds or use as retirement. For example, if I write a $50,000 bond, I will have to pay the surety who provided me with the bond 1.5 percent, or $750, for the bond and another $500 for my build-up fund—whether or not I collect anything on the bond. I may decide that the risk is fair and post a $50,000 bail bond without collecting anything until the following day. If the cosigner and client refuse to pay, then I get stuck paying $1,250 out of my own pocket. Thus, bail bond companies cannot stay in business by "paying for people to get out of jail.")

Arresting bail clients who have not failed to appear in court must be treated somewhat differently than arresting bail clients who have become bail fugitives. A bail client is not a fugitive from the law and therefore has more standing to make a complaint against you. A bail fugitive has less standing because of his criminal flight from prosecution. Of course, a bail agent can surrender a bail client at any time, as long as the bond is still in effect. At the very worst, the bail agent may be ordered to pay back the premium.

Larry drove to the apartment complex where his clients lived, and we walked to his clients' apartment and knocked on the door. When the female client, Linda, answered the door, I could tell immediately that this was going to be a low-key arrest. Linda wasn't a hardened criminal; she had only lied about her ability to pay the bond to get her and her husband out of jail after both being arrested for domestic violence.

Larry and Linda went back and forth for a while. Linda's aunt from upstairs was summoned to watch Linda's kids. We confirmed that Linda's husband, the other bail client, was back in jail on a new domestic violence charge.

Linda called her brother, Lawrence, who was an attorney. Lawrence wanted to speak to Larry, so Linda handed over her cordless telephone. Instead of offering to help his sister, Lawrence threatened Larry with legal action for making a false arrest, which didn't dissuade Larry in the least.

Larry decided to book Linda, but we had no female witness or video camera with us, so we improvised. We had Linda's aunt pat down Linda and recruited a neighbor to drive Linda to the jail. I know this may sound crazy, but Larry and I made a judgment call under the circumstances that Linda, her aunt, and her neighbor could be trusted to do as we asked.

Linda was booked into the local county jail, and Larry surrendered the bond on Linda's husband, who was in jail, thus relieving himself of any responsibility if Larry got out and jumped bail. Linda's neighbor got $50 for her time, and Lawrence never followed through on his threats to sue.

This whole situation was unorthodox, but, as a bail fugitive recovery person, you must be flexible in your methods so that you can thwart liability before it can occur. Since this arrest, I make sure that I have a female team member and video records of every arrest involving a female bail fugitive.

CHAPTER TWENTY-EIGHT

Transporting Bail Fugitives

The chase is over once the bail fugitive is safely placed in your car for transportation to the proper authority, but it is important to realize that the trip to the jail is still a critical part of bail fugitive recovery.

TRANSPORT VEHICLE

The number-one rule for transporting fugitives is that your car must be dependable. Mechanical problems can be incredibly frustrating and perhaps even disastrous. You don't want to be out in the middle of nowhere with a dangerous fugitive, and you also don't want to have to explain to a police officer or an attorney why it took you 10 hours to travel 10 miles and surrender a prisoner.

Before heading out to make an arrest, thoroughly search the back of your car for any contraband. Check under the bench seat if at all possible. You should also check the backseat area of your car after transporting any bail fugitive. The last thing you need is for illegal narcotics or weapons to be found in your car, and bail fugitives, knowing they are about to be strip-searched, may stash illegal items in your car to avoid being caught with them.

My transport vehicle, a Crown Victoria, is equipped with a plastic seat molded so the passenger in the backseat is comfortable while riding handcuffed behind the back. There is a prisoner partition with a Plexiglas spit guard, side bat wings, and antikicking board. The backseat door handles and windows are not operational. This setup is ideal for transporting fugitives.

Initially you may not be able to afford proper transportation equipment, but you will gradually acquire equipment geared to your needs. In any event, you should make every effort to protect yourself from attack and avoid liability while transporting a bail fugitive.

The professional recovery agent is set up to transport bail skips humanely and with strict adherence to agent safety.

SAFETY AND COMFORT OF PRISONER

You will be the one who is ultimately responsible for the bail fugitive's safe arrival at the county jail, so the number-two rule is to buckle the bail fugitive in. This may seem like common sense, but while doing so you must take care not to lean so far over that you are vulnerable to being bitten, head-butted, or accused of sexual assault.

Depending on the distance and time on the road, you should make sure that the bail fugitive is comfortable, within reason. You shouldn't jeopardize security or safety to make the bail fugitive overly comfy, but letting cold wind blow a bail fugitive into hypothermia is a good way to get sued. Use your good common sense. Besides if you treat your prisoner courteously and professionally, he may reciprocate, which will make the journey more pleasant and your job much easier.

"The office." This mobile rig is equipped with nearly everything to do the job on the run: laptop computer with GPS and mobile Internet, file bag, tape recorder, video and audio recorders for liability protection, and a scanner to make sure that information isn't being transmitted over unsecured channels.

LESSON FROM THE STREET

The target house was way out in the sticks. The bail agent and I had taken so many darkened roads that I had become disoriented. Though I looked, I had not seen a traffic or street light for at least 30 miles.

We stopped at a U.S. Post Office that was no

bigger than a toolshed and called the local sheriff's department for assistance. The bail fugitive, Lou, had an extensive history of various violations but nothing indicating a propensity for violence. Nevertheless, we opted to err on the side of caution and involve the local constabulary. About 45 minutes later, two patrol deputies arrived, checked out our story, and agreed to provide a civil standby. I was happy to have them with us since the roads were not matching my map.

The family of the bail fugitive swore on all that was holy that Lou was not at the house and they didn't know where he was. By all accounts, the family appeared to be decent folks living in a well-kept dwelling. Dad owned a construction business, and one of the rooms in the house obviously served as a home office. Mom helped with the business and kept the house up. Lou's wife, who was there, also claimed not to know where Lou was.

The parent's house was the address on the bail application, so we were on firmer ground when it came to searching the residence. However, the deputies and Lou's dad were on a first-name basis, which made the deputies question our need to search the house.

Frankly, I believed the parents and the wife, and I consider myself a good judge of character. After being put at ease, I holstered my weapon, and, while everyone was busily talking over the situation, I casually meandered into a nearby, vacant bedroom that was being used for storage. Boxes and holiday decorations surrounded a dusty treadmill and desk. Out of sheer curiosity, I approached a closet and opened the door to find the six-foot-five, 280-pound bail fugitive with ultrawide shoulders, a van dyke beard, and a mohawk standing there in his underwear.

Startled, I jumped back against the treadmill while at the same time drawing my weapon.

"Let me see your hands!" I yelled and was stunned to see this behemoth complying. "Step out of the closet—do it now!" I demanded.

Everyone rushed to the bedroom door in time to watch me handcuff the big man. The deputies looked at the dad, who just shrugged his shoulders. Mom and the wife were wailing, but, in my opinion, they deserved no sympathy for putting me in a position where Lou could scare the shit out me.

The deputies had no wish to take Lou, which meant that the bail agent and I had to drive him 60 minutes to the neighboring county jail.

It was a brisk night, so I made sure Lou was warm enough. Before leaving his parents' house, I helped him put on his clothes, and I personally put his shoes on for him. His mom handed me a jacket for him. After checking it for weapons, I draped the jacket over Lou's muscular shoulders.

Several miles from Lou's parent's house I pulled into a gas station. I disarmed myself and had the bail agent cover me. I opened the rear door nearer to Lou and told him to stick his feet out. I placed leg shackles on his ankles and told Lou to step out of my sedan. Admonishing him not to be stupid, I removed his handcuffs and used waist chains to restrain him. Then I gave him his cigarettes so that he could smoke one before we hit the road.

"Hey, man, I really appreciate this," Lou began. "Those handcuffs were killing my wrists."

Once on the road, I quickly realized that I was hopelessly disoriented. I asked the bail agent if he knew where we were, and he didn't either. There was no moon, and it was dark. Suddenly from the backseat, Lou volunteered, "You have to go straight for about 25 miles." Lou appreciated the way he was being treated, and in return he provided useful directions until we reached familiar freeways.

The lesson here is that I treated my bail fugitive humanely, and he guided me out of a desolate portion of his county. There was no reason to deny him creature comforts within reason. This is a good example of how to transport a cooperative bail fugitive.

LONG-DISTANCE RIDES

Not all trips to the county jail are short ones. You may arrest a bail fugitive several counties away from where he should be booked in. For longer rides, waist chains and shackles are highly advisable. Long-term use of handcuffs has been associated with nerve damage, so avoid using handcuffs for extended periods.

On long trips you may have to stop for food, fuel, or rest room facilities. Be mindful that any request by the prisoner to use a rest room should be viewed as high risk, so act accordingly.

UNPLEASANTRIES

Some bail fugitives are gregarious while others are silent. One bail fugitive may not give you any problems while another will jump out of a moving car if provided the opportunity to do so.

You may encounter foul-smelling bail fugitives, and some may defecate or vomit in your car out of sheer spite—and then hurl it at you. Spitting is a favorite method of getting back at the recovery agents. You have to figure out a way to deal with this hazard in such a way that you and the bail fugitive remain unharmed. There are spit guards available that fit over the head of a spitter, although I've never used one.

TRANSPORTING FIGHTERS

Try as you might, it is impossible to make every last bail fugitive happy about being plucked from bed in the still of the morning,

handcuffed, and placed in a mobile cage en route to jail to meet his judicial and contractual obligations. Because this usually results in a loss of his freedom or, at the very least, is a tremendous inconvenience for him, you could end up with a fighter on your hands.

Every once in a while, you may find that your newly arrested bail fugitive is given to intemperate, impetuous outbursts, fecal flinging, spitting, kicking, and other disagreeable acts. Nevertheless, it is still in your best interest to ensure the safe arrival of the bail fugitive to the proper authority.

I'm not going to kid you here. It takes an enormous amount of patience to restrain yourself from closing a spitter's foul mouth with pepper spray or subjecting the bail fugitive to a "screen test" (where you fail to buckle the prisoner in securely and then drive really fast and slam on your brakes, thrusting the fugitive's face into the prisoner screen). Hey, we're human too, but we're also expected to act like professionals, and mistreating a bail fugitive can get *you* time in prison.

When you are minutes away from the jail, call the jail where you are heading to advise officers that you have a fighter. You'll find jail staff ready and waiting to assist in making that smooth and harmonious transition of the bail fugitive.

For longer trips, I've had the California Highway Patrol send traffic officers to collect fighters from my cage. They're generally happy to assist, and this shifts the liability from you should the bail fugitive get injured. You will need to have the responding officer sign your arrest form (see Appendix D for a sample of the California form).

LESSON FROM THE STREET

I watched Ahmed in my rearview mirror, staring blankly. Ahmed had been very tough to find because we couldn't get people in his Middle Eastern circles to talk to us. So I had to get resourceful.

Though I don't generally rely too heavily on database searches, a query on Ahmed revealed a cell phone number on his credit heading. I obtained the calls made by that cell phone, and six numbers kept popping up daily. I ran a cross-directory check on all the numbers, which revealed physical addresses. I found that the billing address for what was most likely Ahmed's cell phone, and the location called the most was the same address. Ahmed was soon on his way to jail.

"How did you find me?" Ahmed asked from the backseat.

I looked in my rearview mirror to find Ahmed leaning forward. I didn't want to reveal any trade secrets in case he bailed out and jumped again. "The same way I'll find you if you miss court again."

Ahmed threw his head up and then lowered it back level. "That bitch," he said.

"Ahmed, why is it that every time I pick someone up it's always someone else's fault?" I turned down the radio. "Why can't you guys accept responsibility for your own actions?"

Ahmed yelled something about a jihad and began pounding his head on the Plexiglas portion of the prisoner partition. Then he started pounding the side of his head on the bars covering the side passenger door windows. I radioed for my follow car to pull over, and I pointed the dash cam backward to videotape Ahmed's rather successful attempt at self-inflicted injuries.

Pulling over on the side of a freeway puts you at the mercy of your fellow motorists to keep their vehicles between the lines, and I resented Ahmed for freaking out while we were on the freeway. He could have at least waited until there was a turnoff with a nice, clean gas station.

Ahmed was knocking himself silly, so I pulled him out of my car before he started spilling blood. He screamed that he was a martyr and tried to make me join him. I had sent the other three team members home, so there were only the driver of the follow car and me to deliver Ahmed to jail. Fortunately, my partner had the presence of mind to get the highway patrol response rolling as we were pulling over.

An hour later, I was exonerated from Ahmed's claims that I beat him up by showing the responding officer the dash cam videos from my and my partner's sedans. The officer wanted to take my originals then, but I promised to send him the originals in the morning once I had made copies for my records. With all that done, the officer signed my form and took custody of Ahmed.

It made no sense to keep Ahmed in my car where he was hurting himself. It made perfect sense to transfer the liability for transporting Ahmed to the state.

You should always think in terms of liability to avoid future problems that carry enough weight to cause you ulcers. The solution in this lesson was easy with the aid of video proof. Consider this lesson carefully to determine if dash cams are right for you. Also try to give up your fighter to the first police officer who comes along.

CHAPTER TWENTY-NINE

Booking Bail Fugitives

Booking a bail fugitive is a relatively easy process, provided that you have followed the letter of the law for your area of operation.

When jail personnel ask you for paperwork, you must turn over the *original* documents that gave you your authority to make the arrest: court-certified copy of the bail bond face sheet, authority to arrest defendant on bail bond, affidavit of undertaking, and any court-certified copies of warrants. If you show up without these documents and the warrant isn't in the system, you will have to convince the officers of your right to enforce a private civil contract.

In California, for example, booking a bail fugitive may be as simple as having a deputy take the bail fugitive from you. Some jails require bail enforcement agents to fill out the pre-booking sheets, which are a bit confusing, and medical questionnaires. In Alameda County, I've been told on occasion to take the bail fugitive to the public lobby and wait for a deputy, whereas at other times the person at the lobby desk has directed me to the official booking/intake section reserved for law enforcement. In San Joaquin County, I've been bounced back and forth between the public lobby and the official booking/intake section, depending on which shift was on duty at the time.

You may want to call ahead to the station and ask where you should deposit your bail fugitive.

In cases where you do not fill out and keep a copy of the pre-booking sheet, you should have the intake deputy sign your completed 1301 form (illustrated in Appendix D). Technically, the 1301 shouldn't be signed if the bail fugitive has failed to appear, but most jail personnel won't know this. However, some deputies may refuse to sign the form, instead referring to your apprehension as a "citizen's arrest on the warrant." This is confusing since bail fugitive enforcement agents are not serving warrants. Irrespective of what they want to call it, you have earned your commission either way.

Don't freak out if you can't obtain either the pre-booking sheet or the signed 1301 form. You just need to call the bail agent, who will call the jail and confirm that his bail fugitive was booked on the same case and charges that prompted the forfeiture of bail.

In one situation, a bail agent tried to withhold payment to me on the grounds that the police were present during the arrest; hence, I didn't actually make the arrest and therefore shouldn't be paid. I told the bail agent that I took a picture with the fugitive at the police station where I had to retrieve my handcuffs used to restrain him. I told him that the picture would be exhibit one at the small-claims hearing if he withheld payment. Well, I got paid without having to resort to legal action. The point is that sometimes getting photographic proof of your booking a fugitive does more than just adding pictures to your bail enforcement photo album.

If the bail fugitive resisted arrest and, as a consequence, sustained any injuries from pain-and-compliance techniques or exposure to less-than-lethal devices, or if he is under the influence of a drug such as PCP, then a jail nurse will most likely direct you to take the fugitive to the county hospital for medical clearance before accepting responsibility for him. This is rare, but you want to avoid it if at all possible for liability reasons. One way to avoid having your bail fugitive rejected at the jail for medical reasons is to arrange to have the bail fugitive transported to jail by police officers if possible.

Finally, make sure you and your teammates leave all weapons that aren't allowed in a secure booking area (e.g., firearms, pepper spray, spare ammo, edged weapons) securely locked up in your transport vehicle before entering the station.

By and large, booking a bail fugitive into the county jail where the case originated is relatively easy, but each facility has different procedures. Part of your homework is finding out the process in each jurisdiction you plan to work in.

LESSON FROM THE STREET

We were quickly running out of time on this case since we didn't get it until it was, as is common, an "emergency." Preliminary investi-

gation revealed that our skip could be at any one of four addresses in the same neighborhood where drug dens were rumored to be operational. The plan called for knocking on all four doors simultaneously. Doing so meant that the team had to be to split up, so we requested police assistance and got it. Luckily, our radios would work since all locations were within a square-mile radius.

We all parked several houses away, walked in, set up around the various perimeters, radioed that we were ready to go, and then I radioed the signal to go.

As I struck out for my location, Pat, one of my junior agents, radioed that he, with the help of a police officer, had arrested the skip who had answered the door. The warrant for the skip was for another county, so the police bid us farewell and were off to catch up on calls.

I drove to the Pat's location and found the skip in the backseat of Pat's sedan.

"We got him," Pat said excitedly. Pat was elated because he knew that I had considered the case terminal. His speech was rushed, and he couldn't seem to keep still.

"Good job," I replied. "Who patted him down?"

"Oh, I patted him down," Pat said in passing.

I wasn't satisfied with his dismissive tone, so I instructed, "Pat, Look at me." Pat's smile faded slightly. "Is he clean, or does he need to be checked again?"

"No," Pat said reassuringly, "he's good to go."

The bail fugitive was looking down so I couldn't see his face, but I noticed that he was wearing what appeared to be an old, dirty knit-type cap. "Did you check his hat?" I asked.

Pat looked incredulous and replied, "Yeah, the guy's clean."

With that said, we mounted up and hit the road for the next county to book our bail skip and call the bail agent.

Once in the county that held jurisdiction, I called the jail to find out where they wanted us to drop off the bail fugitive, and the person on the phone plainly told me to take him to the public lobby, which I dutifully relayed to Pat. We walked our bail fugitive into the lobby, where the civilian jail clerk ordered us out and around back to the official booking intake ramp. We quickly complied.

I guess it had been a busy night in intake. About a dozen cops were in line with their perspective suspects waiting to get past the sally port and into the main booking area.

At first the police officers and sheriff's deputies noticed us because we were intentionally in unfamiliar uniforms. One of the officers stepped up close and read my left shoulder patch: "Allied Bail Agencies, Bail Agent," he mumbled to himself. "Who're you guys with?"

"We're bail agents," I responded.

He asked for clarification. I explained who we were, what we did, and under what authority we worked. I then mentioned the names of a couple of officers from his agency who had assisted us in an arrest the previous week.

"That was you guys?" he blurted out. "Hey, Smith, you remember that thing with Sheffield? These are the guys."

Another officer (Smith, I presumed) approached, looked us over, and smiled.

With this introduction, the conversation went all over the place until a jail deputy called for us to bring the bail fugitive—who was looking kind of pale and ill—into the main booking area.

I stood back so that Pat could get experience in booking a bail skip at this particular jail. Pat walked the bail fugitive to one of several windows to begin the booking process. The jail deputy moved quickly through the first part, including reading the medical questionnaire Pat had filled out while we were waiting.

"What's under the cap?" the deputy asked, and this caught my attention. The bail fugitive didn't answer. "Take off your cap," the deputy ordered.

By now the two officers who had been speaking to us had come into the main area with their prisoner. I didn't want to be embarrassed, so I walked over to the bail fugitive where the good lighting revealed a sort of undulating movement in the top left part of the bail fugitive's cap. It looked like it was alive. Pat took off the cap, and several items flew around the booking desk, and they were alive!

"Bend over," the jail deputy ordered the bail fugitive, who wisely complied.

I stepped to where I could see better, and I was shocked to see a swell of maggots milling around the guy's head like they were at a barbecue. Oddly enough, I didn't notice any odor that would have tipped me off to the infestation.

"Nurse!" the jail deputy yelled immediately.

I figured that we'd have to take the bail fugitive to the hospital, but the nurse took him to a sink, washed off the maggots, took his temperature, declared him well on his way to healing, and thus cleared him to be booked.

As we left the jail, Pat got an earful from me for not conducting a proper pat down of the bail fugitive. Indeed, if Pat had missed the gaggle of maggots, it stood to reason that he could have missed a weapon. Moreover, I'm sure the maggot story got all over the local police department before the end of the shift.

The lesson here is be safe with a good pat down before you get to the jail. I've worked a county jail, and I'm telling you that those people will find things that you miss, so avoid the embarrassment and do it right. It will help you the next time you book a fugitive at that jail, as well as at others because officer like to tell stories about what happens at their jails.

Conclusion

Now that you have reached the end of the book, I hope that you have a better understanding of the nature of bail recovery work and the role of the bail fugitive recovery person. At this point you should know how to find out whether your state allows bounty hunting, whether you need a license in your state to recover bail fugitives, and how to research the specific laws that you would be working under, such as your legal right to arrest a bail fugitive. You should also be able to assess your skills and know if you need to add more training to make you more employable to a bail agent. Or if you prefer to work for yourself, I have shown you how to set up your business; select the proper equipment; get your first contracts; apprehend, control, transport, and surrender prisoners; and, most important, how to get paid for your hard work.

As I have reiterated throughout this book, bail recovery can be a dangerous but lucrative field. How dangerous the work is depends on you—what precautions you take in the field, how well you research your fugitives, how careful you are in selecting teammates, and how willing you are to walk away when the odds aren't in your favor. How lucrative the work is also depends on you—how willing you are to work hard at making your business successful, at spending long and frustrating nights tracking down elusive fugitives, and at establishing professional relationships in the industry and among law enforcement personnel so you can get the lucrative contracts and deliver the goods on time and in good condition.

Another lesson is this book is that bail recovery field is constantly changing. From the laws in each state to the technologies available to track down and apprehend felony fugitives, staying informed is essential to the recovery agent. One of the best ways that I found to do this is to trade information and ideas with people in this same business all over the country by telephone, Internet chat forums, and professional associations. This is particularly helpful if you must pursue someone across state lines because what works on the East Coast might be illegal or ineffective on the West Coast or in the heartland.

One final lesson I hope that you have gotten from this book is how rewarding bail recovery can be from a nonfinancial perspective. When you successfully complete a contract, you get the satisfaction of performing a historic function that others have been doing for hundreds of years. You can take pride in knowing that you are performing a vital function in our society. That can mean getting a dangerous criminal off the streets, making certain that a family member doesn't lose the family home because of a ne'er-do-well who skipped town, or simply successfully matching your wits against those of a wanted fugitive. Regardless, you will have great stories to tell your friends and grandkids about the ones who didn't get away!

It takes a lot of moxie to knock on a strange door in the middle of the night in pursuit of a dangerous felon. The job isn't for everyone, but it might be for you. Just remember, watch your back and those of the people backing you up, and good luck on the hunt.

State Laws on Bail Recovery

ALABAMA

Relevant statutes: Code of Alabama Title 15, Criminal Procedure, Chapter 13, Bail, Articles 1–6.

General provisions: Bondsman (or an agent who is duly authorized in writing by the bondsman) has broad authority to arrest defendant anywhere in the state. Bondsman or agent must carry certified copy of the undertaking. Must be resident of state and have no convictions for any felonies or crimes of moral turpitude.

Terminology: "Professional bondsman."

ALASKA

Relevant statues: Alaska Criminal Code, Title 12, Chapter 30; Chapter 60, Section 150; Chapter 70, Sections 170–210.

General provisions: Alaska law does permit private persons to make arrests (AS 12,12.010; 12.25.030). No specific regulations for bounty hunters or bail fugitive recovery agents, but "bail bond limited producer license" required for bond agent.

Terminology: None specified.

ARIZONA

Relevant statutes: Arizona Revised Statutes Annotated 20-282.10

General provisions: License required. Must be fingerprinted and have a criminal background check. No felons or persons convicted of an offense involving the use of a dangerous weapon. Requires written permission to act on behalf of the surety as well as authorization by a licensed bail bondsman in Arizona to arrest a defendant. May not enter a residence without permission and must identify himself as a bail enforcement agent. Prohibited from wearing law enforcement clothing or equipment that makes him appear to be a police officer. Out-of-state recovery agents must work through a licensed Arizona bondsman.

Terminology: "Professional bondsman," "bail bond agent," or "bail recovery agent."

ARKANSAS

Relevant statutes: Arkansas Code Title 17, Criminal Offenses, Subtitle 2, Chapter 19, Bail bondsmen. H.B. 1163, enacted April 15, 1999.

General provisions: Nobody can represent himself as a bounty hunter or bail recovery agent. Only licensed bail agents, private investigators, or law enforcement officers can arrest fugitives. Must be 21 years old and have no felonies. Must notify local police officials of presence in their jurisdiction, as well as providing the defendant's name, charges, and suspected location.

Terminology: None specified.

CALIFORNIA

Relevant statutes: A 243, the Bail Fugitive Recovery Persons Act, passed in September 1999, added section 1299 to the California Penal Code (Part 2, Title 10, Chapter 1, Article 5.5, Section 1299) and Insurance Code, Section 1810.7.

General provisions: Regulates bail fugitive recovery persons (BFRP), who must have written authorization from the depositor of bail to act on his behalf. License required. No felons. Must be 18 years old and have completed a 40-hour power-of-arrest training course; a minimum of 12 hours of classroom education (as proscribed by IC 1810.7 [PC 1299.04(a)(3)]); and training course in the power to arrest pursuant to Section 7583.7 of Business and Professions Code [PC 1299.04)a)(4)]. Requires BFRP to notify local police at least 6 hours before attempting to arrest a defendant. Prohibits BFRP from wearing a badge or other law enforcement apparel or carry a firearm except in compliance with state law. BFRP must carry proof of training certifications when on the job. Must turn in defendant within 48 hours of arrest if in state (or within 48 hours of return to state) and go through extradition process if interstate transport is required.

Terminology: "Bail fugitive recovery person."

COLORADO

Relevant statutes: Colorado Revised Statues Annotated (CRSA) Title 12, Article 7; CRSA Title 13, Chapter 30, Rule 246; CRSA Title 16, Article 4, Part 1.

General provisions: Bail bonds regulated by the Division of Insurance. Fingerprints and background check required. No one with felony conviction in past 15 years. Completion of Peace Officer Standards and Training Board (POST) course from private bail recovery program or accredited school as required by section 24-31-303(1)(h), CRS, not to exceed 16 hours.

Terminology: None specified.

CONNECTICUT

Relevant statutes: Connecticut General Statutes Annotated (CGSA) Title 29, Chapter 533A; CGSA Title 54, Chapter 960; CGSA Title 29, Chapter 533.

General provisions: License required. Must notify local police before any apprehensions attempted and are not allowed to wear any badges, equipment, or apparel that look like law enforcement items. Permit required for firearms. Training (20 hours) and background check required. No felons.

Terminology: "Bail enforcement agent."

DELAWARE

Relevant statutes: Delaware Code Annotated Rules, Title 24, Chapter 55, Sections 5501–5505.

General provisions: License required through the Department of Safety and Homeland Security. Must be 21 years old, of good moral character, and submit to criminal background check. No one convicted of a felony or violent crime, or of having used a firearm in the commission of a crime, can be licensed. No one who has been convicted of possession, use, or sale of illegal substances, or has been committed to a mental facility (unless he can document that he no longer suffers from the mental illness) can be licensed. Before apprehending any defendant, State Police and chief law enforcement agent from applicable municipality must be informed

Terminology: "Bail enforcement agent" or "bounty hunter."

DISTRICT OF COLUMBIA

Relevant statutes: District of Columbia Code 1981, Part 4, Title 903, Chapter 11; Michie's District of Columbia Court Rules Annotated, Superior Court Rules of Criminal Procedure 11, Rule 16.

General provisions: No specific regulations for bail recovery agents, but bail agents must be licensed. The District is not friendly to commercial bail and to bounty hunters. Firearms possession and use restricted.

Terminology: None specified.

FLORIDA

Relevant statutes: Florida Statutes Chapter 648, Chapter 24; Florida Administrative Code, Chapter 4–221.

General provisions: Free-lance bounty hunters are not allowed. No person shall represent himself or herself as a bail enforcement agent, bounty hunter, or other similar title. No person, other that a certified law enforcement officer, shall be authorized to apprehend, detain, or arrest a principal on a bond, wherever issued, unless that person is qualified, licensed, and appointed as provided in this chapter or licensed as a bail bond agent by the state where the bond was written [FS 648.39(4)].

Terminology: "Bail enforcement agent."

GEORGIA

Relevant statutes: Code of Georgia (COG) Title 17, Chapter 6, Article 2, Parts 1 and 2; COG Title 17, Chapter 6, Article 3.

General provisions: Has specific restrictions regarding bounty hunters or bail recovery agents (BRA). Must be 25 years old, a U.S. citizen, have a Georgia firearms permit to carry (if carrying a firearm). If BRA is from out of state he must carry his license or if from a state that requires no license or training he must hire a licensed Georgia agent. BRA must carry ID that contains a description of carrier from bondsman that is signed by bondsman. If apprehension of defendant is scheduled for a private residence, BRA must notify local police; no notification required for public arrests.

Terminology: "Bail recovery agent."

HAWAII

Relevant statutes:	Hawaii Revised Statutes 804-51.
General provisions:	No specific regulations for bounty hunters.
Terminology:	None specified.

IDAHO

Relevant statutes:	Idaho Code (IC) Title 19, Chapter 29, Section 19-2906, 2924; Idaho Criminal Rules (ICR), Rule 46.
General provisions:	No specific provisions for bail enforcement agents in Idaho. Surety or his empowered agent may arrest defendant at any time.
Terminology:	None specified.

ILLINOIS

Relevant statutes:	Illinois Statutes Chapter 725, Section 5/103-9
General provisions:	Bounty hunters illegal. 1963 law effectively eliminated bail bond industry (see *Schilb v. Kuebel*, 264 N.E.2nd 377, 380 (Ill. 1970) aff'd 404 U.S. 357 (1971); Ill. Stat. Ch. 725 Secs. 5/110-7, 5/110-8: "No bail bondsman from any state may seize or transport unwillingly any person found in this State who is allegedly in violation of a bail bond posted in some other state."
Terminology:	None specified.

INDIANA

Relevant statutes:	Indiana Code (IC) 27-10-1 through 10-5-3
General provisions:	License required. Must pass a test given by the state and be 18 years or older, a resident of the state for at least a year (can be waived), a U.S. citizen. Must not have a felony conviction in past 10 years or a misdemeanor conviction in past 5 years. Must notify sheriff in their resident locales of their residency and bond agents must provide a list of all recovery agents to the state. Prohibited from forcibly entering the residence of a third party while trying to apprehend the defendant.
Terminology:	None specified.

IOWA

Relevant statutes:	Iowa Code Annotated (ICA), Title 3, Chapter 80A, Sections 1–16A; ICA Title 16, Chapter 811, Section 8.
General provisions:	License required. Bail enforcement agents (BEA) must notify local police before apprehending defendant. BEA are prohibited from forcibly entering home of a third party or using force against him. Surety may authorize BEA, by written permission on a certified copy of the undertaking, to arrest the defendant at any place in the state. BEA must be 18 years or older and have no criminal record.
Terminology:	"Bail enforcement agent."

KANSAS

Relevant statutes:	Kansas Statutes Annotated Chapter 22, Article 28, 22-2806 – 22-2809.
General provisions:	No specific regulations for bail enforcement agents. Kansas Insurance Department is the regulatory agency for bail bonds. The surety or his designated agent may arrest the defendant and deliver him to the county in which he is charged.
Terminology:	None specified.

KENTUCKY

Relevant statutes: Kentucky Statute §431.510; Kentucky Revised Statute §440.270.

General provisions: Bounty hunters, as well as commercial bail bond businesses, banned. Out-of-state bond agents must get a warrant for bail fugitives who have fled to Kentucky.

Terminology: None specified.

LOUISIANA

*Relevant statutes: Louisiana Statutes Annotated Louisiana Revised Statutes (LSALSR), Title 22, Chapter 1, Part 34; LSALSR, Title 15, Chapter 1, Title 8.

General provisions: License required through the Department of Insurance. Prelicensing and continuing education licensing requirements. Out-of-state bounty hunters must work with licensed Louisiana bail agent. Notification of local law enforcement agents is required for apprehension in private residence. Recovery agents required to wear apparel or equipment identifying the company for which they work.

Terminology: None specified.

MAINE

Relevant statutes: Maine Revised Statutes Title 15, Part 2, Chapter 105-A – 1072, 1094

General provisions: No specific regulations for bail fugitive recovery agents.

Terminology: None specified.

MARYLAND

Relevant statutes: Maryland Rules, Criminal Causes, Rule 4-217 (B)(3)(h)(1)(2)(i)(3) and Rule 722 (h).

General provisions: Surety may surrender defendant before a forfeiture.

Terminology: None specified.

MASSACHUSETTS

Relevant statutes: Massachusetts General Laws Annotated, Part 4, Title 2, Chapter 276.

General provisions: No specific regulations for bail recovery agents.

Terminology: None specified.

MICHIGAN

Relevant statutes: Michigan Compiled Laws Annotated Chapter 765, Section 128.

General provisions: No specific regulations for bail recovery agents. Surety may arrest the defendant and can expect help from relevant law enforcement agencies.

Terminology: None specified.

MINNESOTA

Relevant statutes: Minnesota Statutes Criminal Procedure Chapter 629, Section 63.

General provisions: No specific regulations for bail recovery agents. Surety may arrest defendant or have him arrested. Must notify sheriff before any apprehension.

Terminology: None specified.

MISSISSIPPI

Relevant statutes: Mississippi Code (MS C) Title 83, Chapter 39, Section 3; MS C Title 99, Chapter 5, Sections 27, 29

General provisions: License required. Must be 21 years old, state resident for at least a year, and have

Terminology: "Bail enforcement agent," defined as a person who assists the professional bail agent in presenting the defendant in court when required, or who assists in the apprehension and surrender of the defendant under necessary surveillance.

no felonies or crimes of moral turpitude on his record. Surety, or authorized agent, may arrest defendant anywhere and may request assistance from law enforcement, but must present certified copy of the bond.

MISSOURI

Relevant statutes: Missouri Revised Statutes Title 37, Chapter 544, Section 700.

General provisions: UCEA does not apply in Missouri. Surety or authorized agent may arrest defendant in any county. Surety must have a copy of recognizance from the clerk before surrendering defendant.

Terminology: None specified.

MONTANA

Relevant statutes: Montana Code Annotated Title 46, Chapter 9, Part 5, Sections 503, 510.

General provisions: No specific regulations for bail recovery agents. At any time surety or authorized agent may surrender defendant to court or any peace officer in state.

Terminology: None specified.

NEBRASKA

Relevant statutes: Nebraska Revised Statues, Chapter 29, Section 906.

General provisions: No specific regulations for bail recovery agents. At any time surety or authorized agent may surrender defendant to sheriff in county where bond is held.

Terminology: None specified.

NEVADA

Relevant statutes: Nevada Revised Statutes, Title 57, Chapter 697 et seq.; Title 14, Chapter 178, Section 526.

General provisions: License required. Nevada has some of the most restrictive regulations for bail bond industry and bail recovery agents in the nation. Must be 21 years or older, be a U.S. citizen or able to lawfully work in this country, have no felonies or evidence of moral turpitude on record, have no controlled substance convictions and pass a drug test, submit to a Nevada criminal history background check, be a high school graduate or pass GED, show proof from a licensed Nevada psychiatrist or psychologist that he is fit to work as bail enforcement agent, have completed 80 hours of training. Must notify local police before forcible entering an inhabited residence and immediately after apprehending a defendant to relate his name, name of defendant, and where defendant is being surrendered into custody.

Terminology: "Bail enforcement agent."

NEW HAMPSHIRE

Relevant statutes: New Hampshire Revised Statutes, Title 59, Chapter 597, Sections 7–36.

General provisions: Requires training and certification by a program approved by Professional Bail Agents of the United States. Must register with Secretary of State, who will provide proof of registration. Must notify police in jurisdiction where arrest occurs.

Terminology: "Recovery agent," defined as a person who meets the requirements of paragraph II of this section and who is offered or given any compensation by a bail agent or surety in exchange for assisting the bail agent or surety in apprehending or surrendering any defendant, or keeping the defendant under necessary surveillance.

NEW JERSEY

Relevant statutes: New Jersey Rules of Court, Part 3, Chapter 6, Rule 3:26PS 2A:15-47 or 2A160-26

General provisions: No specific regulations for bail bond recovery agents. Surety can make a civil arrest of defendant, but latter has same legal rights as if arrested for a crime. Defendant must be returned within 20 days after court takes action against surety for nonappearance of defendant.

Terminology: None specified.

NEW MEXICO

Relevant statutes: New Mexico Statutes Annotated, Chapter 31, Article 3, Section 3; Chapter 31, Article 4, Section 14; Chapter 59A, Article 51, Sections 2–19.

General provisions: No specific regulations for bail recovery agents. At any time surety or authorized agent may surrender defendant to sheriff in county where bond is held. Certified copies of order admitting the defendant to bail and of the bond must accompany surrender. Subject to criminal prosecution for armed, unauthorized forcible entry into third-party residences.

Terminology: None specified.

NEW YORK

Relevant statutes: McKinney's Consolidated Laws of New York Annotated Criminal Procedure Law, Chapter 28, Article 68, Section 6802; Criminal Proc. Title P, Division 3, Articles 530.80 and 540.

General provisions: License required. Firearms restricted. Licensing requirements for bondsmen are lengthy, and are overseen by the department of state. Fingerprinting and criminal background check required. Requires either 3 years' experience as a police officer; an investigator in an agency of the state, county, or federal government; or an employee of a licensed private investigator or at a firm, partnership, company, or corporation where one member has been performing the duties described in the definition of bail enforcement agent; OR 20 years' experience as a police officer or fire marshal. If an applicant doesn't have the necessary experience, must complete training course (25 hours).

Terminology: "Bail enforcement agent" shall mean and include only the business of bail enforcement and shall also mean and include, separately or collectively, the engaging in the business of enforcing the terms and conditions of a person's release from custody on bail in a criminal proceeding, including locating, apprehending, and returning any such person released from custody on bail who has failed to appear at any stage of a criminal proceeding to answer the charge before the court in which he may be prosecuted."

NORTH CAROLINA

Relevant statutes: North Carolina General Statutes (NCGS) Chapter 58, Article 71, Sections 25–140; NCGS Chapter 15A, Subchapter 5, Article 26, Part 1, Sections 15A-544.

General provisions: Bail enforcement agents banned. Bail runners can work for only one company at a time. Bail runner must be 18 or older, a resident of North Carolina, have proscribed training or experience in job, provide fingerprints to State Bureau of Investigation for criminal record search. Cannot enter third-party home to search for defendant.

Terminology: "Bail runner," defined as a person employed by a bail bondsman for the purpose of assisting the bail bondsman in presenting the defendant in court when required, or to assist in apprehension and surrender of defendant to the court, or keeping defendant under necessary surveillance, or to execute bonds on behalf of the licensed bondsman when the power of attorney has been duly recorded. Runner does not include, however, a duly license attorney-at-law or a law-enforcement officer assisting a bondsman.

NORTH DAKOTA

Relevant statutes: North Dakota Century Code (Insurance) Title 26.1 – 26.6; North Dakota Rules of Criminal Procedure, Rule 46.

General provisions: No specific regulations for bail recovery agents. At any time surety or authorized agent may arrest the defendant before forfeiture or authorize in writing a peace officer to do so.

Terminology: None specified.

OHIO

Relevant statutes: Baldwin's Ohio Revised Code Annotated, Title 29, Chapter 2937; Ohio Revised Statutes Annotated 2713-22.

General provisions: No specific regulations for bail recovery agents or any specific statutes that give agents the right to arrest defendants. At any time surety or authorized agent (with written authority on certified copy of bond) may arrest defendant.

Terminology: None specified.

OKLAHOMA

Relevant statutes: Oklahoma Statutes Annotated Title 59, Chapter 33, Sections 1301–1332; Oklahoma Statutes (OKS) Title 39, 1328–329, Criminal Procedures 1107 and OKS 1750.14.

General provisions: Oklahoma has extensive provisions on licensing for bondsmen but not for recovery agents or bounty hunters. Out-of-state bounty hunters or bond agents must be accompanied by peace officer or licensed Oklahoma bond agent when apprehending defendant.

Terminology: None specified.

OREGON

Relevant statutes: Oregon Revised Statute §§135.255, .260, .265. ORS, Title 56, Chapter 731 for Insurance. In *State v. Epps*, 585 P 2nd 425 (Oregon 1978), the Oregon Supreme Court abolished the broad common law rights of bounty hunters and bond agents and allied the provisions of the UCEA to bounty hunters taking defendants across state lines.

General provisions: Bail recovery agents and commercial bail banned. Defendants can be released from custody on conditional release, deposit bond, or on his own recognizance (i.e., no surety bonds).

Terminology: None specified.

PENNSYLVANIA

Relevant statutes: Pennsylvania Statutes, Rules of Criminal Procedure, Chapter 4000, Part 3, Rule 4016

General provisions: No specific regulations for bail recovery. Upon receipt of a bail piece from the court, the surety or authorized agent may arrest the defendant whenever and wherever found.

Terminology: None specified.

RHODE ISLAND

Relevant statutes: Rhode Island Court Rules Annotated, Rules 1–13, 46.

General provisions: No specific regulations for bail recovery agents. At any time surety or authorized agent may surrender defendant to court or magistrate of jurisdiction.

Terminology: None specified.

SOUTH CAROLINA

Relevant statutes: Code of Laws of South Carolina 1976 Annotated, Title 17, Chapter 15; S.C. Statute 38-53-80.

General provisions: Free-lance bounty hunters or bail agents banned. Bail runners must be licensed, and each year bondsmen must submit to the clerk of each county wherein he does business a list of all licensed runners who work for him. Runners must be 18 years or older, be a South Carolina resident, have no criminal record for past 10 years, take a training course (20 hours) and pass an exam. Bail runners may work for only one agent at a time.

Terminology: "Bail runner," defined as a person employed by a bail bondsman for the purpose of assisting the bail bondsman in presenting the defendant in court when required, or to assist in apprehension and surrender of defendant to the court, or keeping defendant under necessary surveillance, or to execute bonds on behalf of the licensed bondsman when the power of attorney has been duly recorded. Runner does not include, an attorney or a law-enforcement officer assisting a bondsman.

SOUTH DAKOTA

Relevant statutes: South Dakota Codified Law §§58-22-12 –52.

General provisions: License required. Bail runner must submit fingerprints, have no felonies, and pass examination. Out-of-state runners must notify local police in advance of intended actions and show proof of license in state of residence. Bail agents must provide state with the names of bail runners they employ.

Terminology: "Bail runner," defined as a person employed by a bail bondsman for the purpose of assisting the bail bondsman in presenting the defendant in court when required, or to assist in apprehension and surrender of defendant to the court, or keeping defendant under necessary surveillance, or to execute bonds on behalf of the licensed bondsman when the power of attorney has been duly recorded. Runner does not include, an attorney or a law-enforcement officer assisting a bondsman.

TENNESSEE

Relevant statutes: Tennessee Code Annotated, Title 40, Chapter 11, Parts 1–4.

General provisions: Bounty hunter cannot have a criminal record. Before a bounty hunter takes into defendant into custody, he must present the following to the office of the appropriate law enforcement officer of the political subdivision where the taking will occur: a copy of the applicable warrant, a copy of the bond, and proper credentials from a professional bondsman in Tennessee or another state verifying that the bounty hunter is an agent of a professional bondsman. The surety or his authorized agent may arrest defendant in any place in the state and is entitled to assistance from the sheriff in the county where the apprehension is to take place. The surety or his agent must show the defendant a copy of undertaking when he is arrested.

Terminology: "Bounty hunting" is defined as a person who acts as an agent of a professional bondsman who attempts to or takes into custody a person who has failed to appear in court and whose bond has been forfeited, for a fee, the payment of which is contingent upon the taking of a person into custody and returning such person to the custody of the professional bondsman for whom the bounty hunter works; provided, that "bounty hunting" does not include the taking into custody of a person by a professional bondsman.

TEXAS

Relevant statutes: Occupations Code, Chapter 1704; Code of Criminal Procedures, Chapters 14, 17, and 22; Revised Civil Statutes of State of Texas, Volume 7A, Article 2372p-3.

General provisions: Texas severely restricts actions of bounty hunters. The surety can without force or breach of the peace surrender the defendant at any time. Arrests can be made only by peace officers, security officers, or private investigators licensed in the state of Texas.

Terminology: None specified.

UTAH

Relevant statutes: Utah Code (UC) 1953, Title 53, Chapter 11, Sections 53-11-102 – 53-11-124; UC, Title 77 1953, Chapters 20 and 20b; UC 1953 Title 31A, Chapter 35, Act Part 1.

General provisions: License required. Bail enforcement agents must be 21 or older, a citizen or legal resident of U.S., pass a background check, complete a training course and apprenticeship under a bond agent or law enforcement officer. May not wear any law enforcement–like apparel or badges and must identify themselves as bail enforcement agents. Surety may apprehend defendant at any time or place in Utah. Must notify local police at least 24 hours before entering an occupied structure to make an arrest. Must carry certified copy of the undertaking and provide a copy to peace officer when defendant is surrendered.

Terminology: "Bail enforcement agent."

VERMONT

Relevant statutes: Vermont Statutes Annotated, Title 13, Part 5, Chapter 229, Section 7562; Chapter 125, Sections 3478 and 3484.

General provisions: No specific licensing regulations for recovery agents. Surety gets warrant from justice of the peace, which directs any sheriff or constable to assist in the arrest of the defendant. Then the surety or authorized may arrest defendant at any time.

Terminology: None specified.

VIRGINIA

Relevant statutes: Code of Virginia, Title 19.2, Chapter 9, Article 4, Sections 19.2-152.1; Article 4.

General provisions: No specific regulations for bail recovery agents. Surety may arrest the defendant at any time and surrender him to court.

Terminology: None specified.

WASHINGTON

Relevant statutes: Revised Code of Washington, Title 18, Chapter 18.185. Sections .010, .040, .090, .110, and .170.

General provisions: New legislation enacted in 2004, which becomes effective in December 2005, requires a license for bail fugitive recovery agents. For a license, an applicant must pass an examination determined by the director of the Department of Licensing to measure his or her knowledge and competence in the bail recovery business; be at least 21 years old; be a citizen or legal resident alien of the United States; not have been convicted of a crime in any jurisdiction, if the director determines that the applicant's particular crime directly relates to a capacity to perform the duties of a bail bond recovery agent, and that the license should be withheld to protect the citizens of Washington state; submit a receipt showing payment for a background check through the Washington state patrol and the FBI; and have a current firearms certificate issued by the commission if carrying a firearm in the performance of his or her duties as a bail bond recovery agent.

Terminology: "Bail bond recovery agent," defined as a person who is under contract with a bail bond agent to receive compensation, reward, or any other form of lawful consideration for locating, apprehending, and surrendering a fugitive criminal defendant for whom a bail bond has been posted. "Bail bond recovery agent" does not include a general authority Washington peace officer or a limited authority Washington peace officer.

WEST VIRGINIA

Relevant statutes: West Virginia Code 1966, Chapter 51, Article 10A; Chapter 62, Article 1C; WV H 4481 (enacted April 4, 2000).

General provisions: License required. Bail bond enforcer applicants must register with state police and list at least one bail bondsman for whom he or she is licensed to act; be fingerprinted, certified by an authorized law enforcement agent; provide a full-face photograph; be 21 years of age or older; be a citizen of the U.S.; and have never been convicted of any felony in any state of the U.S.

Terminology: "Bail bond enforcer," defined as a person who on behalf of a bail bondsman enters this state of is present in this state for the purposes of (1) assisting a bail bondsman in presenting the defendant in court when required, (2) assisting in the apprehension and surrender of the defendant to a court, (3) keeping a defendant under surveillance, or (4) executing bonds on behalf of a bail bondsman when a power of attorney has been duly recorded. The term "bail bond enforcer" does not include a duly licensed attorney-at-law or a law-enforcement officer assisting a bail bondsman.

WISCONSIN

Relevant statutes: WS 818.21 (969.14); Wisconsin Statute (WS) 969.12; *Kahn v. McCormack*, 299 N.W.2d 279 (Ct. App. 1980).

General provisions: Bounty hunters or bail enforcement agents banned. WS 818.21 (969.14) gives a surety or his agent (by written authority on a certified copy of the bond) the power to arrest the defendant, but WS 969.12 states: "No surety under this chapter may be compensated for acting as such a surety," which effectively bans the commercial bail industry. *Kahn v. McCormack* upheld WS 969.12.

Terminology: None specified.

WYOMING

Relevant statutes: Wyoming Rules of Criminal Procedure, Rule 46.

General provisions: No specific regulations for bail recovery agents. Surety or his authorized agent may arrest defendant at any time.

Terminology: None specified.

Sample Letters to Bail Agents

Date

Dear Sir or Madam,

As a professional in the bail bond industry for XX years, I know what is required to get the job done and satisfy clients. I think my record shows that I have a firm understanding of the legal liabilities affecting all parties, as well as the foresight to identify potential problem areas, present an effective solution, and implement a successful solution.

I have no doubt that much of my success as a bail bond professional comes from the training and experience I received from my military police, civilian law enforcement, corrections, and bail bond recovery work. The lessons I learned in those real-life fields have enabled me to make a successful transition from law enforcement to private sector contracting. The exceptional qualities I bring to the recovery field are as follows:

- Working knowledge of penal codes that directly pertain to fugitive recovery and applicable case law
- More than 14 years of experience in law enforcement and fugitive recovery
- The ability to work harmoniously with law enforcement professionals when needed
- Full-time dedication toward bail exoneration

In addition, I use state-of-the-art techniques and equipment. For instance, I have a fully equipped four-door sedan with prisoner transport partition, limo-tinted rear windows, fiberglass-molded single-piece seat, and state-of-the-art restraining belts.

Please keep me in mind if you need the services of a dedicated professional bail fugitive recovery person.

Sincerely,

Rex Venator

A more formal example of a letter to a prospective client.

Date

Dear Sir or Madam,

Allow me to introduce myself. I am a seasoned, knowledgeable former bail bond company owner with a strong background in the bail bond industry. I believe that I may be able to help you with your business.

The qualities I bring to the recovery field are as follows:

- Currently licensed as a bail agent
- Current Notary Public Commission
- More than 300 bail fugitive arrests with zero residual liability
- Have personally drafted and filed 83 motions in numerous jurisdictions
- Appeared as an agent for the surety 83 times
- Successfully won 83 court-ordered bond exonerations

I am very interested in meeting with you to discuss how my knowledge, drive, and enthusiasm can benefit your company. I look forward to hearing from you and thank you for your consideration.

Sincerely,

Rex Venator

Another example of a letter to a prospective client that is more straightforward and action oriented. This is ideal for someone who has been in the business for a while and has concrete accomplishments he can emphasize.

Sample Wanted Posters

BAIL FUGITIVE TEAM
1-800-XXX-XXXX

Subject's name and date of birth: John Doe, 1/1/1951
Physical description: Male, Caucasian, 5' 11"
165 lbs., brown hair, brown eyes.

Officer safety advisory: Subject has violent background and is looking at a "third-strike" arrest; he may resist arrest at any cost. Exercise extreme caution.

You may be entitled to a reward for information leading to the arrest of this person.

Front and back of sample business card–sized wanted "poster." Smaller wanted posters are good to hand out one-on-one to merchants, passers-by on the street, neighborhood residents, and others when a full-size poster would be inconvenient. They are also handier to carry around in your pockets or wallet.

John Doe

Wanted For Allegedly:
Trafficking in Illegal Narcotics

Other Information:
$200,000.00
Felony Warrant
Issued by the
Fresno County Superior Court
Case # F019X45PIUN45-A

FUGITIVE ALERT

REWARD FOR INFORMATION LEADING TO THE ARREST OF:

Sex:

Date of Birth:

Height:

Weight:

Eyes:

Hair:

Salients:

Place of Birth:

Race:

Aliases:

WANTED FOR ALLEGEDLY:
COMMITTING LEWD ACT ON A CHILD x 15

$ 500,000.00 FELONY WARRANT
ISSUED BY THE VENTURA COUNTY SUPERIOR COURT
CASE NUMBER

LAST KNOWN ADDRESS:

LAST KNOWN EMPLOYER:

OFFICER SAFETY ADVISORY

ADDITIONAL INFORMATION:

1-800-123-456

CALLERS WITH INFORMATION MAY REMAIN ANONYMOUS.
$ REWARD MONEY AVAILABLE $

*Full-size wanted poster of pending case. These posters are better for posting on bulletin
boards or display windows because they catch the viewer's attention more readily.*

Standard California 1301 Form

IN THE _____ COURT _____ JUDICIAL DISTRICT

COUNTY OF _____ , STATE OF CALIFORNIA

THE PEOPLE OF THE STATE OF CALIFORNIA,
Plaintiff,

vs.

_____
Defendant.

} ss.

RECEIPT ACKNOWLEDGING SURRENDER OF DEFENDANT BY BONDSMAN

Case No. _____

Original Charge(s) _____

I HEREBY CERTIFY that the above named defendant is now in my custody pursuant to the provisions of Section 1300-1301 of the California Penal Code.
(strike one)

SHERIFF FOR THE COUNTY OF _____

DATED this _____ day of _____ 19 ____   By _____
Deputy/Jailor

CHIEF OF POLICE. CITY OF _____

By _____
Jailor

SURRENDER OF DEFENDANT

1300.1 P.C. A certified copy of the undertaking of bail, or a certified copy of the certificate of deposit where a deposit is made, must be delivered to the officer who must detain the defendant in his custody thereon as upon a commitment, and by a certificate in writing acknowledge the surrender.

1301 P.C. Provides the bail may themselves arrest the defendant, or by written authority, endorsed on a certified copy of the undertaking or a certified copy of the certificate of deposit, may empower any person of suitable age and discretion to do so.

FPIC-61   (5/94)

Sample Independent Contractor Agreement

The following six-page document is a sample of an independent contractor agreement that the author uses in his business in California. It specifically addresses do's and don'ts, payment, covenant not to compete, and confidentiality. You should have a local attorney draw up a contract for you to make sure that it is in compliance with local law and that your interests are protected fully under the law.

INDEPENDENT CONTRACTOR AGREEMENT FOR PERSONAL/EXECUTIVE PROTECTION AND/OR BAIL FUGITIVE RECOVERY OPERATIONS

This Independent Contractor Agreement ("Agreement") is made and effective this ___(Date)_____, by and between John Doe (hereafter called "BFRP") and Ultimate Bail Fugitive Recovery Group (hereafter called "Company").

Now, therefore, BFRP and Company agree as follows:

1. ENGAGEMENT
Company hereby engages BFRP, and BFRP accepts engagement, to provide to Company the following services and under the following requirements:
- To provide personal or executive protection services as prescribed by law or to investigate, locate, secure the arrest, and/or surrender of any bail fugitive that BFRP has been authorized to arrest or surrender.
- To ultimately cause the exoneration of associated forfeited bond/s of any bail fugitive that BFRP has been authorized to arrest or surrender as provided under the governing and applicable law of the jurisdiction wherein said forfeiture and subsequent arrest has occurred.

BFRP shall not knowingly misrepresent him- or herself as being a member of any federal, state, or local law enforcement agency to any person, or to conceal any misdemeanor or felony conviction(s), or of being subject to any restraining order that has been issued by any court.

BFRP shall not knowingly misrepresent him- or herself as never having been adjudicated under Welfare and Institutions Codes 8100, 8100(b), 8103(a), 8103(b), 8103(d), 8103(e), or 8103(f)(g).

BFRP shall not possess any weapon that is not legally registered to BFRP, and BFRP shall not be in possession of any weapon or ammunition that is not in full compliance with all applicable laws of the state of California or any other state within the United States.

BFRP shall supply true and correct copies of the following documents prior to field activation/training:
- Completed background investigation documents

165

- Completed 1099 tax form
- Valid private investigator license or 40-hour powers-of-arrest 832 PC certificate
- 12-hour bail agent prelicensing certificate
- Business and Professions 7583.7 certification
- Valid California driver's license,
- Complete and Full Waiver of Liability
- Physician's release
- Applicable contracts

BFRP, prior to field activation, shall successfully pass a physical agility test consisting of the following continuous activities:
- 5 pull-ups palms outward (men), or hang for 30 seconds (women)
- Stand-up contact sparring for 5 minutes
- Run 1 mile in under 12 minutes
- Grapple for 5 minutes

BFRP, after field activation, shall maintain commission standard after successfully passing the quarterly physical agility test consisting of the following activities:
- Cycle 5 miles in a hilly area in 30 minutes or less
- Complete 5 pull-ups palm outward (men) or hang for 30 seconds (women)
- Swim ten 25-yard laps in 15 minutes or less using any stroke

BFRP shall complete the following requirements *prior* to conducting any investigation. (For the purposes of this section, "investigating" is defined as tracking, surveilling, locating, identifying, arresting, and transporting any bail fugitive to the proper authorities within 48 hours of arrest.) BFRP shall obtain a court-certified copy of all applicable bail bonds posted on all bail fugitives' behalf, court-certified copy of any applicable warrants on all bail fugitives if applicable, Authority to arrest form, and a confirmed booking photograph of the bail fugitive. BFRP shall make every effort to ascertain any and all salient characteristics (e.g., scars, marks, tattoos) on each bail fugitive prior to attempting any arrest.

BFRP shall, at all times while attempting the arrest of any bail fugitive, wear National Institute of Justice–approved Level IIIA body armor.

BFRP shall not investigate any bail fugitive while under the influence of any drug either legal or illegal under the laws of the State of California. BFRP shall not consume any alcoholic beverage 24 hours prior to attempting any arrest of any bail fugitive.

BFRP shall, during all attempts to arrest any bail fugitive, carry those documents on his or her person that are required by law:
- Court-certified copy of the bail bond
- Affidavit of Undertaking of Bail for Surrender of Defendant
- Authority to Arrest Form
- 832 PC Certificate
- Business & Professions 7583.7 Powers of Arrest document
- 12-hour prelicensing certificate pursuant to Insurance Code 1810.7

BFRP shall, immediately prior to attempting any arrest or bail surrender, confirm that previously confirmed warrants (if applicable) are still active by checking with the appropriate court, jail, and police/sheriff agencies.

BFRP shall immediately notify the proper law enforcement agency of his or her presence and intentions upon entering any jurisdiction with the intention of investigating any bail fugitive.

BFRP shall not summon or in any other way employ any person who is not in full compliance with the requirements of this contract and all applicable laws pertaining to bail arrest in California, for the purposes of investigating any bail fugitive.

BFRP shall not attempt any arrest of any bail fugitive without the assistance of Company BFRPs or sworn peace officers.

BFRP shall attend all mandatory training at BFRP's expense when Company is unable to arrange for BFRP's tuition of any mandatory training class. Mandatory training shall include, but is not limited to, the following:

- Weapons training and retention
- High-risk handcuffing
- Laws affecting BFRP
- High-risk warrant service
- Control and restraint techniques
- Shoot/don't shoot scenarios
- Paintball training
- Air- or waterborne training

BFRP shall, on each Monday of every week, submit a detailed written report of all activity pertaining to each bail fugitive being investigated by BFRP. BFRP shall also include an activity/time sheet with supporting receipts or other verifiable documents. BFRP shall make certain that Company receives said reports either in person or by facsimile or U.S. mail. BFRP agrees to surrender to Company all material on any file within 24 hours after failing to report as directed.

2. TERM
BFRP shall provide services to Company pursuant to this Agreement for a term commencing on __(Date)_____ and ending upon verbal and/or written notice from the Company. BFRP may terminate this Agreement upon 30 days written notice mailed to the principal office of the Company to the attention of Rex Venator.

BFRP shall immediately notify Company in writing of any circumstance or incident that disqualifies BFRP from performing the services described herein. Circumstance or incident is defined as any occurrence or ongoing condition that is contrary to requirements of this contract either known or unknown to Company or BFRP.

BFRP shall immediately turn in all materials belonging to Company upon written notice.

3. PLACE OF WORK
BFRP shall render services primarily at BFRP's office, but will, upon request, provide the services at Company's office or such other places as reasonably requested by Company as appropriate for the performance of particular services. BFRP shall routinely travel varied distances in a manner consistent with investigating the whereabouts of any bail fugitive that the BFRP has been authorized to arrest, surrender, or assist in arresting or surrendering.

4. TIME
BFRP's daily schedule and hours worked under this Agreement on a given day shall generally be

subject to BFRP's discretion, provided that BFRP and Company anticipate that BFRP shall work a necessary amount of hours per week per contract in the performance of services pursuant to this Agreement. Company relies upon BFRP to devote sufficient time as is reasonably necessary to fulfill the spirit and purpose of this Agreement. BFRP shall surrender any complete file and all copies, originals, or other material should, in the opinion of Company, it be determined that BFRP is not working the necessary amount of time on any case, contract, or investigation.

5. PAYMENT

Company shall pay BFRP 2.5 percent of total commission received for personal or executive protection services payments made to Company, or 1 percent of total commission received for actually assisting in a physical arrest for each bail fugitive, or 1 percent for causing a court-ordered vacating of forfeiture conducted within the spirit of this agreement, or 2.5 percent of total commission received if BFRP is solely responsible for causing any exoneration of any bond to include another 0.5 percent of actual commission received if BFRP is in compliance with physical agility requirements as set forth by Company, or 1 percent of actual commission received for in-custody location of any bail fugitive assigned to BFRP. While assisting Company during physical arrests, Company shall pay physical-agility-compliant BFRP 1 percent and noncompliant BFRP 0.5 percent of actual commission received upon actual arrest of any bail for services performed pursuant to this Agreement and according to proof (activity logs and supporting documents). All payments shall be made within 7 working days upon receipt of payment to Company. Receipt of payment to Company generally occurs within 21 days of submitting all necessary documents for payment. BFRP shall bear all of BFRFs expenses incurred in the performance of this Agreement.

BFRP shall obtain, complete, and submit all necessary original documents from Company prior to receipt of payment. The necessary documents include, but are not limited to, the following:

- Activity log(s)
- Incident report
- Recovery agent updates
- Supplementary report
- Body receipt
- In-custody affidavit
- 1301 PC Surrender form

BFRP shall not receive a commission for cases found to be reinstated.

6. COVENANT NOT TO COMPETE

During the term of this Agreement and for a period of 5 years thereafter, BFRP shall not within Santa Clara, Alameda, Contra Costa, San Francisco, San Mateo, San Joaquin, Stanislaus, Sacramento, El Dorado, Placer, Amador, Calaveras, and Tuolumne Counties, directly or indirectly, either for his own account, or as a partner, shareholder, officer, director, employee, or agent; or otherwise own, manage, operate, control, be employed by, participate in, consult with, perform services for, or otherwise be connected with any business the same as or similar to the business conducted by Company. In the event any of the provisions of this Section 6 are determined to be invalid by reason of their scope or duration, this Section 6 shall be deemed modified to the extent required to cure the invalidity. In the event of a breach, or a threatened breach, of this Section 6, Company shall be entitled to obtain an injunction restraining the commitments or continuance of the breach, as well as any other legal or equitable remedies permitted by law.

BFRPs providing personal or executive protection services for non-Company clients are exempt from this section to the extent that Company did not, in any way, establish the business relationship between BFRP and his or her existing or new client(s). This exemption does not apply to any bail bond support services.

7. CONFIDENTIALITY

During the term of this Agreement, and thereafter in perpetuity, BFRP shall not, without the prior written consent of Company, disclose to anyone any confidential information. "Confidential information," for the purposes of this Agreement, shall include Company's proprietary and confidential information such as, but not limited to, customer lists, business plans, marketing plans, financial information, designs, drawing, specifications, models, software, source codes, and object codes. Confidential information shall not include any information that:

- Is disclosed by Company without restriction
- Becomes publicly available through no act of BFRP
- Is rightfully received by BFRP from a third party

8. TERMINATION

This Agreement may be terminated by Company as follows:
- If BFRP is unable to provide the bail fugitive recovery services by reason of temporary or permanent illness, disability, incapacity or death
- Breach or default of any obligation of BFRP pursuant to Section 6, Covenant Not to Compete, or Section 7, Confidentiality, of this Agreement.
- Breach or default by BFRP of any other material obligation in this Agreement, which breach or default is not cured within 5 days of written notice from Company.

BFRP may terminate this Agreement as follows:
- Breach or default of any material obligation of Company, which breach or default is not cured within 5 days of written notice from BFRP
- If Company files protection under the federal bankruptcy laws, or any bankruptcy petition or petition for receiver is commenced by a third party against Company, any of the foregoing of which remains undismissed for a period of 60 days

9. INDEPENDENT CONTRACTOR

BFRP is and throughout this Agreement shall be an independent contractor and not an employee, partner, or agent of Company. BFRP shall not be entitled to, nor receive, any benefit normally provided to Company's employees such as, but not limited to, vacation payment, retirement, health care, or sick pay. Company shall not be responsible for withholding income or other taxes from the payments made to BFRP. BFRP shall be solely responsible for filing all returns and paying any income, Social Security, or other tax levied upon or determined with respect to the payments made to BFRP pursuant to this Agreement.

10. TOOLS AND SUPPLIES

Unless otherwise agreed to by Company in advance, BFRP shall be solely responsible for procuring, paying for, and maintaining any computer equipment, software, paper, tools, or supplies necessary or appropriate for the performance of BFRP's services hereunder.

BFRP shall, prior to conducting any field operations, *legally* obtain and maintain the following necessary equipment:
- Level IIIA body armor
- Legal firearm
- Level II or better holster

- Spare ammunition with ammo holders affixed to duty belt
- Identifiable clothing as required

11. CONTROLLING LAW
This Agreement shall be governed by and construed in accordance with the laws of the State of California.

12. HEADINGS
The headings in this Agreement are inserted for convenience only and shall not be used to define, limit, or describe the scope of this Agreement or any of the obligations herein.

13. FINAL AGREEMENT
This Agreement constitutes the final understanding and agreement between the parties with respect to the subject matter hereof and supersedes all prior negotiations, understandings, and agreements between the parties, whether written or oral. This Agreement may be amended, supplemented, or changed only by an agreement in writing signed by both of the parties.

14. NOTICES
Any notice required to be given or otherwise given pursuant to this Agreement shall be in writing and shall be hand-delivered, mailed by certified mail return receipt requested, or sent by recognized overnight courier service as follows:

If to BFRP	**If to Company**
John Doe	Ultimate Bail Fugitive Recovery Group
1852 West 11th Street #412	123 Any Street
Any Town, CA 95123	Tracy, CA 95376

15. SEVERABILITY
If any term of this Agreement is held by a court of competent jurisdiction to be invalid or unenforceable, then this Agreement, including all of the remaining terms, will remain in full force and effect as if such invalid or unenforceable term had never been included.

IN WITNESS WHEREOF, this Agreement has been executed by the parties as of the date first above written.

John Doe   John Smith
Ultimate Bail Fugitive Recovery Group

STATE_____COUNTY OF_____
ON_____before me_____

personally known to me or proved to me on the basis of satisfactory evidence to be the person(s), whose name(s) is/are subscribed to the within instrument and acknowledged to me that his/her/their authorized capacity(ies), and that by his/her/their signatures(s) on the instrument the person(s), or entity upon behalf of which the person(s) acted, executed instrument.

WITNESS my hand and official seal.

My commission expires _____

_____
Notary Public

Complete and Full Waiver of Liability

I, _____ (Hereafter called "First Party") who resides at

_____ located in the City of _____,

and of the County of _____, State of *California*, hereby release(s) and

forever discharge(s) _____ (Hereafter called "Second Party"), _____

(Hereafter called "Third Party"), _____ (Hereafter called "First Company"),

_____ (Hereafter called "Second Company"), _____

(Hereafter called "Third Company"), and their/its agents, heirs, executors, administrators,

assigns and successors in interest of and from any and all claims, demands, damages,

causes of action and debts whatsoever, in law or in equity, which, may or may not occur

either directly or indirectly, through the course of any fugitive arrest(s) and/or bail

surrender activities as described within California Penal Code Sections 834, 837, 839,

841, 844, 1300(a)(1), 1301, 1301(a)(1), and 1299 through 1299.11.

First Party understand/s that any and all activities described above are of a hazardous

nature and may result in injury or death to his, her, or their person, relative or child/ren.

First Party and his/her/ their heirs, spouse, former spouse(s), legal representatives,

assigns, and anyone else claiming under him/her/them family, friends, relatives, business

associates, or any other person shall not, in any way, hold any future claim, whatsoever in

reserve for any injury, physical or emotional, that First Party now has (have), or may

hereafter have, whether known, unknown, suspected, for, upon, or by reason of matter,

cause or thing whatsoever.

This is intended as a full and complete waiver of liability of any and all claims as

hereinabove described.

COMPLETE AND FULL WAIVER OF LIABILITY WITH TWO PAGES TOTAL

First Party voluntarily and knowingly execute(s) this waiver of liability with the express intention of eliminating Second Party, Third Party, and Companies (1) one through (3) three from any and all liability as described below.

First Party hereby and forever releases Second Party, Third Party, and Companies (1) one through (3) three from all claims, known or unknown that have arisen or may arise from any and all occurrences including but not limited to fugitive arrest(s) and/or bail surrender activities performed anywhere within the United States of America. ----------

This waiver of liability was executed on _____ ,
20_____

at _____
            city/town/county state

_____
signature of First Party

STATE OF_____
COUNTY OF_____
On_____before me_____
personally appeared_____
personally known to me or proved to me on the basis of satisfactory evidence to be the person(s), whose name(s) is/are subscribed to the within instrument and acknowledged to me that he/she/their executed the same in his/her/their authorized capacity(ies), and that by his/her/their signatures(s) on the instrument the person(s), or entity upon behalf of which the person(s) acted, executed the instrument.

WITNESS my hand and official seal.

_____
Notary Public
         My commission expires_____

Sample Policy on the Use of Force and Restraints

BAIL ARREST POLICY

Effective Date: May 2005
Subject: The Use of Force and Restraints
Policy: Recovery agents will use only that minimum amount of force and restraint reasonably necessary to control a principal who displays violent, threatening, or resistive behavior.

FORCE DEFINED

- Overcoming resistance by the exertion of strength, weight, and power.

PROCEDURE

- In no event is physical force justifiable as punishment.
- Recovery agents shall establish and maintain control of any principal who uses aggressive gestures or violently resists arrest.
- In every case in which force is necessary, the recovery agent must use good judgment in selecting the degree and type of force applied.

ESCALATION OF FORCE

- After identification is made, the degree of force is as follows:

    1. Verbal direction
    2. Show of force
    3. Leading by the arm
    4. Koga-style arrest and control techniques
    5. Oleoresin Capsicum pepper spray
    6. Taser
    7. Any means necessary to defend against immediate, life-threatening aggression by any person who attempts to use lethal force to the extent that the recovery agent(s) may suffer great bodily injury or death.

    Recovery agents shall use only that amount of force necessary to gain and maintain control of the situation in a manner that minimizes injuries to all concerned.

USE OF RESTRAINTS

- As a precaution, the use of restraint shall be used as a means to prevent escape; for the safe movement of any principal considered a special security risk; to prevent the principal from injuring himself or others, or damaging property; or for medical or mental health reasons.

Use of Restraints Prohibited

- When applied in such a manner as to cause the restrained principal unnecessary discomfort, pain, or injury.
- For the purpose of punishment or for a longer period than is reasonably necessary.

Instruments of Restraints

- Handcuffs
- Leg shackles with chain
- Handcuffs with waist chain
- Plastic flex cuffs

COMMENTS

_____
_____
_____
_____
_____

I have thoroughly read and understand the policy regarding the use of force to effect arrests of principals; moreover, I have been instructed in the use of force and restraints as it applies to this policy. I further understand that I shall submit a written report subsequent to any use of force incident that occurs while I am arresting a principal.

_____ _____ _____
Print name   Sign name   Date

I have personally instructed the above-named person in matters directly related to the application of the use of force policy as it pertains to fugitive recovery; furthermore, the person named above has demonstrated his/her ability to apply the use of force in a manner consistent with this policy.

_____ _____ _____
Print name   Sign name   Date

COMMENTS

_____
_____
_____
_____

Examples of Official Forms and Documents

AMERICAN BANKERS INSURANCE COMPANY
OF FLORIDA
BAIL BOND DIVISION
5 Hutton Center Drive, Suite 800, Santa Ana, CA 92707

ANDREW LACEY'S BAIL BONDS
230 E. MAIN ST.
STOCKTON, CA 95202
(209) 941-0798

(PLACE BAIL AGENT'S ADDRESS STAMP HERE)

BAIL BOND

NO. *A25-0026454*
(POWER OF ATTORNEY WITH THIS NUMBER MUST BE ATTACHED.)

IN THE *Municipal* _____ COURT OF THE *Lodi* _____ JUDICIAL DISTRICT,
COUNTY OF *San Joaquin* _____ STATE OF CALIFORNIA

THE PEOPLE OF THE STATE OF CALIFORNIA,

Plaintiff,

vs.

Defendant.

Case No. _____

Div. No. _____

Defendant _____
(NAME OF DEFENDANT)

A96-3952
(BOOKING NO.)

having been admitted to bail in the sum of *Eleven Thousand Six Hundred Sixty Six* Dollars ($ *11,666.00/100*) and ordered to appear in the above-entitled

court on *1-10 @ 8:30A* 19 *97*, on *11379 H&S - 11377(A) - 11357(A) H&S* charge/s:
(DATE OF APPEARANCE) (STATE MISDEMEANOR OR FELONY)

Now, the AMERICAN BANKERS INSURANCE COMPANY OF FLORIDA, a Florida Corporation, hereby undertakes that the above-named defendant will appear in the above-named court on the date above set forth to answer any change in any accusatory pleading based upon the acts supporting the complaint filed against him/her and as duly authorized amendments thereof in whatever court it may be prosecuted, and will at all times hold him/herself amendable to the orders and process of the court, and if convicted, will appear for pronouncement of judgment or grant of probation; or if he/she fails to perform either of these conditions that the AMERICAN BANKERS INSURANCE COMPANY OF FLORIDA, a Florida Corporation, will pay to the people of the State of

California, the sum of *Eleven Thousand Six Hundred Sixty Six* *00/100* dollars
($ *11,666.00/100*).

If the forfeiture of this bond be ordered by the Court, judgment may be summarily made and entered forthwith, against the said, AMERICAN BANKERS INSURANCE COMPANY, for the amount of its undertaking herein as provided by Sections 1305 and 1306 of the Penal Code.

THIS BOND IS VOID IF WRITTEN FOR AN AMOUNT GREATER THAN THE POWER OF ATTORNEY ATTACHED HERETO, IF MORE THAN ONE SUCH POWER IS ATTACHED, OR IF WRITTEN AFTER THE EXPIRATION DATE IF SPECIFIED ON THE ATTACHED POWER OF ATTORNEY.

AMERICAN BANKERS
INSURANCE COMPANY OF FLORIDA
(a Florida Corporation)

By _____ (SEAL)
ATTORNEY-IN-FACT

I certify under penalty of perjury that I am a licensed bail agent of the AMERICAN BANKERS INSURANCE COMPANY and that I

am executing this bond on *12-7-96*
(DATE)

at *Lodi*
(LOCATION)

_____
(SIGNATURE OF LICENSED AGENT)

THE PREMIUM CHARGED FOR
THIS BOND PER ANNUM IS: $ *1,176.60*

Approved this _____ day of _____, 19 ____
(TITLE)

NOTE: This is an Appearance Bond and cannot be construed as a guarantee for failure to provide payments, back alimony payments, FINES, or Wage Law claims, nor can it be used as a Bond on Appeal.

I hereby certify that the foregoing instrument is a true and correct copy of the original on file in this office.

ATTEST Date *May 6*, 19 *97*

GLENDA D. GORDON, Clerk, Municipal Court
Lodi Judicial District

By *L Nichols*, Deputy Clerk

Bail bond face sheet

Court clerk stamp.

The foregoing instrument is a correct copy of the original on file in this office.
ATTEST:

KIRI TORRE
Chief Executive Officer/Clerk
Superior Court of CA County of Santa Clara
By: _____ DEPUTY

SUPERIOR COURT OF CALIFORNIA, COUNTY OF SAN BERNARDINO
Rancho District, 8303 N Haven Ave, Rnch Cucamonga, 91730

Perdidy Bin 32

NOTICE OF FORFEITURE OF
BAIL BOND

TO: Surety or Depositor

███████ CO C/O ███████ ████
███████ ██████

To: Bail Agent or Solicitor

███████ ████████
███████ ███████ ██
███████

Defendant: ████████████

Case Number: ████████   Bond Number: ███████
                               Bond Amount: $10,000.00
Date Forfeited: 03/30/00

Please take notice that the surety bond posted by you in behalf of the named defendant has been ordered forfeited by the court pursuant to Penal Code Section 1305. Your contractual obligation to pay this bond will become absolute on the 181st day following the date of mailing of this notice unless the court shall sooner order the forfeiture set aside and the bond reinstated. If payment is not received, summary judgment will be requested pursuant to Penal Code 1306 upon the expiration of the time allowed by law.

The 180th day is: 10/02/00

Clerk/Administrator
By: _____
         Deputy Clerk

CERTIFICATE OF SERVICE BY MAIL
I hereby certify that I am over the age of 18 years, a citizen of the United States, a resident of the above-named County & State, and not a party to nor interested in the proceedings named in the Notice of Forfeiture of Bail Bond. I am a deputy clerk in the above-named County. On the date shown below, I deposited a sealed envelope addressed as shown above which contained a true copy of this notice for collection and mailing, following ordinary business practice, at the location shown above.

Executed on 3/31/00 at San Bernardino, California.

Clerk/Administrator
By: _____
         Deputy Clerk

Notice of forfeiture form San Bernardino County, California.

SUPERIOR COURT OF CALIFORNIA
COUNTY OF SANTA CLARA

ENDORSED

FILED

JUN 1 2 2002

KIRI TORRE
Chief Executive Officer/Clerk
Superior Court of Santa Clara
DAMON OTWELL
BY _____ DEPUTY

THE PEOPLE OF THE STATE OF CALIFORNIA,

Plaintiff,

▬▬▬ ▬ Defendant.

NOTICE OF BAIL FORFEITURE

NO.

▬▬▬▬

To: _____ and _____

PLEASE TAKE NOTICE that Bail Bond No. ▬▬▬▬▬▬▬

in the sum of $ 100,000.00 _____ was forfeited on __6-12-02__

the defendant having failed to appear before Judge ▬▬▬▬▬

for Arraignment

The forfeiture will become final in 180 days (plus 5 days mailing), to wit: _____12-13-02_____

unless the defendant is surrendered to the court or to custody before 180 days pursuant to Penal Code Section 1305.

THE UNDERSIGNED SAYS THAT: I AM A CITIZEN OF THE UNITED STATES, OVER 18 YEARS OF AGE, EMPLOYED IN SANTA CLARA COUNTY AND NOT A PARTY TO THE WITHIN ACTION. THAT MY BUSINESS ADDRESS IS COURT HOUSE, SAN JOSE, CALIFORNIA. THAT I SERVED THE WITHIN NOTICE BY CAUSING TO BE PLACED A TRUE COPY THEREOF IN AN ENVELOPE ADDRESSED TO PARTIES SHOWN WHICH ENVELOPE WAS THEN SEALED AND POSTAGE FULLY PREPAID THEREON, AND THEREAFTER WAS DEPOSITED IN THE UNITED STATES MAIL AT SAN JOSE, CALIFORNIA, ON DATE SHOWN BELOW: THAT THERE IS DELIVERY SERVICE BY THE UNITED STATES MAIL AT THE PLACE SO ADDRESSED, OR REGULAR COMMUNICATION BY UNITED STATES MAIL BETWEEN THE PLACE OF MAILING AND THE PLACE SO ADDRESSED" AS SHOWN.

I certify (or declare) under penalty of perjury, that the foregoing is true and correct.

CHIEF EXECUTIVE OFFICER

Executed on _____6-12-02_____
at San Jose, California

By _____ DAMON OTWELL _____

Damon Otwell *Deputy Clerk*

▬▬▬▬▬ Bail Bonds
▬▬▬▬▬ , CA ▬▬▬▬

🅢 2656 REV 2/94

Notice of forfeiture form Santa Clara County, California.

Insurance Company:

Street:

City, State & Zip Code

Office Telephone:

Office Facsimile Number:

AUTHORITY TO ARREST DEFENDANT ON BAIL BOND

KNOW ALL MEN BY THESE PRESENTS:

That I/we, _____ State License No._____ , do hereby authorize and

empower _____ , whose principal

office is located at _____ , as its representative and in its

stead, to *lawfully* arrest and detain _____ , the

defendant named in _____ Bail Bond No._____ ,
Insurance Company

wherever he/she may be found in the UNITED STATES OF AMERICA, pursuant to any applicable

laws of any sovereign state, and to hold said defendant in custody and surrender said defendant to the

_____ City of Judicial District County of

_____State of _____

wherein proceedings are now pending against said defendant described in said Bail Bond.

This Authorization expires on the _____ *day of* _____ , _____

By —————————————————————
signature bail agent licensee

address:_____

_____

_____

telephone: _____

Generic authority to arrest form.

```
                    COUNTY OF TUOLUMNE SHERIFF'S DEPARTMENT
                    TUOLUMNE COUNTY JAIL  -  BOOKING PUBLIC LOG


Name  :                                        Commit # :
        20237 SPARROW LANE                     Booking #:
        SONORA          CA 95370               Case #    : 02-2389
Sex: M Race: W Hgt: 509 Wgt: 170 Eyes: BLU Hair: BRO   Event #   : 02-13040
                                               Orig Bk #:   20003006
DOB: 11/16/1964     Occupation: CARPENTER
```

```
Arrest Date/Time: 09/03/2002 - 15:20    Booking Date/Time: 09/03/2002 - 16:39

Arresting Officer: ROMEO, SGT. JOE        Agency: TUOLUMNE COUNTY SHERIFF
Court    :  TUOLUMNE SUPERIOR.DEPT 3&4    Bail   :        $3,000.00
Warrant #:                  Local

Location of Arrest: 20237 SPARROW LANE #A, SONORA
```

Charges	Qty	Section	Description	M/F
	1	11358 H&S	PLANT/CULTIVATE MARIJUANA	F
	1	11357(c) H&S	POSSESS MARIJUANA OVER 1 OZ/ 28.5 GRAMS	M

```
            ┌─────────────────────────────────────────┐
            │ Released :            at                 │
            │ To:  -                                   │
            └─────────────────────────────────────────┘
```

DISTRIBUTION: PRESS RELEASE ( )   BAIL BONDSMAN ( )

14   12/2/02 @ 815

Bench warrant.

FILED

SEP . 2 2003

Superior Court of California

K. West

IN THE SUPERIOR COURT OF CALIFORNIA
COUNTY OF TUOLUMNE
41 W. Yaney Ave.
Sonora, California [CA] 95370

People of the State of California)
   Plaintiff,)
)
)   Case No.   CRF9770
VS.)
)
)   NOTICE OF ENTRY OF FORFEITURE OF BAIL
   Defendant.)
_____)

BOND NO.: s05-00589724
Date forfeiture was entered into minutes of Court: 09-22-03
Amount of Surety Bond: $ 3000.00

    You are hereby notified that the above-named defendant having failed to appear on **09-22-03**, your surety bond in the amount shown above was ordered forfeited. This forfeiture may be set aside under the terms set forth in Penal Code section 1305 if, within 180 days of the date of mailing this Notice of Forfeiture, the defendant appears and satisfactorily excuses his or her neglect, or shows to the satisfaction of the court that his or her absence was not with the connivance of bail.

    Should you wish to obtain an order setting aside this forfeiture for any reason expressed in Penal Code Section 1305, the notice of motion must be filed within 185 days of the date of mailing this Notice of Forfeiture and must be heard and determined within 30 days thereafter.

    If this order of forfeiture is not set aside, summary judgment shall be entered against each bondsman named in the bond in the amount for which the bondsman is bound.

Date: September 24, 2003   Tuolumne County Superior Court Clerk

                               By: _K. West_
                                       Deputy Clerk

Declaration of Mailing
I declare under penalty of perjury of the laws of the State of California that I am over the age of 18 years and not a party to this action. On the date shown below, I mailed the above document to the parties named below by depositing a true copy thereof in an envelope, first class postage prepaid and depositing the same in the Court mail basket for mailing in the United States Mail at Tuolumne, California.

Ramirez Bail Bonds, 2900 Standiford Ave. # 16B #253, Modesto, CA 95350
Seneca Insurance Company, Inc.. 160 Water St. # 16th Floor, New York, NY 10038

Date: September 24, 2003   By: _K. West_
                                      Deputy Clerk

Bench warrant.

Addr: 20237 Sparrow Lane
        Sonora, CA 95370
Race: White   Ht: 5'9"
Sex: Male   Wt: 170 pounds
DOB: 11/16/1964   Eyes: Blue
DL#: CA U0083717   Hair: Brown

Issued To: Tuolumne Sheriff's Office

SUPERIOR COURT OF CALIFORNIA, COUNTY OF TUOLUMNE
60 North Washington Street, Sonora CA 95370

People vs.

CASE NUMBER   CRF9770

BENCH WARRANT

The People of the State of California, to any Peace Officer of this State:
The defendant   is charged of the following crimes in this Court

     Misdemeanor: HS11357(C)
     Felony: HS11358
and having failed to appear at a regularly scheduled calling of this proceeding, you are therefore ordered to arrest the defendant forthwith and bring him/her before this court for judgment and /or further proceedings.

ENDORSEMENT FOR NIGHT SERVICE

     For good cause shown, I direct that this warrant be served at any hour of the day or night.

_____
(Judge's Endorsement)

     Bail is fixed in the total sum of No Bail.

Dated: _9-24-2003_____

_____

RETURN OF PEACE OFFICER

     I certify that I received the above warrant and that I served the same by arresting the defendant on

_____ and
(Date)

(Check by Applicable Box)

[ ] bringing him before a judge of the _____ District, County of _____

_____, on_____.
(Date)

[ ] booking him at the _____ Jail, County of _____,

on _____.
(Date)

Dated _____   By_____
                                              Officer/Deputy

BENCH WARRANT

Bench warrant with night service.

SENECA INSURANCE COMPANY, INC.
OF NEW YORK
BAIL BOND DIVISION
160 Water Street, 16th Floor
New York, NY 10038-4922

Ramirez Bail Bonds
PMB 253
2900 Standiford Ave. # 16B
Modesto, CA 95350-6575
(209) 544-3779 • (888) 243-8688

(PLACE BAIL AGENT'S ADDRESS STAMP HERE)

BAIL BOND

NO. _____
(POWER OF ATTORNEY WITH THIS NUMBER MUST BE ATTACHED.)

IN THE _____ COURT OF THE _____ JUDICIAL DISTRICT,

COUNTY OF _____ STATE OF CALIFORNIA

THE PEOPLE OF THE STATE OF CALIFORNIA,

Plaintiff,   Case No. _____

vs.

Div. No. _____

_____ Defendant.

Defendant _____   _____
                    (NAME OF DEFENDANT)   (BOOKING NO.)

having been admitted to bail in the sum of _____

_____ Dollars ($ _____) and ordered to appear in the above-entitled

court on _____ 20 ___ , on _____ charge/s:
        (DATE OF APPEARANCE)   (STATE MISDEMEANOR OR FELONY)

Now, the SENECA INSURANCE COMPANY, INC. OF NEW YORK, a New York Corporation, hereby undertakes that the above-named defendant will appear in the above-named court on the date above set forth to answer any charge in any accusatory pleading based upon the acts supporting the complaint filed against him/her and as duly authorized amendments thereof in whatever court it may be prosecuted, and will at all times hold him/herself amendable to the orders and process of the court, and if convicted, will appear for pronouncement of judgment or grant of probation; or if he/she fails to perform either of these conditions that the SENECA INSURANCE COMPANY, INC. OF NEW YORK, a New York Corporation, will pay to the people of the State of

California, the sum of _____ dollars

($ _____).

If the forfeiture of this bond be ordered by the Court, judgment may be summarily made and entered forthwith, against the said, SENECA INSURANCE COMPANY, for the amount of its undertaking herein as provided by Sections 1305 and 1306 of the Penal Code.

| THIS BOND IS VOID IF WRITTEN FOR AN AMOUNT GREATER THAN THE POWER OF ATTORNEY ATTACHED HERETO, IF MORE THAN ONE SUCH POWER IS ATTACHED, OR IF WRITTEN AFTER THE EXPIRATION DATE IF SPECIFIED ON THE ATTACHED POWER OF ATTORNEY. | SENECA INSURANCE COMPANY, INC. OF NEW YORK (a New York Corporation) (SEAL) By _____ ATTORNEY-IN-FACT |

I certify under penalty of perjury that I am a licensed bail agent of the SENECA INSURANCE COMPANY and that I

am executing this bond on _____
                                        (DATE)

at _____
        (LOCATION)

_____
(SIGNATURE OF LICENSED AGENT)

| THE PREMIUM CHARGED FOR THIS BOND PER ANNUM IS: $ _____ | Approved this _____ day of _____ , 20 _____ (TITLE) |

NOTE: This is an Appearance Bond and cannot be construed as a guarantee for failure to provide payments, back alimony payments, FINES, or Wage Law claims, nor can it be used as a Bond on Appeal.

Bail bond face sheet.

Surety Company:

Street:

City & State:

Office Telephone:

Facsimile:

AFFIDAVIT of UNDERTAKING of BAIL for SURRENDER of DEFENDANT
Pursuant to California Penal Code Section 1300(a)(1)

The following information represents a true and correct statement of facts as they pertain to the bail bond posted on:

Defendant's Name: _____
                 Last   First   Middle

AKA: _____ D.O.B. _____

Court: _____ Judicial District: _____

County: _____ State: California Case No. _____

Bond Amount: $_____ Bond Number: _____

Original Charge(s): _____

Check One: ☐ Misdemeanor   ☐ Felony

Bail Agency: Name: _____
             Address: _____
             Telephone: _____

Person(s) authorized to apprehend and surrender Defendant:

_____

_____

I, _____, declare that I am a California bail licensee doing business

as _____ License No. _____. I further declare, under

the penalty of perjury under the laws of the State of California that the foregoing is true and correct.

This Affidavit of Undertaking of Bail Surrender of Defendant was executed on _____, 20_____

at _____
    city/town   county   state

            Affiant's Signature: _____
                                signature of bail licensee

STATE OF _____
COUNTY OF _____
On _____ before me _____
personally appeared _____
personally known to me or proved to me on the basis of satisfactory evidence to be the person(s), whose name(s) is/are subscribed to the within instrument and acknowledged to me that he/she/their executed the same in his/her/their authorized capacity(ies), and that by his/her/their signature(s) on the instrument the person(s) or entity upon behalf of which the person(s) acted, executed instrument.

Witness my hand and official seal.

_____ My commission expires _____
           Notary Public

Affidavit of undertaking of bail for surrender of defendant (may be used in lieu of a bail bond face sheet for arrest purposes only).

REQUEST BY INDEMNITOR FOR SURRENDER
OF PRINCIPAL AND SUBSEQUENT INDEMNITY
AGREEMENT

DEFENDANT_____

BOND#_____AMOUNT $_____

SURETY - FRONTIER PACIFIC INSURANCE COMPANY

AGENCY -

COURT/CASE #_____ / _____

CHARGES_____

INDEMNITOR'S NAME_____

ADDRESS_____

PHONE # (   )_____

I _____,
the indemnitor in the above mentioned undertaking posted on behalf of

_____,
in the matter of the PEOPLE OF THE STATE OF CALIFORNIA v.

_____
hereby request that my liability as indemnitor on this undertaking be terminated herewith,
or as soon as possible, via the surrender of the principal by the surety. Said surrender and
termination of liability is desired by the undersigned indemnitor due to the conviction of
the undersigned indemnitor that there has been a substantial increase in the risk and hazard
of the undertaking.

The undersigned indemnitor further states and agrees that the surety herein, or any of his
employees, agents, general agent and/or surety companies, shall be, and are, held harmless
and fully indemnified by the undersigned indemnitor for said surrender, and that said
indemnification shall include, but not be limited to, investigative fees, court costs,
attorney's fees, civil judgments and any return of premium that may be ordered by the
court pursuant to the California Penal Code, the regulations of the California Department
of Insurance, or any other regulation or law.

The undersigned indemnitor further understands and agrees that his/her liability on the
subject undertaking shall continue in full force and effect until the subject bond is ordered
exonerated by the court, and said liability is pursuant to the terms and conditions of the
bail agreement, signed by the undersigned indemnitor, and incorporated and made part
hereof by reference. Indemnitor agrees to fully assist said surety in the arrest,
apprehension and surrender of said principal, and agrees that should such efforts fail,
indemnitor remains fully liable for said undertaking.

SIGNED THIS _____ DAY OF _____, 19____, AT

_____, CALIFORNIA.

INDEMNITOR SIGNATURE   INDEMNITOR NAME (Typed or Printed)

_____   _____

Request by the indemnitor for a surrender of principal.

SUPERIOR COURT, CNTY OF FRESNO
COUNTY OF FRESNO, STATE OF CALIFORNIA
CENTRAL DIVISION
Fresno, CA 93724

DEFENDANT: _____
CASE NO: <u>F00907172-1</u>
BOND NO: <u>BD11142716</u>

Dave Tomlinson Bail Bonds
3089 N. TRACY BLVD. PMB#120
TRACY, CA 95376 7769

<u>BAIL FORFEITURE NOTICE</u>

Bail in the sum of $<u>20000.00</u>, posted for the release of above named defendant, was forfeited on <u>08/02/2000</u> when defendant failed to appear in court. Issuance of bench warrant stayed to 08-08-00.

If, within 185 days of the time of forfeiture, defendant surrenders to Court or is brought to Court by bailor, and is able to offer sufficient reason for failure to appear as cited, the Court may consider setting aside the forfeiture. However, at the expiration of 185 days, this is due and payable to the Court.

Dated: 08/02/2000

By _____
L. Aguilar, Deputy Clerk

CERTIFICATE RE SERVICE OF NOTICE OF FORFEITURE OF BAIL

I do hereby certify under penalty of perjury that I am not a party to the above-entitled action; that on <u>08/02/2000</u> I served a Notice of Forfeiture of Surety Bond in said case upon the bail depositor by enclosing said Notice in a sealed, postage pre-paid envelope and depositing same in the United States mail at Fresno, California, addressed as above.

By _____
L. Aguilar, Deputy Clerk

CC:
LEGION INSURANCE COMPANY
525 PENN STREET
READING, PA 19601

(bail_forfeit_bwstay 96v1)

Always check to see if a principal has more than one bond written on him. This principal
had three separate bonds, and the bail agent or surety may not tell you this up-front.

SUPERIOR COURT, CNTY OF FRESNO
COUNTY OF FRESNO, STATE OF CALIFORNIA
CENTRAL DIVISION
Fresno, CA 93724

DEFENDANT: _____
CASE NO: <u>F00907172-1</u>
BOND NO: <u>BD11096450</u>

Dave Tomlinson Bail Bonds
3089 N. TRACY BLVD. PMB#120
TRACY, CA 95376 7769

BAIL FORFEITURE NOTICE

Bail in the sum of $<u>2000.00</u>, posted for the release of above named defendant, was forfeited on <u>08/02/2000</u> when defendant failed to appear in court. Issuance of bench warrant stayed to 080800.

If, within 185 days of the time of forfeiture, defendant surrenders to Court or is brought to Court by bailor, and is able to offer sufficient reason for failure to appear as cited, the Court may consider setting aside the forfeiture. However, at the expiration of 185 days, this is due and payable to the Court.

Dated: 08/02/2000

By _____
     L. Aguilar, Deputy Clerk

CERTIFICATE RE SERVICE OF NOTICE OF FORFEITURE OF BAIL

I do hereby certify under penalty of perjury that I am not a party to the above-entitled action; that on <u>08/02/2000</u> I served a Notice of Forfeiture of Surety Bond in said case upon the bail depositor by enclosing said Notice in a sealed, postage pre-paid envelope and depositing same in the United States mail at Fresno, California, addressed as above.

By _____
     L. Aguilar, Deputy Clerk

CC:
LEGION INSURANCE COMPANY
525 PENN STREET
READING, PA 19601

(bail_forfeit_bwstay 96v1)

SUPERIOR COURT, CNTY OF FRESNO
COUNTY OF FRESNO, STATE OF CALIFORNIA
CENTRAL DIVISION
Fresno, CA 93724

DEFENDANT: _____
CASE NO: F00907172-1
BOND NO: BD11120327

Dave Tomlinson Bail Bonds
3089 N. TRACY BLVD. PMB#120
TRACY, CA 95376 7769

BAIL FORFEITURE NOTICE

Bail in the sum of $10000.00, posted for the release of above named defendant, was forfeited on 08/02/2000 when defendant failed to appear in court. Issuance of bench warrant stayed to 08-08-00.

If, within 185 days of the time of forfeiture, defendant surrenders to Court or is brought to Court by bailor, and is able to offer sufficient reason for failure to appear as cited, the Court may consider setting aside the forfeiture. However, at the expiration of 185 days, this is due and payable to the Court.

Dated: 08/02/2000

By _____
L. Aguilar, Deputy Clerk

CERTIFICATE RE SERVICE OF NOTICE OF FORFEITURE OF BAIL

I do hereby certify under penalty of perjury that I am not a party to the above-entitled action; that on 08/02/2000 I served a Notice of Forfeiture of Surety Bond in said case upon the bail depositor by enclosing said Notice in a sealed, postage pre-paid envelope and depositing same in the United States mail at Fresno, California, addressed as above.

By _____
L. Aguilar, Deputy Clerk

CC:
LEGION INSURANCE COMPANY
525 PENN STREET
READING, PA 19601

(bail_forfeit_bwstay 96v1)

AGREEMENT FOR SURETY BAIL BOND

Offense _____ Case # _____ Bond # _____ Amount _____

Offense _____ Case # _____ Bond # _____ Amount _____

I have read and explained to me an understand the following terms and conditions of Frontier Pacific Insurance Company (herein after called FPI) executing the above listed Surety bail bonds on my behalf:

1. FPI shall have control and jurisdiction over me during the term for which my bail bond(s) is executed and shall have the right to apprehend and surrender me to the proper officials at any time for violation of my bail bond(s) obligations to the Court and FPI as provided by law.

2. It is understood and agreed that any one of the following actions by me shall constitute a breach of my obligations to FPI and that FPI and/or its Agent shall have the right to forthwith apprehend and surrender me in exoneration of my bail bond(s):
   a. If I depart the jurisdiction of the Court without written consent of the Court and FPI, or its Agent.
   b. If I shall move from one address to another or change my phone number without notifying FPI, and/or its Agent
   c. If I commit any act which shall constitute reasonable evidence of my intention to cause a forfeiture of my bail bond(s).
   d. If I am arrested and incarcerated for any offense other than a minor traffic violation.
   e. If I make any material false statement in my Bail Bond Application and Contract with FPI.

3. If I depart the jurisdiction of the Court wherein my bail bond(s) is posted by FPI for any reason, and I am captured by FPI and/or its Agent, or any other law enforcement agency, in a State other than the one which my bail bond(s) is posted, I hereby agree to voluntarily return to the State of original jurisdiction, and I hereby waive extradition proceedings and further consent to the application of such reasonable force as necessary to effect such return.

4. I hereby waive any and all rights I may have under Title 28 Privacy Act - Freedom of Information Act, Title 6, Fair Credit Reporting Act, and any such local or State law. I consent to an authorize FPI and/or its Agent, to obtain any and all private or public information and/or records concerning me from any party or agency, private and governmental (local, State, Federal), including but not limited to Social Security records, criminal records, civil records, driving records, telephone records, medical records, school records, workers compensation records, employment records. I authorize without reservation, any party or agency, private or governmental (local, State, Federal), contacted by FPI, and/or its Agent, to furnish any and all private and public information and records in their possession concerning me to FPI, and/or its Agent.

_____   _____   _____
SIGNATURE OF DEFENDANT   DATE OF BIRTH   SOCIAL SECURITY NUMBER

_____   _____
PRINTED FULL LEGAL NAME   ADDRESS

_____   _____
SIGNATURE OF WITNESS   CITY, STATE, ZIP CODE

STATE OF   _____
COUNTY OF   _____
On _____ before me _____
personally appeared _____
personally known to me or proved to me on the basis of satisfactory evidence to be the person(s), whose name(s) is/are subscribed to the within instrument and acknowledged to me that he/she/their executed the same in his/her/their authorized capacity(ies), and that by his/her/their/ signature(s) on the instrument the person(s), or entity upon behalf of Witness my hand and official seal.

_____ My commission expires _____
NOTARY PUBLIC

A sample agreement for surety bail that is designed to acquire information otherwise private if a client jumps bail.

Date_____

Defendant_____

Jail_____

Bail Amount $_____
Premium Amount $_____
Amount Paid Down $_____
Unpaid Balance $_____
Cash Collateral $_____

INDEMNITOR/GUARANTOR CHECK LIST

_____ 1. I have read and received a copy of the standard surety bail bond agreement.

_____ 2. This check list is intended to explain and clarify the standard bail agreement, which is the entire contract with the bail agency. There are no additional terms nor are there any exemptions to the contract, either in writing or verbally, that limit my responsibility under the bail agreement.

_____ 3. I understand I am required to pay the amount of the bail premium every year, in advance hereafter, until the surety is legally discharged from all liability on the bonds posted. (Renewal premiums charged on California bonds only.)

_____ 4. If the premium has been paid in part, with a balance owing, I understand that having obtained a bail bond release for the defendant that the indemnitor(s) agree to pay $_____ as premium on the bond(s). $_____ upon or before posting of the bond(s). The remaining $_____ will be paid in regular payment of $_____ occurring every _____ starting on _____. (This section regarding payment structure is not applicable, by law, in the state of Indiana.)

_____ 5. The premium paid on the bond is fully earned upon the posting of the bond or bonds with the proper authorities. I further understand in the event that a detainer prevents a defendant from being released from the custody of another jurisdiction, the premium is still fully earned, and is non-refundable. I understand I am responsible to make the payments for money due on the premium as described above. Finance charges are computed on unpaid balances on the 30th day of each month at a rate of ten percent per annum. There is a ten percent late fee on all scheduled payments not received within five days of the due date.

_____ 6. I understand I am responsible for paying the full amount of the bond posted if the defendant does not appear in court, for every appearance and any other time ordered by the court, until the defendant is sentenced or the case is dismissed by the court, and verification is received by bail agency from the court that the bond is exonerated.

_____ 7. A forfeiture of the bail will be entered by the court if the defendant fails to make any court appearance. I understand that if the bond is ordered forfeited and it is not ordered reinstated, or exonerated, that I must pay the full amount of the bail forfeited to the bail agency, in addition to the costs described in paragraphs seven (7), eight (8) and nine (9).

_____ 8. That the indemnitors will cooperate with the company or its representatives in the apprehension of the defendant should he fail to appear on his or her bond(s). This includes, but is not limited to allowing the company's agents to search their place of residence, if it becomes necessary to revoke the defendants bond, under the terms of this agreement. I also understand that if the defendant becomes incarcerated after his release on bail, indemnitors will notify the company immediately.

_____ 9. I understand I am responsible if it becomes necessary to arrest and surrender the defendant. That I am responsible for paying for investigation, location and apprehension time; this is billed at a rate of $100.00 per hour per investigator plus expenses. Investigation costs will begin to accrue after a court forfeiture or when any co-signer requests the defendant be placed back in custody or when any condition exists as defined in the bail bond agreement, specifically, but not limited to Sections Five and Eleven. If no investigation costs have been incurred prior to a voluntary surrender of defendant at the jail facility of the court specified on the bail receipt there will be no Investigation cost charged. Reasonable court costs, as described in Paragraph 8 of this checklist will be charged if applicable and a receipt will be provided.

_____ 10. I understand that if the bail is ordered forfeited by the court, that I am responsible to pay court costs and any reasonable fees (a minimum of $150.00) to the bail agency for the associated costs of requesting the court any of the following: (1) Order to Reinstate; (2) Order to Vacate Judgment; and (3) Order to Exonerate.

_____ 11. That any and all collateral deposited under this agreement may at the discretion of the company, be sold, transferred, or disposed of in any manner, and for an amount that the company deems adequate for the expeditious repayment of any unpaid premium balances, or any other balances arising from this agreement. That the company is not responsible to try to obtain an amount greater than the balances due under this agreement if it becomes necessary to liquidate the collateral deposited in connection with the posting of the bond(s). That the indemnitors are responsible to pay the following any and all storage fees in connection with physical collateral deposited with the company as described herein.

_____ 12. I understand that substitution of collateral is done at the discretion of the surety and the bail bonding agency. There are no agreements to substitute collateral at a future date.

_____ 13. I understand that it is my responsibility to request return of any collateral provided. There may be a delay of return of collateral until the bail agency has researched the exoneration date and verified the bail bond status with the appropriate courts. This process may be done faster if I obtain written verification of the bond exoneration from the court and provide it to the bail agency.

_____ 14. That any collateral deposited with the company cannot be returned until 20 business days after such time as the company receives written notice from the clerk of the court verifying the exoneration of the bond(s), and all obligations under this agreement have been fulfilled. Collateral return is performed during normal business hours, Monday through Friday.

_____ 15. I understand that if I breach the bail bond agreement, by non payment or any other action as defined by the bail agreement, I am responsible for collection actions taken, including attorney fees and costs. Attorney's fees are a minimum of $150.00 an hour. If any collection actions are required, a minimum $25.00 fee will be charged.

_____ 16. I understand the obligation under this agreement is joint and several. This means that I may be held solely and individually liable for up to the full amount owed for any and all charges, even if there are other cosigners on the agreement.

_____ 17. That all claims which might arise out of my signing any agreements with the company as indemnitor upon the bail bond, issued by the company on behalf of the defendant, shall be litigated in the State of _____, in the appropriate court of competent jurisdiction. That by signing this document, the indemnitor is expressing his or her intent to submit to the jurisdiction of the courts of the State of _____, for the resolution of any claims arising out of this agreement. That Indemnitors agree to accept and be bound by any service of process, via regular and or certified mail, address to the home address, which I have indicated on the bail bond application.

_____ 18. I declare that all statements made on the application and financial statement are true. That any violation of this agreement, or any false information provided by the indemnitors, or the defendant, to the company, can result in the immediate revocation of the bond(s) posted by the company. I agree to notify the bail agency, in writing within 48 hours of any changes, including but not limited to any change of address or employment of either myself or the criminal defendant.

I/WE HAVE READ AND AGREE WITH THE ABOVE DECLARATIONS

Signature:_____

Name (print): _____

Signature:_____

Name (print): _____

I/we have received a copy of this Checklist :_____ _____

70742

GBB-108 (3/98)

Sample indemnitor/guarantor checklist.

Example of Bail Bond Application

D.O.B. _____ Sex _____			Exec. Date _____
Race _____ Moustache _____			Arr. Date _____
Height _____ Weight_____	**APPLICATION AND AGREEMENT**		Booking #_____
Hair _____ Eyes _____	**FOR SURETY BAIL BOND**		Where Held _____
	Bond No. _____ AMT. $ _____		
I.D. Marks _____ Glasses _____ Where Born _____			Arr. By _____
S.S.# _____ D.L.# _____ C.I.I.# _____			F.B.I.# _____

Booking Name _____ A.K.A. _____

Charges_____ Case #_____ Date to Appear _____ Time _____

Court _____ Jud. Dist. _____ Div. or Dept. _____ County _____

St. Add. _____ City _____ Phone _____ How Long _____

Former Add. _____ City _____ State _____ How Long _____

Years in City _____ County _____ State _____ Last County _____ Last State _____

Employed By _____ Occupation _____ Work Phone _____ How Long _____

Employer's Add. _____ Superior _____ Mo. Income _____ Shift_____

Previous Employer _____ Address _____ City _____ When_____

Previous Arrest Charge _____ Court_____ County _____ When_____

Disposition _____ Previous Bail _____ With Who _____ Amount $ _____ Case Pending? _____

On Probation? _____ Where_____ Probation Officer _____

Vehicle – Make_____ Model_____ Year _____ Color _____ License # _____

Military Branch _____ Serial # _____ Discharge Date _____ Union _____ Local # _____

Where Arrested _____ Co-Defendants _____

Credit Ref. & Acct. #'s_____

Spouse_____ Add. _____ Phone _____ How Long _____

Employed By _____ Add. _____ City _____ Work Phone_____

Occupation_____ Superior _____ Mo. Income _____ How Long _____

Married? – When_____ Where _____ Spouse's Maiden Name _____ D.O.B. _____

Spouse's Vehicle – Make _____ Model _____ Year _____ Color_____ License #_____

Previous Spouse _____ Add. _____ City _____ Phone _____

Children – Name & Age _____ School_____

Mother _____ Add. _____ City _____ Phone _____

Father_____ Add. _____ City _____ Phone _____

Spouse's Mother _____ Add. _____ City _____ Phone _____

Spouse's Father_____ Add. _____ City _____ Phone _____

Def. Brother _____ Add. _____ City _____ Phone _____

Def. Sister _____ Add. _____ City _____ Phone _____

Best Friend_____ Add. _____ City _____ Phone _____

Defendant's Attorney _____ City _____ Phone _____

Indemnitor _____ Add. _____ City _____ Zip _____

Social Security # _____ D.L. # _____ D.O.B. _____ Relation to Def. _____ Phone _____

Employed By _____ Add. _____ Phone _____

Occupation _____ How Long _____ Superior _____ Mo. Income _____

Bank _____ Branch _____ Account # _____ Type _____ Balance _____

Spouse _____ Add. _____ Phone _____

Employed By _____ Add. _____ Phone _____

Occupation _____ How Long _____ Superior _____ Mo. Income _____

Vehicle – Make _____ Model _____ Year _____ Color _____ License # _____

Registered Owner _____ Legal Owner _____ Liens _____

Real Property _____ In Who's Name _____ How Long _____

Lot _____ Block _____ Tract _____ Maps in Book _____ Page _____

Value _____ Equity _____ Financed By _____ A.P. No. _____

Credit Ref. & Acct. #'s _____

I certify that the above is true and correct. I further understand this is an application for a type of credit, and authorize review of my credit history via credit reporting agency checks.

_____ _____
DATE   SIGNATURE OF INDEMNITOR

STATEMENT OF INFORMATION REQUIRED BY SECTION 2100, CALIFORNIA REGULATORY CODE, WHICH MAY BE REQUIRED IN OTHER STATES

Full Name of person supplying information	Name of person negotiating bail	Name of person receiving information
Address	Address	Date and time information received
Connection or relationship to defendant	Connection or relationship to defendant	Manner in which information received
If same was defendant, how did he communicate?	Name of licensee who negotiated transaction	Name of other agent involved and commission paid

If writ _____
Name of Attorney

_____
Name and sum paid unlicensed persons and service performed

Was consideration other than money received? YES ☐ NO ☐ If yes, explain in detail and attach statement.

FPIC-10 (Rev. 3/97) Ω

Field Interview Card

Last Name			First Name		Middle	Sex M F	CAPAA No.

Nickname?AKA	Address		DOB

Race	Height	Weight	Build	Hair Color	Hair Length	Hair Style	Eye Color

Soc. Sec. & D.L. Nos	Tattoos, Scars, Marks Tracks, Glasses, Facial Hair, Other ID	PED. DRIV. PASS.

Veh. Make	Veh. Model	Body Style	Year	Veh. Colors(s) /	License No.

Location of Stop	Beat	Date	Time	Badges(s)

(NOTE: Complete back in all cases)

Front of card.

Clothing		Telephone

Occupation/School	Employer/Parents

Veh. Cond.	Damage Location	Modified Suspension	Non-Stand Tires	Non-stand Wheels
Windows	Stickers?Decals	Modified Paint	Interior	Other

Notes	Reason for Stop	Disposition
	Copy To: _____	

Back of card

State-by-State Statutory Surrender Time on Forfeited Bonds

State	Surrender Time	State	Surrender Time
Alabama	30 days	Montana	30 days
Alaska	10 days	Nebraska	90 days
Arizona	30 days	Nevada	90 days
Arkansas	Court discretion	New Hampshire	Court discretion
California	180 days	New Jersey	Court discretion
Colorado	30 days	New Mexico	Court discretion
Connecticut	30 days	New York	30–60 days
Delaware	30 days	North Carolina	30 days
District of Columbia	Immediately	North Dakota	30 days
Florida	30 days	Ohio	30–90 days
Georgia	45 days	Oklahoma	30 days (some counties 0)
Hawaii	1/2 day	Oregon	No bail
Idaho	20 days	Pennsylvania	Court discretion
Illinois	No bail	Rhode Island	Immediately
Indiana	180 days	South Carolina	Court discretion
Iowa	10 days	South Dakota	Court discretion
Kansas	45 days	Tennessee	180 days
Kentucky	No bail	Texas	20 days
Louisiana	180 days	Utah	60–150 days
Maine	Court discretion	Vermont	30 days
Maryland	90 days	Virginia	30 days
Massachusetts	90 days	Washington	60 days
Michigan	30 days	West Virginia	10 days
Minnesota	Immediately	Wisconsin	No bail
Mississippi	Immediately	Wyoming	30 days
Missouri	Immediately		

You should verify the summary judgment in each state because of the ever-changing laws.

Bail Fugitive Recovery Payment Agreement

BAIL FUGITIVE RECOVERY PAYMENT AGREEMENT
2 pages total

I _____ (hereafter called "Client") am entering into a contract

with _____ (hereafter called "BFRP) that is designed to bring about the

lawful arrest of _____ (hereafter called "Fugitive") or

exoneration of bail bond(s) _____

BFRP agrees to track, locate, identify, arrest, transport, and surrender Fugitive to

Client, the proper authority, or, alternatively, cause the exoneration of the/those bail

bond(s) posted by Client or person authorized to post bail bonds on Client's behalf to

secure the release of Fugitive.

Client agrees to pay Tuamaveras, Inc. **3 %** of the face value of the/those bail bond(s)

posted by Client or person authorized to post bonds on Client's behalf to secure the

release of Fugitive once BFRP has, in any way, reported to Client that Fugitive is in the

custody of any law enforcement agency or has been in the custody of any law

enforcement agency.

Client agrees to pay Tuamaveras, Inc. **5%** of the face value of the/those bail bond(s)

posted by Client or person authorized to post bonds on Client's behalf to secure the

release of Fugitive when Fugitive actually *Self Surrenders* to Client, indemnitors or any

law enforcement agency after BFRP has made one or more attempt or attempts to arrest

Fugitive.

Client agrees to pay Tuamaveras, Inc. **10%** of the face value of the bail bond(s) within

48 hours after the arrest of Fugitive by BFRP or law enforcement personnel who were

directed to Fugitive by BFRP prior to the date of summary judgment or cause the

BAIL FUGITIVE RECOVERY PAYMENT AGREEMENT
2 pages total

exoneration of the/those bail bond(s) put up by Client or person authorized to post bail bonds on Client's behalf to secure the release of Fugitive.

If Client fails to pay Tuamaveras, Inc. as described in paragraph 5, Client agrees to pay Tuamaveras **20%** of the face value of the bail bond(s) 72 hours after the arrest of Fugitive by BFRP or by law enforcement personnel who were directed to Fugitive by BFRP or cause the exoneration of the/those bail bond(s) put up by Client or person authorized to post bail bonds on Client's behalf to secure the release of Fugitive.

If Client fails to pay Tuamaveras, Inc. in full any amount that is due and owing after (7) calendar days subsequent to Fugitive's arrest by BFRP, arrest by law enforcement personnel who were directed to Fugitive by BFRP, BFRP's discovery of Fugitive being in-custody, BFRP's discovery of Fugitive having been in the custody of any law enforcement agency after the date of forfeiture and before the date of summary judgment or if Fugitive Self Surrenders to Client or any law enforcement personnel or BFRP causes the exoneration of those bail bond(s) posted by Client or a person authorized to post bonds on Client's behalf, Client agrees that the proper jurisdiction to have suit filed and heard shall be Calaveras County within the State of California and that such suit may be filed after the thirtieth day of non-payment in full by Client to Tuamaveras, Inc..

_____   _____
CLIENT SIGNATURE   DATE

_____   _____
BFRP SIGNATURE   DATE

Law Enforcement Agency's Notification of Attempts to Arrest Bail Fugitive

ALLIED BAIL AGENCIES
1852 West 11th Street # 412
Tracy, CA 95376-3736
1-877-726-9092

LAW ENFORCEMENT AGENCY'S NOTIFICATION OF ATTEMPT TO ARREST BAIL FUGITIVE

Method of Notice: Hand Delivered To:_____ Date:_____ Time:_____

Facsimile: Number:_____ Contact Person:_____

*Please **do not** transmit this Notice via any unsecured means (radio) as doing so may result in undesirable action by the bail fugitive and/or associates of the bail fugitive.*

BAIL FUGITIVE INFORMATION

Fugitive Name:_____ DOB _____

Sex: ____ Height: ____ Weight ____ Eyes ____ Hair ____ Salient(s):_____
Fugitive's Last Known Vehicle: _____ Tag: _____
Subject May Be In The Company of: _____ DOB: _____

Bail Forfeited: Yes ___ No ___ Warrant Issued: Yes ___ No ___ Night Service: Yes ___ No ___
Warrant Information: _____
Good Cause for surrender of the defendant may be established by facts other than defendant's failure to appear in court   If "No" is checked, arrest is made
People v. Smith, (1986) 182 Cal. App. 3d 1212; 228 Cal Rptr. 277   pursuant to California Penal Code Sec.1300.

Suspected Address 1 :_____ Contact Time: _____
Suspected Address 2 :_____ Contact Time: _____
Suspected Address 3 :_____ Contact Time: _____

BAIL FUGITIVE RECOVERY PERSON(S) ATTEMPTING BAIL FUGITIVE ARREST

Name: _____ Vehicle: _____ Tag: _____ Cell: _____
Name: _____ Vehicle: _____ Tag: _____ Cell: _____
Name: _____ Vehicle: _____ Tag: _____ Cell: _____
Name: _____ Vehicle: _____ Tag: _____ Cell: _____

The above listed agents are qualified pursuant to California Penal Code Sections 1299 - 1301. Each agent is wearing clothing that is clearly identifiable. Dispatch will be contacted before and after each attempt to arrest the above listed Bail Fugitive pursuant to CPC 1299.08(a). See back for more information.

Formally Requesting Assistance to Preserve the Peace: YES ___ NO ___
Agency Response to Request For Assistance: Granted ___ Denied ___ Check Reason if denied:
_____ Providing Civil Standbys Is Against Department Policy
_____ No NCIC Warrant For Above Described Bail Fugitive Located
_____ Unable To Spare Personnel For The Time Frame Requested
_____ Assisting Bail Fugitive Recovery Persons Is Against Department Policy

Officer Safety Advisory: Yes ___ (see below) No ___

_____

Pursuant to California Penal Code Section 11105.6, I am requesting the following information pertaining to the above listed Bail Fugitive: known aliases, violent felony convictions.
Yes _____ No _____ Agency Response: _____

OPERATION SUMMARY
_____
_____
_____
_____
_____

Nearest Hospital / Trauma Center: _____ Phone: _____

This Notice Prepared by: _____ Date: _____ Time: _____

Contract Enforcement Services Activity Times Sheet

Contract Enforcement Services
Activity Time Sheet

Defendant _____

Depositer of Bail _____

Summary Judgment Date _____

Date	Time Started	Description of Investigative Activity And Supporting Document/s	Time End	Total Time
				Total Case Time

Agent _____

$100.00 Per Hour Investigation Rate billable to Indemnitor(s)

Page _____ of _____

Sample Activity Log

Activity Log

Case:

Last Known Address:

Directions:

Date	Time	

In-House Incident Report

CONFIDENTIAL

CODE		CASE NUMBER

TYPE OF INCIDENT ARRESTED FOR:	LOCATION OF OCCURRENCE	CITY	CROSS STREET

CASE CONTACT:	RELATIONSHIP:	ADDRESS	COLLATERAL

INFORMATION: TRADE, HOBBIES, ASSOCIATES, LOVER, ETC.

RES. PHONE

BUS. PHONE

RES. PHONE

CONTACT:	RELATIONSHIP	ADDRESS	BUS. PHONE

INFORMATION:

BAIL AGENT	BUSINESS ADDRESS:	BAIL AMMOUNT

DAY/DATE/TIME OCCURRED:	REPORTED TO:	DATE/TIME REPORTED	FOREITURE DATE

PRINCIPAL	DOB	SSN	DL/NO.	BOOKED ☐	CITED ☐

ADDRESS USED	SEX/RACE	HT/WT	HAIR/EYES	MARKS/SCARS/TATOOS

SPECIAL CIRCUMSTANCES (PRINCIPAL PROPENSITY TOWARDS VIOLENCE, WEAPONS, GAMES ETC.

PRINCIPAL LEVEL		REASON:

ARREST DETAILS:

Supplementary Report

SUPPLEMENTARY REPORT

PAGE_____ OF_____

ASSISTANT NAME_____ DATE_____

PRINCIPAL_____ TELEPHONE_____

CASE NUMBER

DETAILS: (WHO, WHAT, WHERE, WHEN, WHY)

_____

_____

_____

_____

_____

_____

_____

_____

_____

_____

_____

_____

_____

_____

_____

_____

_____

_____

_____

_____

_____

_____

_____

Glossary

- **bail**—the system of guaranteeing that a person released from jail will appear in court when scheduled to do so.
- **bailspeak**—lingo or jargon peculiar to the trade of writing bonds and enforcing civil contracts on bonds. Where applicable, it is my intent in this book to familiarize the reader with peculiar words or phrases used in the bail community for the purpose of enhancing communication between the aspiring bail fugitive recovery person and his potential client(s).
- **bail agent**—a person or entity licensed by the state (in California by the Department of Insurance) to transact bail for an insurance company and is backed by the same surety/insurance company (sometimes referred to as bail).
- **bail or appearance bond**—by executing a surety bond with one or more commercial bond companies, defendants enter into a contract with the company/ies to appear in court as agreed.
- **bail bond premium**—the fee charged to the bail fugitive by the bondsman to post the bond; this fee is paid directly to the bondsman and is not refundable.
- **bail bondsman**—a person who files with the state to transact bail without a surety and does so with his own assets.
- **bail enforcement agent**—commonly viewed by the media and public at large as a bounty hunter. *Bail* signifies what area of law the private citizen is working under, *enforcement* characterizes what type of action is employed, and *agent* is taken directly from case cites and codified law(s). Most professionals shy away from being identified as a bounty hunter, preferring the term *bail enforcement agent*.
- **bail fugitive**—the defendant who is out of jail on bail.
- **bail fugitive recovery person (BFRP)**—someone who receives written authorization by the bail or depositor of bail and is contracted to investigate, surveil, locate, and arrest a bail fugitive for surrender to the appropriate court, jail, or police department; or any person who is employed to assist a bail or depositor of bail.
- **bail runner**—in those states that specifically prohibit free-lance bounty hunters or bail enforcement agents, a bail runner, who works for only one bail agent at a time, is often permitted. A bail runner is contracted to investigate, surveil, locate, and arrest a bail fugitive for surrender to the appropriate court, jail, or police department. Most states require bail agents to provide a list of all bail runners they employ.
- **bond**—money or something of value put up for a defendant to guarantee his appearance in court; if the defendant misses his court appearance, the judge will order the bond forfeited.
- **bounty hunter**—historically, private citizens who sought out wanted criminals for cash rewards were called bounty hunters, and, today, some people continue to identify themselves as bounty hunters—primarily on reality television shows. California law describes a person who is qualified to enforce private civil contracts as a "bail fugitive recovery person," BFRP for short.
- **cash bond**—by depositing cash or securities in the amount of the bond, defendants (or a representative) can secure their own release.

- **cite and release**—used for minor offenses. Defendant is booked and released after signing a "cite and release" form and promising to appear as directed.
- **collateral**—something of value, such as property or bonds, put up by the defendant or someone acting on his behalf to secure a bond; if the defendant doesn't appear as required, the collateral is forfeited.
- **depositor of bail**—a person or agency that has deposited money or security to secure the release of a defendant
- **exoneration**—the term used by the court to describe a bond that is free and clear of any further liability; this usually happens when the defendant's case is fully adjudicated to the court's satisfaction. It is sometimes necessary to file a motion that is designed to exonerate a forfeited bond on a technicality and not based on surrendering the defendant.
- **human intelligence**—information gained from fieldwork versus theory.
- **indemnitor**—commonly called a cosigner, this person signs the bail bond contracts and other documents, wherein he is personally guaranteeing the appearance of the accused and agrees to be responsible for the total penal amount of the bond or bonds and all necessary expenses.
- **independent contractor**—bail fugitive recovery person; (a bail agent or bondsman is authorized through a state license to transact bail bonds, whereas a bail fugitive recovery person who is not a licensed bail agent cannot bail people out of jail but can enforce the private contract between the parties by physically arresting a bail bond client and returning that person to the proper authority: city, county jail, or court).
- **loose-bail**—bailspeak for posting bonds with little or no money down, unreliable cosigners, and no collateral.
- **summary judgment**—the term used to describe a bail bond that has been forfeited longer than 180 days or past the date of any previously ordered extensions.
- **own recognizance**—by agreeing to appear at a specified time and place, defendants who are not considered flight risks are released without posting security.
- **surety**—California Civil Code §2787 defines *surety* as one who promises to answer for the default of another, and it is defined similarly in other states.
- **three-strikes law**—a law that requires mandatory sentences for three-time repeat felony offenders.
- **zero postoperation residual liability**—bailspeak for never having been arrested or sued because of actions taken on the job.

Resources

WEB SITES

http://www.uenforcebail.com. Check out the author's Web site for the latest information on bail fugitive recovery in California, as well as books and DVDs he offers to the novice and veteran recovery agent. It also offers employment opportunities for aspiring bail enforcement agents.

http://wwwfugitive-recovery.com. The Fugitive Recovery Network is an excellent national reference for bail fugitive recovery agents. It presents detailed descriptions of state laws, as well as links to recovery agencies, books about recovery, discussion forums, and current fugitive listing.

http://chesapeake-bailbonds.com/html/bailenforcement.html. This is Scott McClean's Web site. McClean is a bona fide professional who does bail enforcement, private investigation, bail bonds, and he runs a bail enforcement school that is highly regarded. I've spoken with him over the telephone, and the man knows his stuff.

http://bailrecovery.proboards25.com/index.cgi. The Fugitive Recovery Message Board provides a new forum for those in the recovery business to exchange information about bail enforcement, bail bonding, training, existing and pending state bail legislation, and more.

http://www.tacticalforums.com/cgi-bin/tacticalubb/ultimatebb.cgi. This Web site contains forums on various aspects of related trades with lots of experienced people who are extremely professional and willing to answer questions.

http://www.courtservices.org/thetoolbox/modules.php?name+Forums. This Web site contains a bail enforcement–specific forum where new people can go to get questions answered or just converse with professionals.

http: //www.allbounty.com/bondshome2.php. This Web site contains a forum for bail bonds, private investigators, and bail enforcement agents to correspond with hard-core professionals, who are there to help new people and provide advice.

http://www.usatrace.com/Forum/index.php?. This Web site is for private investigators to share their experiences and thoughts and to converse with one another.

http://lacounty.info/. This Web site enables certain records checks, which might be helpful during an investigation.

http://www.publicdata.com/. I've never used this service, but ostensibly one can run license plates in states where doing so is legal. This service isn't available in California, as far as I know.

http://licgweb.doacs.state.fl.us/weapons/index.html. People can apply by mail for a concealed weapons permit in Florida that is good for several other states that have a reciprocal understanding with Florida.

http://www.lvmpd.com/Permits/ConcealedFirearmsPermit.html. This Las Vegas Metropolitan Police Department Web site contains information about obtaining a concealed carry permit from Nevada that is also good for other states with a reciprocal arrangement.

http://www.anywho.com/rl.html. Any information obtained from this site should be double-checked for accuracy, but listed numbers may yield a reverse directory that reveals the billing address.

http: //appl.lasd.org/icc/agis_search.cfm. More and more entities are setting up Web sites like this one from Pomona. This is a great way to close a case by determining that the fugitive is already in jail, which may result in your obtaining a commission commensurate with the amount of work you put in.

http://www.sdsheriff.net/csb/. San Diego County offers a way to check a suspect for warrants. This helps with a second check to make sure a fugitive is still wanted or to get other information.

http://www.policevehicles.com/. A bail enforcement agent can pick up reconditioned police vehicles or other equipment from this site.

http://galls.com/. This is a great place to start acquiring equipment, uniforms, badges, vehicle signage, and other specialized gear for public safety professionals. It is perfect for bail fugitive recovery work.

http://www.bailsupply.com/. Pacific Law Enforcement Supply bills claims to have the largest selection in the world of fugitive recovery and bail enforcement gear, gadgets, clothing, badges, identification badges, and much more. It also offers training courses.

http://www.atf.treas.gov. The official Web site of the Bureau of Alcohol, Tobacco, Firearms, and Explosives contains federal legislation spelling out who can and cannot legally possess firearms.

http://www.leaa.org. This Law Enforcement Alliance of America Web site contains information about firearms issues, particularly the new Law Enforcement Officer's Safety Act signed into law in July 2004, which allows off-duty and retired law enforcement officers to carry a concealed weapon in any state, subject to the restrictions of the legislation.

http://www.paladin-press.com. Check out the Paladin Press online store for hundreds of books and videos on such topics as bounty hunting, investigations, firearms, martial arts, self-defense, law enforcement, and military science.

BOOKS AND VIDEOS

Investigations and Bail Enforcement

1. Burton, Bob. *Bail Enforcer: The Advanced Bounty Hunter.* Boulder: Paladin Press, 1990.
2. ———. *Bounty Hunter.* Boulder: Paladin Press, 1990. These two action-packed books by Bob Burton represent an older school of bail enforcement and provide a good introduction to and colorful anecdotes about bounty hunting.
3. Christensen, Loren. *Gangbangers: Understanding the Deadly Minds of America's Street Gangs.* Boulder: Paladin Press, 1999. Written by a police officer who headed a gang enforcement team in a large northwest city, this is the best book available for analyzing the threat presented by gang members, especially to anyone who tries to arrest one of them.
4. Jillett, Bud. *Private Investigation in the Computer Age: Using Computers to Revolutionize Your Work and Maximize Your Profits.* Boulder: Paladin Press, 2003. This modern approach to investigations is just the thing for the modern bail recovery agent who wants to use computer technology to help him hunt down felony fugitives.
5. Sankey, Michael L., and Peer J. Weber, eds. *Public Records Online: The National Guide to Private and Government Online Sources of Public Records, 5th Edition.* Tempe, Ariz.: Facts on Demand Press, 2004. Find what you need on the Web quickly and easily by this invaluable compilation of references of more than 10,000 government and private sources for retrieving information about anyone anywhere.
6. Scott, Robert. *The Investigator's Little Black Book 3: Hundreds and Hundreds and Hundreds of Inside*

Sources for Investigative Professionals, Updated and Expanded Edition. Beverly Hills, Calif.: Crime Time Publishing Co., 2002. This indispensable reference is used by thousands of real-life investigators and cops to track down deadbeats and felons by accessing bank accounts, criminal histories, employment records, and other telltale information.

Physical Apprehension and Self-Defense Tactics

1. Christensen, Loren W. *Far Beyond Defensive Tactics: Advanced Concepts, Techniques, Drills, and Tricks for Cops on the Street.* Boulder: Paladin Press, 1998. This book teaches that self-defense should be made simple because fights are too fast, furious, and fraught with danger to rely on complicated maneuvers. Learn how to disarm attackers, prevail against multiple attackers, use the ground to your advantage, deal with people under the influence of drugs, and much more.
2. ———. *Restraint and Control Strategies: State-of-the-Art Defensive Tactics for Law Enforcement and Security Professionals* (video). Boulder: Paladin Press, 2002. Christensen synthesizes the skills he gained from 30 years as a martial artist and 28 years as a cop into a restraint and control system that is efficient, easy to learn, and legally defensible. It is especially useful for aikido or jujitsu practitioners who want to make their wristlocks more street realistic.
3. Grover, Jim. *Street Smarts, Firearms, and Personal Security: Jim Grover's Guide to Staying Alive and Avoiding Crime in the Real World.* Boulder: Paladin Press, 2000. Required reading for anyone who has to work on the streets, this book shows you how to survive if you have to fight by using your mental and physical tools. Especially useful to recovery agents are the sections on firearms, nonlethal weapons, and unarmed combat.
4. Hatmaker, Mark. *Gladiator Conditioning: Fitness for the Modern Warrior* (video). Boulder: Paladin Press, 2003. This state-of-the-art conditioning program will help you to develop the kind of functional strength and endurance that help you win in real fights.
5. Johnson, Willie "The Bam." *Willie "The Bam" Johnson's Street Combat Workout* (video). Boulder: Paladin Press, 2002. A supercharged self-defense–based workout program for functional fitness.
6. Lewis, Edward. *Hostile Ground: Defusing and Restraining Violent Behavior and Physical Assaults.* Boulder, Paladin Press, 2000. Get a graduate course in proper defusing and restraint techniques from a veteran who learned as part of a professional restraint team at a mental health facility and on the streets as a private investigator.
7. Vale, Bart, and Mark Jacobs. *Shootfighting: The Ultimate Fighting System.* Boulder: Paladin Press, 2001. Combine wrestling moves with such martial arts as judo, karate, and Muay Thai to get the ultimate fighting system to keep you in peak physical condition and give you the winning edge if you have to fight.

Firearms

1. Campbell, R.K. *Holsters for Combat and Concealed Carry.* Boulder: Paladin Press, 2004. Find out how to choose the best holster for your firearm for easy access, safe retention, concealability, durability, and more.
2. Clapp, Wiley. *Concealed Carry: The Shooter's Guide to Selecting Handguns.* Boulder, Paladin Press, 2002. If you are thinking about carrying a concealed weapon, get the opinion of an expert about such things as models, calibers, holsters, and much more.
3. Grover, Jim. *Combative Pistol: Jim Grover's Guide to Extreme Close-Quarters Shooting* (video). Boulder: Paladin Press, 2002. This video combines Grover's hard-hitting unarmed tactics with his state-of-the-art shooting techniques for a brutally effective program that will enable you to strike, draw, shoot, and win at arm's length and closer.

4. ———. *Jim Grover's Defensive Shooting Series* (video). Boulder: Paladin Press, 1995. Learn every aspect of employing a firearm as a fight-stopping defensive weapon, including grip, stance, trigger control, use of cover, low-light shooting, and more.

5. Suarez, Gabriel. *The Tactical Pistol: Advanced Gunfighting Concepts and Techniques.* Boulder: Paladin Press, 2001. A former cop draws from his hands-on experience to teach you the most vital lessons, tactics, and techniques for firing your weapon in a life-or-death situation.

About the Author

Rex Venator is the pseudonym for the owner of a bail fugitive recovery agency in California, which he has operated since 1992. Before getting into private contract recovery work, Rex served for eight years as a corrections officer for a county sheriff's department and as a military policeman for the U.S. Army Reserves. He also has experience as a private investigator and a bail agent, and was a special agent with California Judicial Enforcement. His training includes combat shooting, firearms, less-than-lethal weapons, hazardous materials, drug labs, martial arts, and close-quarter combat. You can contact him at his Web site www.uenforcebail.com.